Richard Willes

The History of Trauayle in the West and East Indies,

and other countreys lying eyther way, towardes the fruitfull and ryche Moluccaes.

As Moscouia, Persia, Arabia, Syria, Aegypte, Ethipoia, Guinea, China in Cathayo, and Giapan

Richard Willes

The History of Trauayle in the West and East Indies,
and other countreys lying eyther way, towardes the fruitfull and ryche Moluccaes. As Moscouia, Persia, Arabia, Syria, Aegypte, Ethipoia, Guinea, China in Cathayo, and Giapan

ISBN/EAN: 9783744797160

Printed in Europe, USA, Canada, Australia, Japan

Cover: Foto ©ninafisch / pixelio.de

More available books at **www.hansebooks.com**

THE
History of Trauayle in the

VVest and East Indies, and other countreys lying eyther way, towardes the fruitfull and ryche *Moluccaes.*

As

Moscouia, Persia, Arabia, Syria, Ægypte, Ethiopia, Guinea, China in *Cathayo,* and *Giapan*: VVith a discourse of the Northwest passage.

In the handes of our Lorde be all the corners of the earth. Psal. 94.

Gathered in parte, and done into Englyshe by Richarde Eden.

Newly set in order, augmented, and finished by Richarde VVilles.

Imprinted at London by Richarde Iugge. 1577.

Cum Priuilegio.

To the ryght noble and excellent Lady, the Lady Brigit, Countesse of Bedforde, my singuler good Lady and Mystresse.

AL studies haue theyr speciall tymes (Ryght noble Lady) all good partes, and singuler qualities of the mynde are holden vp, and maynteyned with honour. The seely chylde learneth in his tēder age how to speake, to reade, to write: yoūg laddes bestowe theyr tyme in the study of other liberall sciences: as yeeres come on, and wyt encreaseth, so finally, the whole course of learnyng is runne ouer. Agayne, the arte of Grammer is wont erst to be learned, and than Logike afterwarde: naturall Philosophie goeth not before eloquence in our schooles: Geometry is first read, & than Geography. So that the studies of good letters haue their times in respecte of mans age, they haue theyr tymes in the order of learning: yea they haue a tyme, that maketh vs all to bestowe therein our tyme, and to studie eche facultie in due tyme, I meane that speciall tyme they floryshe in. I may not denye but that learnyng hath at all tymes ben well accompted of, in most countreys the skyll of dyuers languages well thought of, & learned men to haue ben alwayes rewarded. what is than that speciall tyme wherin all studies doe flooryshe? Learnyng may bee ryght well compared vnto the floures & fruites of the earth, and the speciall tyme of learnyng, vnto theyr singuler seasons. In May, floures: in Iune, Cheries: at Haruest, corne: in September, Grapes: so fareth it in the study of good letters. There was a tyme whā the arte of grammer was so muche esteemed, that Gramariens proceeded masters thereof as woorshypfully, as other professours now doe in any other facultie. Than was it honourable to be a Poet: honourable I say, for that the Poet Laureate enioyed the honour of a Palatine, that tyme is paste. There was a tyme whan Logike & Astrology onely so weeried the heades of young schollers, yea and busied olde age also, that true Philosophie in deede was almost forgotten, eloquence defaced, the languages exiled, that tyme is past. Not long since happy was he that had any skil in the greke tongue, he was thought a great scholler that could make a greeke verse. Nowe a dayes, who studieth not rather the Hebrue language? VVhere haue you almost any greeke aucthour printed? Geography laye hydden many hundred yeeres in darkenesse and obliuion, without regarde and price: of late who taketh not vppon him to discourse of the whole worlde, and eche prouince thereof particulerly, euen by hearesay, although in the first principles of that arte, he bee altogeather ignorant and vnskylfull? This tyme is now. So long as Poetry was esteemed, the arte of grammer accompted of, Logike muche made of, Astrology well thought of: Diuine Poets, good Gramariens, perfecte Logiciens, excellent Astronomers no where wanted.

A Virgile can you neuer want where one Mecenas is. Honour & promotion bestowed vppon the maynteyners of controuersies in religion, hath brought gray heares from endlesse Sophistry, from Scotus formalites, from Buridan and Burley, from Holcot, from Bricot, from Vademecum, from Dormi secure, and taught yonger yeeres rather to passe through Aristotle and his interpreters, than euer to dwell therein: caused them to studie the scriptures, to reade ouer the fathers, to conferre the counseyles, to learne the greeke and Hebrue languages, to searche the Chalday Paraphraste, to peruse the olde Doctours, to translate the newe wryters, to heape vp common places, to discourse of sectes, to wryte cunningly, to preach eloquently: and made them to be, for braulyng Sophisters, graue Philosophers, for formal Dunses, plaine doctors, for rude questionaries, diuine Orators, for vnskilful schoolemen, eloquent and graue diuines.

It is nowe almost one hundred & fiftie yeeres agoe, that Don Henrico, sonne of Iohn the fyrst of that name Kyng in Portugale, and Nepheu vnto our Kyng Henry the fourth, made his vyage after the conquest of Septa to the Canaries, and encouraged the Portugales to searche the coastes of Africa, and to seeke the landes thereabout not spoken of to fore. His grande Nepheu Iohn the seconde, so furthered this enterpryse, that the Portugale shyppes halled the Cape of good hope, discouered Æthiopia, and sayled where antiquitie denyed passage, beyond all Africa into the Indian seas. He sent also expert and cunning traueylers into Ægypt, and the redde sea coastes to espye what way the Portugales might looke for beyond the Cape of good hope to Calecut in India: the which viage in his sonne Emanuell his tyme, was prosperously taken in hand by Vasquez Gama, the nienth day of Iuly, in the yeere of our Lorde. 1497. & happely ended in Iuly againe, two yeeres after, to his great credit and preferment, to the immortal fame & honour of his Prince and countrey. Here began the studie of Geographie, that euer since Ptolomeus raigne laye troden vnder foote, & buried in dust and ashes, to spring vp agayne, and by the relations of skilful traueylers in Europe, Affrike, & Asie: through the discouery of the far Indies, the Moluccaes, & new founde landes, of late so to be wondred at, as no other facultie more. I dare be bold to say, that generally all Christians, Iewes, Turkes, Moores, Infidels, & Barbares be this day in loue with Geographie. The wylde and rogishe Tartares myght for famine perishe in the winter, if they in the sommer skylfully followed not the sunne. The heathen Giapans diuided the worlde into three partes: Afrike was described by a Moore. The Iewes report the estates of all countreyes to the Turkes. The Turkishe Basshaes gouerne the sweetest prouinces in Europe, Afrike, and Asia, no men greater traueylers than Christians. VVho but Geographers doe teach vs what partes of the earth be cold, warme, or temperate? Of whom doe we learne howe to diuyde the world into partes, the partes into prouinces, the prouinces into shyres? of Geographers. vnto

whom

whom haue wee to make recourse for Mappes, Globes, tables, and Cardes, wherein the dyuers countreys of the worlde are set downe? vnto Geographers. Set Geographie asyde, you shal neyther be able to get intelligences of the situation and strength of any citie, nor of the limites and boundes of any countrey, nor of the rule and gouernement of any kingdome, nor be able wel to trauayle out of your owne doores. wil you see what wise and experte traueylers, skilful in geometry and Astronomy, (for that is to bee a Geographer in deede) be able to doe? Looke you on the King of Portugales title: the two partes, of the three therein, were atchiued by Vasques Gama, and other traueylers aduentures. Consider the fruites, the drugges, the pearle, the treasure, the millions of golde and siluer, the Spanyardes haue brought out of the VVest Indies since the first viage of Columbus: The great commodities our nation reapeth by the traueyle of our countreymen into Barbary, Guiny, and Moscouia, wil be a sufficient testimony vnto all vs Englishmen, what it is to be a skilful traueyler, what to bee a paineful Geographer, and learned. Desire of rule breedeth victories, victories come by cōquestes, conquestes are furthered by traueyle, traueyle can not bee maynteyned without great wealth, wealth maketh all traueyle pleasant. The Northwesterne vyage, be it neuer so full of difficulties, will become as plausible as any other iourney, if our passengers may returne with plentie of siluer, silkes, and pearle. Let Columbus, Americus, Cortesius, be as wel set foorth againe, and bountefully

Kyng of Portugale & Algarbs, Lorde of Guinea, of the cōquest, nauigation, and trafike into Ethiopia, Arabia, Persia, & India.

 fully

ly rewarded, you ſhal heare of other newe found landes yet altogeather vnknowen. Let Gama be ſet in place, and Gama will tell you the ſituation, the maners, the force and wealth of forreyne nations, for Gama his endeuor was, not onely by his friend Cœlius to deſcrye the countrey wherſoeuer he came, but alſo to learne him ſelfe the riches, ſtrength, and conditions of the people. Honour maynteyneth arte: and the ſkill in Geography, as all other ſciences, hath but a tyme of preferment, the whiche than chiefly myght bee looked for, whan it is moſt eſteemed. This in the noble mynde of Cadamuſt bred that earneſt deſire, after Don Henrico his example, to traueyle, to pen his owne aduentures into the Southeaſt and Eaſt partes, to make the nauigation of Gama and his companions knowen vnto the worlde. The occaſions, the good ſucceſſe, the great commodities wherof, Barros a counſeller of the Portugale Kyng, paynted out long agoe in manye bookes, Oſorius of late, hiſtorically hath written the ſame in fewe. This made Marcus Paulus Venetus a courtier in Tartary, Hayton the Armenian to become a Frenchman, Lewes Vartomanne a traueyler in Ethiopia, Brocardus an inhabiter of Iury, & eche one of them to leaue his painful iorney with poſteritie in wrytyng. This enflamed the Spanyardes to take vppon them the diſcouery of the VVeſt and Southweſterne landes, done and written by Columbus, Pinzonus, Alfonſus, Corteſius, and Americus, of whom that region America hath name. VVhoſe long letters and tedious reportes of thinges there brought to

paſſe

passe in the conquest of that halfe worlde, the straunge beastes, the sundry sortes of fruites, the ioyes and riches the whiche that countrey yeeldeth, the manners and fashions of the people, their cities, and princely palaces, theyr nobilitie, their maner of gouernement, their warres, theyr seruile estate vnder the kynges of Spayne, their conuersion vnto the Christian fayth, P. Martyr a learned and graue man, borne at Angleria in the duchy of Milane, then President of the Spanish kinges counsell for the west Indies, gathered into one volume, and leauing a side all superfluous narrations, made thereof, as it were, one briefe and continuall historie. This volume deuided he into eyght Decades, after the Greeke worde, so calling the sundry parcels thereof, for that eche one conteyneth in it ten particuler bookes or chapters. R. Eden our countreyman dyd into English, whan K. Philippe was in Englande, the three first Decades, and the fourth also, though vnder a wrong title, according to the Dutche Printers edition, wherin the fifte, sixte, seuenth, and eight Decades were lefte out. He translated moreouer Gonzales Ferdinandus Ouiedus breuiary of the west Indies, & geathered togeather out of many myghty and huge workes, some other prety pamflettes concernyng the Spanyardes and Portugalles voiages into the late discouered lands, adding thereto certeine discourses of the north partes. These his aforesayde doinges, as fewe mennes workes at the first come exactly abrode, this paynefull translatour mynded, if not to amende, at the least to augment, by puttyng thereunto in Engliſh Lewes Vartomannus Nauigation into Ægypte, Arabia, Siria, Perſia, and India, with our Merchantes Moſcouian and Perſian trauelles: but death preuented his purpoſe, not ſuffryng him to accompliſh his deſire.

Chriſtian charitie therefore vnto the party departed, cauſed me to helpe his workes forwarde: Nature moued me to take ſome paynes in placing orderly, that whiche he had confuſely gyuen out, the better to direct, and the more to profit the reader: My profeſſion enforced me to cut of ſome ſuperfluous tranſlations, and to fill vp the reſt of his doinges with P. Martyrs other writinges, and finally to furniſhe his want with my owne ſtore. Hoping and perſwading with my ſelfe, that if God likewiſe call me from theſe worldly Nauigations, and earthly deſcriptions, before my other trauell in this facultye, taken long ſince in hande, be ended: ſome other profeſſor of Coſmography wil ſo rewarde me after my death, as preſently of this dead man I doe deſerue. Other credite ſeeke I none therefore, I loke for no prayſe, I hope not for honor, I gape for no gayne by this kind of ſtudie. I knowe this day no place, no preferment, no publike chayre, no ordinarie lecture, no commune ſtipende, no ſpecial reward due vnto the ſtudentes in Geography: no not at this time, when this faculty was neuer more ſet by: no not in this realme, where yt neuer more floriſhed. The honorable name of a Chriſtian, and the infallible fruites thereof, euer inclined me, euen from my tender

yeeres,

yeeres, for the smal portion of learning that god hath lent me, to do good, if I could, vnto many: and specially to make those my friendes and wel doers knowen vnto the worlde, by whose beneuolence & fauour I doe liue, and am mainteined. In the smal number whereof, for amongst many wel willers I finde but few well doers, your Honor (right noble Lady) my Lorde & you, his noble children and yours, since my first returne from beyond the seas, must I confesse to haue stoode me chiefly in steede: & humbly acknowledge, the first yeerely pension I euer was assured of in England, to haue ben by your Ladiship bestowed on me. VVherefore as I will most willingly yeelde vnto many other of your Honors gẽtlemẽ to come of great houses, to haue welthier friendes, larger possessions & reuenues than I, to be more actiue, more comely, more wyse, politike, learned, & to haue seene more: so in hũble duety, loyal seruice, sincere affection & good wil to your Honor, I may, I can, I wyl contende with any of them all, euen to the vttermust force and power of my hart, head, body, life, blood, mynd, & soule. In testimony wherof, and full assurance of my seruice vnto you for euer, these last doings of R. Eden newly encreased, my first labours in our language, his history & mine of trauel in the west & East Indies, altogeather in one volume, ductifully do I present vnto your Honour, with al humility praying & most earnestly requesting your good Ladiship, that you will vouchsafe it, & by leysure, in this iourney, the whiche my

Lorde and you haue determined into the west countrey, to let your page reade them ouer to your Honours recreation, as one of the principall causes wherefore at this tyme they were set foorth. If varietie of matter, occurrents out of forraigne countryes, newes of newe founde landes, the sundry sortes of gouernement, the different manners & fashions of diuers nations, the wonderfull workes of nature, the sightes of straunge trees, fruites, foule, and beastes, the infinite treasure of Pearle, Golde, Siluer, & ioyes may recreate and delight a mynde trauelled in weighty matters, & weeried with great affayres: credit me, good Madam, in listning vnto this worke, shall you haue recreation, you shall finde delight in reading ouer these relations, wherein so newe, so straunge, so diuers, so many recreations and delightes of the mynd are expressed.

Your Honours good lykyng thereof, wyll be to me no small contentation for this worke paynefully doone, a good occasion spedyly to finish the rest of my owne labours concerning this faculty, a great encouragement and comfort to bestow my whole time hereafter only in that study, wherewith all my former knowledge in Philosophy and Geography may ende. The whiche, conueniently now, I am in good hope to perfourme, with my Lorde and your Ladyshyps good leaue, and continuance of my duety and effectuall desire to doe your Honours the better seruice. *At London the 4. day. of July. 1577.*

Your Honors seruaunt humbly at commaundement.

Richarde Willes.

R. VVilles Preface vnto the Reader, wherein is set downe a generall summe as it were of the whole worke.

This greate and large volume consisteth principally of foure partes, agreeable vnto those foure corners of the worlde, whereunto the skilfull seamen and merchauntes aduenturers of late yeeres haue chiefely traueiled, and yet specially are wont to resorte. The first part conteyneth foure Decades, *The first part, the first Decade* written by *P. Martyr*, a learned & graue counseller of Charles the Emperour fifte of that name, concernyng the Spanyardes voyages Southwestwarde, & theyr famous exploites doone in these newly discouered partes of the worlde, the whiche usually wee now call the west *Indies*. Hereunto haue we added *Gonzalus Ferdinandus Ouiedus* breefe historie touching the same matter, so that the first part of our volume hath fiue particular bookes. In the first whereof cap 1.2.3 4 and 5. *P. Martir* describeth *Columbus* first and second nauigations and discoueries of certaine Ilandes made by hym specially and his brother. In the 6 chapter or booke thereof (for both names we finde) is set foorth *Columbus* third voiage, and the discouery of *Peru*, in the maigne west *Indish* lande. In the seuenth, his troubles both in the west *Indies*, and retourne into Spaigne with his brother, being both prisoners. The 8. is of *P. Alfonsus* voyages that same way. In the 9. are declared the trauailes of *Vincent* and *Peter Tinzoni*, and other Spaniards likewise thither from *Palos*. The 10. is a conclusion of the whole Decade, with particuler mention of some special nouelties, & *Colonus* fourth voiage beganne. So that in the first Decade you haue historically set downe the discouerye of the west *Indies*, taken in hande about the yeere of our Lorde. 1492. by *Columbus* and his companions, vntill the yeere 1510. as *P. Martir* witnesseth fol 8.43 47 and 54. This worthy trauayler and skilfull seaman died at [illegible] in Spaigne. [illegible] 1506. as *Lopez* reporteth cap 25. in his generall historie [illegible] *Indias*.

The second Decade conteyneth [illegible] matters, entituled by *P. Martir*, [illegible], that is a continent or maigne lande, as *The second Decade.*

in deede it is of it selfe with the rest of *America*, in lyke maner as Europe, Affryk, & Asia, be one continent or maigne lande vnited togeather. In the fyrst and seconde chapters of this Decade, shall you reade the voyages of *Fogeda* and *Nicuesa*, to *Dariena*. In the thyrd, *Colmenaris* trauayles, *Nicuesa* his death, and the *Indishe* kyng *Comogrus* beneuolence: In the fourth, *Vasquez Nunnez* voyages in *Vraba* gulfe. His conquest of rebellious Barbarian kyngs in the fifte. In the syxt *Quicedus* & *Colmenaris* ambassage out of *Dariena* to *Hispaniola*, and the religion of king *Commendator* in *Cuba*. The seuenth booke conteineth *Petrus Arias* iorney to *Paria* in *Peru*. The. 8. the dissention betwixt the Spaniardes and Portugales for theyr boundes, and makyng of fyue Bishops in these newely founde partes of the worlde. In the 9 are shewed the ryuers of *Darien*, and philosophically the causes of so great waters there. That countrey is described in the. 10 and the extreme hunger abydden by the companions of *Nicuesa*, set forth.

The thyrd Decade.

In the fyrst, second, and thyrd chapters of the thyrde Decade, is conteyned an abridgement of *Vascus Nunnez* relations, concernyng his voyage to the south sea, for it lyeth south from *Darien*, vsually termed nowe a dayes *Mar del zur*, and may also be called the wyde east Indyshe Ocean. The discouery thereof made by *Nunnez*, the kyng subdued by hym, especially kyng *Commogrus* christenyng by the name of Charles, and the wynnyng of kyng *Tumanama* or *Tubanama* and his countrey. In the fourth chapter shal you fynd *Columbus* fourth vyage, began *An. do.* 1502 to the mayne west Indyshe lande, with the description of some part therof, lyinge betwyxt our Atlantike or westerne Ocean, and the aforesayde *Mar del zur*, as *Vraba*, and *Beragua*. In respecte of the history and course of yeeres, this booke myght haue been placed before the seconde Decade, but it shoulde seeme that these reporters came no sooner to *P. Martyr* his handes, wherefore he began this fourth booke ryght well thus. I was determined. &c. The fyfth booke conteyneth *P. Arias* iorney mentioned dec. 2 lib. 7. to the north syde of *Peru*, wherein *Carthagena* and *S. Martha*, two famous hauens, do stande, with a description of the countrey and people thereof. In the syxt you haue a disputation touchyng the Leuant streame or easterne surge of the sea, the discouery of *Baccalaos* done by *Cabot*. *P. Arias* arriuall in Darien, the buildyng of *S. Maria antiqua* there, with other fortresses, finally the commodities and vnwholesomnesse of *Darien*. In the .7. 8. & .9 bookes, shal you haue a description of *Hispaniola*, *Cuba*, and other Ilandes thereabout, done by *Andreas Moralis*. And in the .10 shall you reade of the Ilande *Diues* in *Mar del zur*, of the kyng therof subdued by *Andreas Morilis*, of *Pearles* & the findyng therof, of *Petrus Arias* Captaynes doinges agaynst the Canibales, of the Barbares fowlyng, & the manner of the gatheryng of gold in *Dariena*.

The fourth Decade, for so was it named in the Spanyardes edition of *P. Martyr* his workes set forth at *Alcala* in Spayne *An. do.* 1530. though the *Basile* and *Cullen* printers haue entituled it, *De insulis nuper inuentis*, that is, of Ilandes lately found out, to wyt, after *Columbus* voyages: this booke I say was by *P. Mar.* culled out of the Indian registers, conteynyng speciall notes that seemed vnto hym most meete to be publyshed: as the discouery of certayne Ilandes and crekes, namely *Iucatan* (done by *Fernandes* of *Corduba* & his companions) *Cozumella*, the Ilande of Sacrifice, the Ilandes of women, the prouince *Coluacan* and *Palmaria* &c. by *Iohn Grijalua* & his felowes: the *Iucatans* captiuitie and discouery of *Florida* made by those Spanyardes which *Diegus Velasquez* sent out of *Cuba* and *Ferd. Cortesius* fyrst nauigation, wherein he conquered *Potanchana* in newe Spayne, the death of *Valdiuia*, ŷ execution of *Viscus Nunnez*, king *Muteezũa* his presentes to Charles the Emperour, his bookes, letters, and superstitions, finally the ruine of *Hispaniola*, and vtter decaye thereof, if heede shoulde not be taken in tyme.

The fourth Decade.

Last of al *Gonzalus Ferdinandus Oviedus* historie conteineth in .18. seuerall chapters (eche one whereof hath his proper title) a briefe declaration of the west Indysh nauigation, of the metals the which are found in those lately discouered landes, of the maners of the people, rites, customes, and ceremonies, of the beastes, foules, byrdes, wormes, fyshes, seas, riuers, sprynges, trees, plantes, hearbes, & diuers other thinges that are engendred there both on the land & in the water. To this haue we added certaine speciall reportes of new Spaine or *Mexico*, of [illegible] of [illegible] & the countrey lying therunto, of the [illegible] with the discouering of [illegible] and thus make [illegible] ende [illegible] of this volume.

The

To the Reader.

The seconde part.

The seconde part of this worke appeareth what it is, by the title thereof set downe. Fol. 230. to wyt, a discourse to proue that there is a passage to the *Moluccaes* by the northwest, the whiche presently *M. Cap. Furbisher* attempteth, with certayne reportes of the prouince *China* in *Cathayo*, where he hath to strike in his voyage, and thyrdly of *Giapan*, and other Ilandes by the way. The whiche seconde part, wherein matter concernyng the northwest is handled, is so much the shorter, by how much the fyrst part seemed ouerlong: besydes that the particularities of this corner of the worlde are not yet so throughly knowen, but that other writers shal doubtlesse in more ample maner employe theyr labour therein after the returne of our northwesterne trauaylers. The which I wyshe to be most happie and prosperous, as they most valiantly & painefully, to the renowne of our Englyshe nation, do shewe to haue taken it in hande.

The thyrde part.

In the thyrd part shal you fynd a discription of the northeasterne frostie seas and kingdomes lying that way: as *Moscouia*, *Scondia*, or *Denmarke*, *Groenlande*, *Islande*, *Laponia*, *Norway*, *Suecia*, or *Swetlande*, *Bothnia*, and *Gothlande*: out of *Zeiglerus*, *Paulus Iouius*, *Haiton*, and *Sebastian* free lord or Baron of *Herbestein*, with the countreys as well north and northeast beyond *Moscouia*, namely *Petzora*, *Iubra*, and other prouinces of the Tartars: as also the voyages made through *Moscouia* by the merchauntes of London into *Persia*, conteinyng many speciall thynges woorth the knowledge, both of the countrey it self, the commodities thereof, the manners of the people and the priuiledges graunted unto our merchauntes by the *Sophi* or *Shaugh* the *Persian* kyng.

The fourth part.

Finally in the fourth par are set downe our merchauntes voyages into *Guinea*, and the other parcelles of Affrike lying towardes the Southeast, *Lewes Vertomannus* nauigations into Egypte, *Ethiopia*, *Arabia*, *Syria*, *Persia*, and east *India*, euen to the fruitefull *Moluccaes*, with the prices of drugges and other wares brought from thence. Whereto for a conclusion, haue we added partly out of *Maximilian* [illegible] a letter wrytten unto the Cardinall of [illegible] of *P. Martyrs* other woorkes that famous [illegible] about the whole world: the contention betwene [illegible] and Spanyardes for the [illegible] the [illegible]

[illegible]

Pope Alexander the syxt: and last of all the abridgement of .*P. Martyrs* foure last Decades, wherein especially that noble and gloryous conquest of *Mexico* is wrytten. Generally this much of the foure partes of this large volume. The lesser parcelles and speciall matter conteyned in eche part, you haue so exactely rehearsed in the table of the Decades. Fol. 173. and in the resydue of the whole worke before eche chapter so euidently set downe, that any particular table thereof at al the reader greatly needeth not, if so be that he be able to remember in what region of the worlde, East, West, North, or South, that be, the which he looketh for.

Nowe concernyng .R. Edens owne doynges, syncerely to say what I thynke, and curteously to yeelde hym that due prayse the whiche worthyly these his labours deserue, yet not to flatter hym neither, where any faulte hath ben committed: as hyghly he was to be commended for Englyshyng so straunge, so wonderfull, so profitable histories as these are, nothyng inferior to the bookes of auncient writers, far exceedyng the multitude of foolysh commentaries and friuolous translations, to to licentiousely vsed in our tyme: So may the gentle reader forbeare his ouersyghte, in so great a worke, where some Spanyshe prouerbe, harsh latine phrase, or vncleane speache may seeme hardly Englyshed, or any rashe note to shame the texte. I woulde excuse hym for translatyng the dayes by the latine names, as Fol. 12. *Non. April.* thus. At the Nones of Apryll *item, 3. Idus Octobris.* thus. The thyrd daye of the Ides of October *item. Fol. 17 tertio Kalend. Maij.* thus. The thyrd daye before the Kalendes of Maye: meanyng in deede, the fyfth daye of Aprill, the 13 day of October, the 29 of Aprill: but therein it shoulde seeme that he folowed his owne humor, for he obserueth the same phrase of translatyng throughout. P. *Martyrs* whole worke. Many of his Englyshe woordes cannot be excused in my opinion for smellyng to much of the Latine, as *Dominatore.* Fol. 5. [illegible] Fol. 3. *Dominators.* Fol. 5. [illegible] S. [illegible] *inseparable.* Fol. 387. [illegible] Fol. 90. [illegible] Fol. 390. [illegible] 87. [illegible] Fol. 276.

To the Reader.

Prodigious. Fol. 279. with other such lyke: in the stede of Lords, weyghtie, subiectes, wonderfull, auncient, lowe, carefull, dueti-full, manslaughter, drunken, noysome, monstrous. &c. the which faultes he confesseth in other his owne verses, wrytyng thus of hym selfe.

I haue not for euery worde asked counsayle
of eloquent Eliot, or Sir Thomas Moore:
Take it therefore as I haue intended,
the faultes with fauour may soone be a mended.

Certayne Preambles here folowe, geathered by R. Eden, for the better understanding of the whole worke.

Of the fyrst discouerynge of the west Indies

A Certayne Carauel saylyng in the West Ocean, about the coastes of Spayne, had a forcyble and continuall wynde from the East, wherby it was dryuen to a land unknowen, and not described in any map or carde of the sea, and was dryuen styl along by the coaste of the same for the space of many dayes, untyll it came to a hauen, where in a shorte tyme the most part of the maryners, beyng long before very weake and feble by reason of hunger and trauayll, dyed: So that onely the Pilot, with three or foure other, remayned alyue. And not only they that dyed, dyd not inioye the Indies whiche they fyrst discouered to theyr misfortune, but the resydue also that lyued had in maner as litle fruition of the same: not leauyng, or at the least not openly publysshyng any memorie thereof, neyther of the place, or what it was called, or in what yeere it was founde: Albeit, the faulte was not theyrs, but rather the malyce of other, or the enuie of that which we call fortune. I do not therfore maruayle, that the auncient histories affyrme, that great thynges procede and increase of small and obscure begynnynges, syth we haue seene the same veryfied in this fyndyng of the Indies, being so notable and newe a thyng. We neede not be curious to seeke the name of the Pilot, syth death made a shorte ende of his doynges. Some wyl, that he came from *Andaluzia*, and traded to the Ilandes of *Canaria*, and the Iland of *Madera*, when this large and mortal nauigation chaunced unto hym. Other say that he was a *Byscanne*, and traded into Englande and Fraunce. Other also, that he was a Portugale, & that either he went or came from *Mina* or *India*: which agreeth well with the name of these newe landes, as I haue sayd before. Agayne, some there be that say that he brought the Carauel to Portugale, or to the Iland of *Madera*, or to some other of the Ilandes called *De los Azores*. Yet do none of them affyrme any thyng, although they al affirme that the Pilot dyed in the house of *Christopher Colon*, with whom remayned all suche writynges and annotations as he had made of his voyage in the sayd Carauell, aswell of such thynges as he obserued both by land and sea, as also of the eleuation of the pole in those landes whiche he had discouered.

A harde begynnyng.

The Pylot that fyrst founde the Indies.

Mina.

The Table.

Of the fruitefull citie of Bisinagar in the kyngdome of Narsinga. Cap. 8. Fol. 384
Of the Docilitie, agilitie and wytte of Elephantes. Cap. 9. Fol. 385
Of the ingendryng of Elephantes. And of the magnificence and ryches of the kyng of Narsinga. Cap. 10. Fol. 386

[illegible]

Of the famous and ryche citie of Calecut. Cap. 1. Fol. 387
Of the kyng of Calecut: And of theyr Idolatrye. Cap. 2. Fol. 387
Of the maner whiche the kyng useth at his meate. Cap. 3. Fol. 388
Of the Priestes of Calecut named Bramini. Cap. 4. Fol. 388
Of the diuers sectes of Idolatours in the citie of Calecut. Cap. 5. Fol. 398
The apparell of the kyng, queene, and the inhabitantes of the citie of Calecut: And of theyr maner of feedyng. Cap. 6. Fol. 389
Of theyr custome after the death of the kyng. Cap. 7. Fol. 389
Of theyr changyng of wyues. Cap. 8. Fol. 390
The maner of feedyng of the common people of the Idolaters: And of there Iustice. Cap. 9. Fol. 390
Of their honouryng of Idoles. Cap. 10. Fol. 390
Of their maner of warre. Cap. 11. Fol. 391
Of theyr shyppes and maner of saylyng on the sea. Cap. 12. Fol. 391
The palace and courte of the kyng of Calecut. Cap. 13. Fol. 392
The Spices of Calecut. Cap. 14. Fol. 392
The foules and byrdes of Calecut. Cap. 15. Fol. 393
Of a most fruitefull tree of all the worlde. Cap. 16. Fol. 393
Howe they sowe Ryse. Cap. 17. Fol. 394
Howe theyr Phisitions visit the sicke folkes. Cap. 18. Fol. 394
Of theyr exchaungers, bankers, and brokers. Cap. 19. Fol. 395
Of thinhabitantes of Poliar and Hiraua. Cap. 20. Fol. 395
Of foure footed beastes, foules, and byrdes of Calecut. Cap. 21. Fol. 395
Of certayne Serpentes whiche are seene in Calecut. Cap. 22. Fol. 396
Of the lyghtes and lampes whiche are seene in the palace of the kyng of Calecut. Cap. 23. Fol. 396
The great multitude of Idolaters whiche resorte to Calecut [illegible] pardon of theyr sinnes. Cap. 24. Fol. 396

¶ [illegible]

Of the citie of Caicolon and Colon. Cap. 1. Fol. 397
Of Cyromandel a citie of India. Cap. 2. Fol. 397
Of the Ilande of Zailon, and the [illegible] there. Cap. [illegible] Fol. [illegible]
Of the tree of Cinamome [illegible]
Of Paleachet, a citie of India. [illegible]
Of Tarnasari, a Citie of India. [illegible]
Of the wylde and [illegible]
The maner whiche the [illegible]
[illegible]
The maner of burnyng [illegible]
Tarna[illegible]
The Iustice wh[illegible]
Howe the [illegible]
Tarna[illegible]
The [illegible]

The Table.

Of the Rubie. Fol. 423
Of the Rubies whiche growe in the Ilande of Zeilam. Fol. 423
Of the kynde of Rubies called Spinelle. Fol. 424
Of the Rubies called Balasini. Fol. 424
Of the Diamondes of the olde mine. Fol. 424
Of Saphires. Fol. 425
Of Topasies. Fol. 425
Of Turquesses. Fol 425
Of Iacinthes. Fol. 426
Of Smaragdes or Emeraldes. Fol. 426
Of dyuers kyndes of spices, where they growe, what they are woorth in Calecut, and whyther they are caryed from thence. And fyrst of Pepper. Fol. 426
Of Cloues. Fol. 427
Of Cinamome.
Of Ginger called Beledi.
Of Ginger Mechino. Fol. 427
Of greene Ginger in conserues.
Of the Apothecaries drugges, and of what price they are in Calecut and Malabar. Fol. 428
Of the weyghtes of Portugale and India, and how they agree. Fol. 429
Of the vyage made by the Spanyardes rounde about the worlde. Fol 42[illegible]
Maximilian Transiluanus letter thereof to the Cardinall of Saltzburge. Fol 4[illegible]
The debate and strife, betweene the Spaniardes and Portugales for the diuision of the Indies, and the trade of Spices, and the Molucaes out of Lopez de Gomara. Fol [illegible]
The repartition and diuision of the Indies and [illegible] betweene the Spanyardes and the Portugales. [illegible]
The cause and aucthoritie whereby they deuided the Indies. [illegible]
Howe and by what occasion the Emperour [illegible] to pledge to the kyng of Portugale. [illegible]
Pope Alexander the .6. his Bull touchyng the [illegible] Indies, Latine and Englyshe. [illegible]
An abridgement of .P. Martyrs [illegible] of F. C. conquest of [illegible]

FINIS

Imprinted [illegible]

A Certayne Carauel [illegible] coastes of Spayne, had a [illegible] from the East, wherby it was [illegible] and not described in any map or carde of the [illegible] [dri]uen styl along by the coaste of the same for the space of [ma]ny dayes, untyll it came to a hauen, where in a shorte tyme the most part of the maryners, beyng long before very weake and feble by reason of hunger and trauayll, dyed: so that onely the Pilot, with three or foure other, remayned alyue. And not only they that dyed, dyd not inioye the Indies whiche they fyrst discouered to theyr mysfortune, but the resydue also that lyued had in maner as litle fruition of the same: not leauyng, or at the least not openly publysshyng any memorie thereof, neyther of the place, or what it was called, or in what yeere it was founde: Albeit, the faulte was not theyrs, but rather the malyce of other, or the enuie of that which we call fortune. I do not therfore marueyle, that auncient histories affyrme, that great thynges procede and increase of small and obscure begynnynges, syth we haue seene the same verified in this fyndyng of the Indies, being so notable and newe a thyng. We neede not be curious to seeke the name of the Pilot, syth death made a shorte ende of his doynges. Some wyll, that he came from *Andaluzia*, and traded to the Ilandes of *Canaria*, and the Iland of *Madera*, when this large and mortal nauigation chaunced vnto hym. Other say that he was a *Byscanne*, and traded into Englande and Fraunce. Other also, that he was a Portugale, & that either he went or came from *Mina* or *India*: which agreeth well with the name of these newe landes, as I haue sayd before. Agayne, some there be that say that he brought the Carauel to Portugale, or to the Iland of *Madera*, or to some other of the Ilandes called *De los Azores*. Yet do none of them affyrme any thyng, although they al affirme that the Pilot dyed in the house of *Christopher Colon*, with whom remayned all suche [illegible] annotations as he had made of his voyage in the [illegible] thynges as he obserued both by land [illegible] of the pole in those landes whiche [illegible]

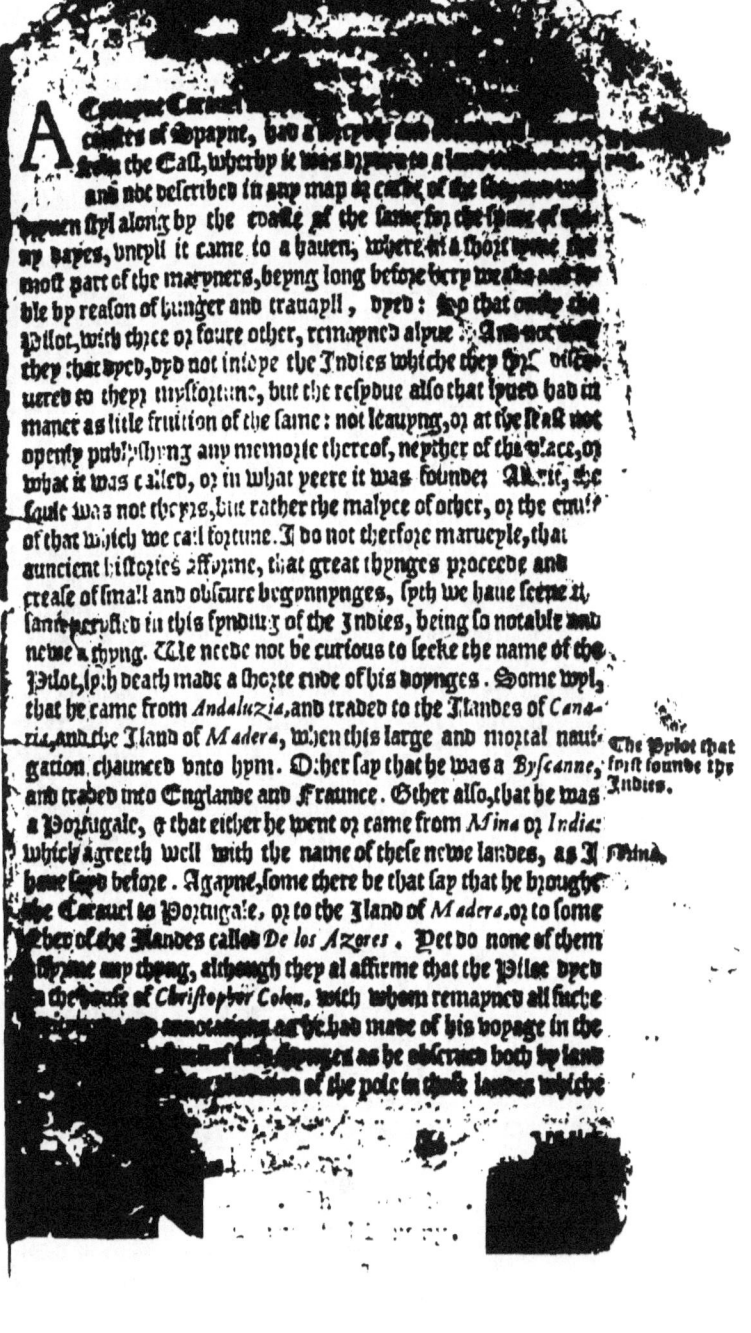

The Pylot that first founde the Indies.

Mina.

VVhat [illegible] of man Christopher Colon (otherwyse called Columbus) was, and how he came fyrst to the knowledge of the Indies.

Christopher *Colon* was borne in *Cugureo*, or (as some say) in *Nerui*, a vyllage in the territorie of *Genua* in Italie. He descended as some thynke, of the house of the *Pelestreles* of *Placentia* in *Lumbardie*. He beganne of a chylde to be a maryner: of whose arte they haue great exercise on the ryuer of *Genua*. He traded many yeres into *Suria*, and other partes of the East. After this, he became a maister in makyng cardes for the sea, whereby he had great vantage. He came to Portugale to know the reason & description of the south coastes of Affrica, and the nauigations of the Portugales, thereby to make his cardes more perfecte to be solde. He maryed in Portugale, as some say: or as many say, in the Ilande of *Madera*, where he dwelt at suche tyme as the sayd Carauell aryued there, whose [illegible] soiourned in his house, and dyed also there, bequeathyng to [illegible]on his carde of the description of suche newe landes as he had [illegible]und, whereby *Colon* had the fyrst knowledge of the Indies. Some haue thought ye *Colon* was wel learned in ye Latine tongue and the science of Cosmographie: and that he was thereby fyrst moued to seeke the lands of *Antipodes*, and the rych Ilande of *Cipango*, wherof *Marchus Paulus* wryteth. Also that he had redde what *Plato* in his dialoges of *Timeus* and *Cricias*, wryteth of the great Ilande of *Atlantide*, and of a great land in the west Ocean undiscouered, beyng bygger then Asia and Affrica. Furthermore that he had knowledge what *Aristotell* and *Theophrastus* saye in theyr bookes of maruayles, where they wryte that certayne merchauntes of Carthage, saylyng from the streyghtes of *Gibraltar* towarde the West and South, founde after many dayes a great Ilande not inhabited, yet replenyshed with al thynges requisite, and hauing many nauigable ryuers. In deede *Colan* was not greatly learned: yet of good understandyng. And when he had knowledge of the sayde newe landes by the information of the dead Pilot, made relation thereof to certayne learned men, with whom he conferred [illegible] mentioned of olde autours. He [illegible]

[illegible] was not [illegible]learned.

[illegible] conferres

[illegible] chiefely [illegible] fryer, named *Iohn Perez of Marchena*, that dwelt in the [illegible] of *Rabida*. So that I verily beleeue, that in maner all that he [illegible], and many thynges more that he left vnspoken, were written by the sayde Spanyshe Pilot that dyed in his house. For I am verily [illegible] if *Colon* by science atteined to the knowledg of the [illegible] long before haue communicat this [illegible] men the *Genueses* that trauayle all the worlde [illegible] not haue come into Spayne for this purpose. But doubtelesse he neuer thought of any such thyng, before he chaunced to be acquainted with the sayde Pilot, who founde those landes by fortune, accordyng to the saying of Plinie, *Quod ars docere non potuit, casus inuenit.* That is, That [illegible] teache, chaunce founde. Albeit, [illegible] opinion [illegible] that God of his sing[illegible] prouidence and infinite goodnesse, at the length with eyes [illegible] compassion as it were lookyng downe from heauen vppon the sonnes of Adam, so long kept vnder Sathans captiuitie, intended euen then (for causes [illegible] knowen) to rayse those wyndes of [illegible] Carauell (herein most lyke vnto the shyppe of [illegible], wherby the remnante of the [illegible] world was saued, as by this Carauel this newe worlde receyued the fyrst hope of theyr saluation) was dryuen to these landes. But we wyll now declare what great thynges folowed of this small begynnyng, and howe *Colon* [illegible] this matter, reuealed vnto hym not without Gods prouidence.

VVhat labour and trauayle Colon tooke in attempting his fyrst voyage to the Indies.

After the death of the Pilot & maryners of the Spanyshe Carauell that discouered ye Indies, *Christopher Colon* purposed to seeke the same. But in howe muche more he desyred this, the lesse was his power to accomplyshe his desyre. For, besyde that of hym selfe he was not able to furnyshe one shyppe, he lacked also the fauoure of a kyng, vnder whose [illegible]

And seyng the kyng of Portugale occupied in the conquest of Africa, and the Nauigations of the East, whiche were then fyrst attempted, the kyng of Castyle lykewyse no lesse busyed in the warres of *Granada*, he sent to his brother *Bartholomewe Colon* (who was also pryuie to this secrete) to practise with the kyng of Englande (Henry the seuenth) beyng very ryche and without warres, promisyng to bryng hym great ryches in short tyme, if he woulde shewe hym fauour, and furnyshe hym with shyps to discouer the newe Indies, whereof he had certayne knowledge. But neyther here beyng able to bryng his sute to passe, he caused the matter to be moued to the kyng of Portugale *Don Alonso*, the fyfth of that name: at whose handes he founde neither fauour nor mony, forasmuch as the Licenciat *Calzadilla* the bishop of *Viseo*, and one master *Rodrigo*, men of credite in the science of Cosmographie, withstoode hym, and contended that there neither was nor coulde any golde or other ryches be founde in the west, as *Colon* affirmed. By reason whereof he was very sad and pensiue: but yet was not discouraged, or despaired of the hope of his good aduenture, which he afterwarde founde. This doone, he tooke shyppyng at *Lisburne*, and came to *Palos* of *Moguer*, where he communed with *Martin Alonso Pinzon*, an expert Pilot, who offered hym selfe vnto hym. After this, disclosyng the whole secretes of his mynd to *Iohn Perez* of *Marchena* (a fryer of the order of saint Frances in *Rabida*, & well learned in Cosmographie) and declaryng vnto hym howe by folowyng the course of the Sunne by a temperate voyage, ryche and great landes myght be founde: the fryer greatly commended his interpryse, and gaue him counsayle to breake the matter to the Duke of *Medina Sidonia*, *Don Enrique* of *Guzman*, a great lorde, and very ryche: and also to *Don Luis* of *Cerda*, the Duke of *Medina Celi*, who at that time had great prouision of shyps wel furnyshed in his hauen of *Santa Maria*. But whereas both these Dukes tooke the matter for a dreame, and as a thyng deuised of an Italian deceyuer, who (as they thought) had before with lyke pretence deluded the kynges of Englande and Portugale, the fryer gaue hym courage to go to the courte of the Catholyke princes *Don Ferdinando*, and lady *Isabell* princes of Castyle, affyrmyng that they woulde be ioyful of suche newes: And for his better furtherance herein, wrote

Kyng Henry the seuenth.

Barnarde knewe not all thynges.

mence by hym to fryer *Ferdinando of Talavera* the queenes confessor. *Christopher Colon* therefore, repayred to the courte of the Catholyke princes, in the yeere .1486. and delyvered unto theyr handes the petition of his request, as concernyng the discoveryng of the new Indies. But they beyng more carefull, and applyinge al theyr mynde howe they myght dryve the Moores out of the kyngdome of *Granada*, whiche greate enterpryse they had alredy taken in hande, dyd lyttle or nothyng esteeme the matter. But *Colon* not thus discouraged, founde the meanes to declare his sute to suche as had sometymes private communication with the kyng. Yet because he was a straunger, and went but in simple apparell, nor otherwyse credited then by the letter of a gray frier, they beleeved hym not, neyther gave eare to his woordes, whereby he was greatly tormented in his imagination. Onely *Alonso of Quintanilia*, the kynges chiefe auditour, gave hym meate and drynke at his owne charges, and hearde gladly such thynges as he declared of the landes not then founde: desyryng hym in the meane tyme to be content with that poore entertaynment, and not to despayre of his enterpryse: puttyng hym also in good comforte that he shoulde, at one tyme or other, come to the speache of the Catholyke princes. And thus shortly after, by the meanes of *Alonso of Quintanilia*, *Colon* was brought to the presence and audience of the Cardinall *Don Pero Gonzales* of *Mendoza*, archbishop of *Toledo*, a man of great revenues and authoritie with the kyng and queene, who brought hym before them, after that he well perceived and examined his intent. And by this meanes was his sute hearde of the Catholyke princes, who also redde the booke of his memorials whiche he presented unto them. And although at the fyrst they tooke it for vayne and false that he promysed, neverthelesse they put hym in good hope that he shoulde be well dispatched when they had fynyshed the warres of *Granada* whiche they had nowe in hande. With which answere, *Colon* began to revyve his spirites, with hope to be better esteemed, and more favorably to be hearde among the gentelmen & noble men of the courte, who before tooke hym onely for a craftie felowe and deceyver: and was nothyng dismayde or discouraged whensoever he debated the matter with them, although many iudged hym phantasticall, as is the maner of ignorant men, to cal all

All

The conquest of Granada.

The archbishop of Toledo.

suche as attempt any thyng beyonde theyr reache, and the compasse of theyr knowledge, thynkyng the worlde to be no bygger then the regions wherein they are brought up and bred. But to returne to *Colon*. So hotte and urgente was the siege of *Granada*, that they presently graunted hym his demaunde to seeke the newe landes, and to brynge from thence golde, syluer, pearles, precious stones, spices, and suche other ryche thynges. They gave hym also the tenth part of all the reuenues and customes due unto the kyng, of all such landes as he shoulde discouer, not doyng preiudice in any thyng to the kyng of Portugale. The particulars of this agreement were made in the towne called *Sancta Fe*: and the priuiledge of the rewarde in *Granada* the .xxx. daye of Apryll, the same yeare that the citie was woonne. And whereas the sayde Catholyke princes had not mony presently to dispatch *Colon, Luis* of .S. *Angel*, the kynges secretary of accomptes, lent them syxe *Quentes* of *Maraz*, whiche in a grosse summe make .xvi. thousande ducades.

In the scutcheon of armes geuen to *Columbus* by *Don Ferdinando* and queene *Isabella*, these verses were written.

Por Castella, y por Leon. Nueuo mondo hallo Colon.

For *Castile* and for *Leon*.

A newe worlde founde was by *Colon*.

VVhy they were called Indies.

The colour of the East Indians.

SOme thynke that the people of the newe world were called Indians, bycause they are of the colour of the east Indians. And although (as it semmeth to me) they dyffer much in colour and fashions, yet is it true that of India they were called Indians. India is properly called that great prouince of Asia, in the whiche great Alexander kepte his warres, and was so named of the ryuer *Indus*: and is diuided into many kyngdomes confinyng with the same. From this great India (called the East India) came great companyes of men, as wryteth *Herodotus*, and inhabited that part of Ethiopia that lyeth betweene the sea *Bermeia* (otherwyse called the red sea, or ẏ goulfe of *Arabia*) and the ryuer of *Nilus*: all whiche regions that great Christian prince *Prester Iohn* doth nowe possesse. The said Indians [illegible] the customes and

maners

[illegible] of that lande, and called it India: by reason whereof, Ethiopia also hath of long tyme ben called India. And hereupon came it that *Aristotle, Seneca*, and certayne other olde authours sayd, that India was not farre from Spayne. After this also, of later dayes our west India was so called, of the sayde India of *Prester Iohn* where the Portugales had theyr trade: For the pilot of the Carauell that was fyrst dryuen by forcible wynde to an unknowen lande in the west Ocean, called the same India, because the Portugales so called such landes as they had lately discouered eastward. *Christopher Colon* also, after the sayd Pilot, called the west landes by the same name: Albeit some that take *Colonus* for an expert Cosmographer, thynke that he so named them of the East India, as to be the furthest and unknowen ende thereof, reachyng into the West, under the other hemisphere or halfe globe of the earth beneath us: affirming that when he fyrste attempted to discouer the Indies, he went chiefly to seeke the ryche Ilande of *Cipango*, whiche falleth on the part of great *China* or *Cathay*, as wryteth *Marcus Paulus Venetus*, and other. And that he shoulde sooner come thyther by folowyng the course of the Sunne Westward, then agaynst the same.

Of the colour of the Indians.

One of the marueylous thynges ye God useth in the composition of man, is colour: whiche doubtlesse can not be consydered without great admiration, in holdyng one to be whyte, and an other blacke, beyng colours utterly contrary: some lykewyse to be yealowe, whiche is betweene blacke and white: and other of other colours, as it were of diuers liueries. And as these colours are to be marueyled at, euen so is it to be considered, howe they dyffer one from an other, as it were by degrees, forasmuch as some men are whyte after dyuers sortes of whitnes, yelowe after diuers maners of yelow, [illegible] after dyuers sortes of blacknes: & how from white they go to yelow by discolouring to browne & red, and to blacke by ashe colour, & [illegible] somwhat lighter then blacke, & tawny like unto the [illegible] [illegible] whiche are altogether [illegible] lyke vnto sodde Quinses, or of the colour of Chestnuttes or Olyues, which colour is to them naturall: and not by theyr goyng naked, as many haue thought: albeit theyr nakednesse haue somewhat helped therevnto. Therefore in lyke maner, and with suche diuersitie as men are commonly whyte in Europe, and blacke in Affrike, euen with lyke varietie are they tawney in these Indies, with diuers degrees diuersly inclinyng more or lesse to blacke or whyte. No lesse marueyle is it to consider, that men are white in Siuile, and blacke at the cape of *Buena Speranza*, and of Chestnut colour at the ryuer of *Plata*, being all in equall degrees from the Equinoctiall lyne. Lykewyse, that the men of Affrike and Asia, that lyue vnder the burnt line (called *Zona Torrida*) are blacke: and not they that lyue beneath, or on this syde the same lyne, as in *Mexico, Iucatan, Quauhtema, Lian, Nicaragua, Panama, Santo Domingo, Paria, Cape Sainct Augustine, Lima, Quito*, and other landes of *Peru*, which touche in the same Equinoctiall. For in all the tracte of these coastes, certayne blacke men were founde only in *Quarequa*, when *Vascbus Nunnez* of *Balboa* discouered the sea of *Sur*. By reason whereof it may seeme, that such varietie of colours proceedeth of man, and not of the earth: which may wel be, although we be al borne of Adam & Eue, & know not the cause why God hath so ordeyned it, otherwise then to consider that his diuine maiestie hath done this, as infinite other, to declare his omnipotencie and wisedome, in such diuersities of colours, as appeare not only in the nature of man, but the like also in beastes, byrdes, and floures, where diuers and contrary colours are seene in one litle feather, or the leaues growyng out of one litle stalke.

Gods wysedome & power is seene in his workes.

An other thing is also greatly to be noted, as touching these Indians: and this is, that their heare is not curld, as is the Moores and Ethiopians that inhabite the same clime: neyther are they balde, excepte very seldome, and that but litle. All whiche thynges may gyue further occasions to Philosophers to searche the secretes of nature, and complexions of men, with the nouelties of the newe worlde.

A most auncient testimonie of the VVest Indies, by the writing of the diuine Philosopher Plato.

PLato in his famous and diuine Dialogue, named *Timeus*, where he entreateth of the vniuersall nature and frame of the whole worlde, taketh for his principle the moste auncient hystorie of an Ilande, in tyme of great antiquitie, named *Athlantides*, makyng also mention of the kyng, people, and inhabitantes of the same: and that they kept warre agaynst the *Atheniens*, and were ouercome of them. *Plato* also there inducing the sayde hystorie to be rehearsed by one named *Critia*, who affirmed that he had often hearde it of his Uncle, who was in the tyme of *Solon*, one of the seuen sages of the Grekes. This *Critia* declared, that when *Solon* went into Egypt to a certayne citie named *Saim*, situate vpon the riuer of *Nilus*, where the diuision and recurryng of the riuer, maketh the Ilande *Delta*, he there spake with certayne learned priestes, very skylful in knowledge of antiquities of many worldes past. Insomuch that they made mention of manye thinges that were before the flood of Noe, or *Deucalion*, and also before the vniuersal conflagration or burning of the worlde in the tyme of *Phaeton*, forasmuche as the warres betweene the people of the sayde Ilande of *Athlantides* and the *Atheniens*, was long before the general flood, and the conflagration aforesayde. *Plato* induceth the priest, speaking to *Solon* in maner as foloweth.

Thinges most marueylous and true (O *Solon*) remayne in auncient writynges and memorie of our predecessours, and olde ages long before our tymes. But aboue all thynges, one exceedeth al admiration for the greatnesse and singularitie thereof, whiche is this: It is in our recordes of moste antiquities, that in times past your citie of *Athens* hath oftentymes kepte warres agaynst an innumerable multitude of nations whiche came from the sea *Athlantike*, in maner into al *Europe* and *Asia*: whereas nowe appeareth no suche nation, forasmuche as the sayde sea is nowe al ouer nauigable: And yet at that tyme it in the mouth, and as it were in the entrie (where you place the Columnes of Hercules) an Ilande whiche was sayd to be much greater then al *Africa* and *Asia*, and that from thence was passage to many other Ilandes neare thereabout, and from the sayde Ilandes to the continent or fyrme lande, whiche was right ouer agaynst it neare vnto the sea: Yet, that within the mouth, there was a litle gulfe with a porte: the deepe sea without, was the true sea, and the lande without was the true continent. This Ilande was named *Athlantides*, and in it was a kyng of marueylous great power and myght, who had the dominion of the sayde Ilande, and many other, and also a great part of the continent lande whereof we haue spoken, and muche more towarde our partes also, forasmuche as they were dominatours of the thyrde part of the worlde conteynyng *Africa*, *Egypt*, and *Europe*, euen vnto the sea *Tirrhenum*. The power therefore of them beyng then so great, they came to inuade both your countrey and ours, and all other that are within the Columnes of Hercules. Then (*O Solon*) the vertue of your citie shewed it selfe famous in magnanimitie and feates of armes, with the assemblance of the other Grecians, in resystyng theyr great power, vntyl you had driuen them out of our lands, and restored vs to our libertie. But shortly after that this enterprise was atchiued, befel a marueylous great earthquake, and exundation or ouerflowing of the sea, which continued for the space of one day and nyght: In the whiche the earth opened it selfe, and inglutted all those valiant and warlike men, and the sayde Ilande *Athlantides* sunke into the bottome of the sea, whiche was the occasion that neuer from that tyme forwarde, any shyp coulde sayle that way, by reason of the great mudde and slyme whiche remayned of the drowned Ilande.

This is the summe of those thynges whiche olde *Critia* sayde he had vnderstoode of *Solon*. And certaynely these wordes of *Plato* of the said Iland, haue caused great contention among many great Philosophers, which haue written commentaries vpon the sayde Dialogue of *Timeus* composed by *Plato*: Insomuche that the same in those dayes being vtterly vnknowen, many haue taken this narration of *Solon* for an allegorical fable, and haue interpreted the same in diuers senses and meaninges. But it may nowe well appeare the true meanyng hereof to be this: that *Plato* intendyng to wryte of the uniuersall frame of the worlde, the whiche he knewe to be made an habitation for the diuine best man, and also beholdyng therin the great ornament and beautie of the heauen and starres, whereby man myght knowe his God and creatour, it myght seeme to hym a thyng to farre from reason, that only two partes thereof shoulde be inhabited, and the other part desolate and depriued of men: and that the Sunne and starres might seeme to shewe theyr lyght only halfe theyr course without profite, shining only upon the sea and desolate places, destitute of man and other liuing creatures. And therefore *Plato* had in great admiration the hystorie of the sayde Egyptian priest, makyng mention of an other part of the worlde besyde *Asia, Europa,* and *Africa,* and thought it worthy to be rehearsed in the beginning of his diuine Dialogue aforesayde. We ought therefore certainely to thinke our selues most bounde unto God, that in these our tymes it hath pleased hym to reueale and discouer this secrete in the fyndyng of this newe worlde, whereby we are certaynely assured, that under our Pole starre, and under the *Equinoctial* line, are most goodlye and ample regions, as well and commodiously inhabited, as are other partes of the worlde best knowen unto us.

The testimonie of the Poet *Seneca* in his Tragedie *De Medea,* where by the spirite of Poetical furie, he sayth.

Venient annis
Secula seris, quibus Oceanus
Vincula rerum laxet, et ingens
Pateat tellus, Typhisque nouos
Detegat Orbes,
Nec sit terris, ultima Thyle.

Whiche may be thus Englished.

When *Typhis* nauigation newe worldes shal fynde out,
Then shal not Thyle for last be left out.
For then shal the Ocean dissolue his large bandes,
And shewe foorth newe worldes, regions, and landes.

Thyle is ...ilande.

To the moste noble prince and catholike kynge, Charles, Peter Martyr of Angleria wisheth perpetual felicitie.

The largenesse of the Ocean unknowen to this day.

The diuine prouidence, from the time that he fyrst created the worlde, hath reserued vnto this day the knowledge of the great and large Ocean sea: In the whiche tyme he hath opened the same, chiefly vnto you (moste mightie Prince) by the good fourtune and happie successe of your grandfather by your mother syde. The same prouidence (I knowe not by what destenie) hath brought me out of my natiue countrey of Milane, and out of the citie of Rome (where I continued almost .x. yeeres) into Spaine, that I myght particularlye collecte these marueilous and newe thinges, which shoulde otherwyse perhappes haue lien drowned in the whirlepoole of obliuion, forasmuche as the Spanyardes (men worthy great commendation) had only care to the generall inuentions of these thinges. Notwithstanding, I do not chalenge vnto me only, the thankes of the trauaile bestowed herein, whereas the chiefe rewarde therof is due to Ascanius, vicount Cardinal, who perceauyng that I was wyllyng to departe out of the citie to be present at the warres of *Granatum*, dissuaded me from my purpose: But seeing that I was fully resolued to departe, exhorted & required me to write vnto him suche newes as were famous in Spaine, & worthy to be noted. I toke therfore my iourney into Spayne, chiefely for the desyre I had to see the expedition whiche was prepared agaynst the enimies of the fayth, forasmuche as in Italye, by reason of the dissention among the Princes, I [illegible]

Cardinal Ascanius.

The warres at Granatum agaynst the Moores.

of thynges. I was therefore presente at the warres, from whence I wrytte to Cardinal Ascanius, and by sundry epistles certifyed hym of such thinges as I thought most woorthye to be put in memorie. But when I perceiued that his fortune was turned from a naturall mother to a stepdame, I ceassed from wrytyng. Yet after I sawe, that by thouerthrowe of the enimies of our fayth, Spayne was pourged of the Moores, as of an euil weede plucked vp by the rootes, lest I shoulde bestowe my slippery yeares in vnprofitable idlenesse, I was mynded to returne to Italie. But the singuler benignitie of both the Catholyke kyng and queene nowe departed, and theyr large promises towarde me vpon my returne from my legacie of Babylon, deteyned me from my purpose. Yet doth it not repent me that I drewe backe my foote, aswel for that I see in no other place of the worlde at this tyme the lyke woorthy thinges to be done: as also that in maner throughout all Italie, by reason of the discorde of Christian Princes, I perceiued all thynges to runne headlong into ruine, the countreys to be destroyed and made fatte with humane blood, the cities sacked, virgins and matrones with theyr goods and possessions caried away as captiues, and miserable innocentes without offence to be slayne vnarmed within theyr owne houses. Of the whiche calamities, I dyd not onely heare the lamentable outcryes, but dyd also feele the same: For euen the blood of myne owne kinsfolkes and frendes, was not free from that crueltie. As I was therefore musyng with my selfe of these thynges, the Cardinal of Arragone, after that he had seene the two fyrst bookes of my Decades wrytten to Ascanius, required me in the name of kyng Frederike his vncle, to put foorth the other eyght epistle bookes. In the meane tyme also, whyle I was voyde of al care as touching the matters of the Ocean, the Apostolicall messengers of the byshop of Rome, Leo the tenth (by whose holsome counsayle and auctoritie we trust the calamities of Italy shalbe fynished) raysed me as it were from sleepe, & encoraged me to procede as I had begun. To his holynesse I wrytte two Decades, comprysed in shorte bookes, after the maner of epistles, and added them to the fyrst, which was printed without mine aduise, as shal further appeare by the preface folowyng. But nowe I returne to [illegible]

Italy disquieted with warres.

The sequeles of warre.

Kyng Frederike.

noble Prince) from whom I haue somwhat digressed. Therfore wheras your grandfather by your mothers side, haue subdued al Spaine vnder your dominion, except only one corner of the same, and haue also lefte you the kingdome of Naples, with the fruteful Ilands of our seas, it is surely a great thing and worthy to be noted in our cronacles. But not offendyng the reuerence due to our predecessours, whatsoeuer from the begynnyng of the worlde hath been doone or wrytten to this day, to my iudgement seemeth but lyttle, yf we consyder what newe landes and countreys, what newe seas, what sundry nations and toungеs, what golde mynes, what treasuries of perles they haue lefte vnto your hyghnesse, besyde other reuenues. The whiche, what they are, and howe greate, these three Decades shall declare. Come therfore most noble Prince elected of God, and enioye that hyghe estate of thinges not yet vnderstode to men. We offer vnto you the *Equinoctiall* lyne hytherto vnknowen, and burnte by the furious heate of the sonne, and vnhabitable after the opinion of the olde wryters, a fewe excepted: but nowe founde to be most replenished with people, faire, fruitefull, and most fortunate, with a thousande Ilandes crowned with golde and bewtifull pearles, besydes that greate portion of earth supposed to be parte of the firme lande, excedyng in quantitie three Europes. Come therfore and embrase this newe worlde, and suffer vs no longer to consume in desyre of your presence. From hence, from hence I say (most noble young Prince) shal instrumentes be prepared for you, wherby al the worlde shalbe vnder your obeysance. And thus I byd your maiestie farewell: to whose taste if I shal perceaue the frutes of this my tyllage to be delectable, I wyll heareafter do my endeuoure that you may receaue the same more abundantly. From Madrid, the day before the Calendes of October, In the yere of Christ M.D.XVI.

Spayne subdued from the Moores.
The kyngdome of Naples.
The temperatenesse of the Equinoctiall vnknowen to the olde wryters.
Continent or firme lande as bygge as three Europes.
Riches are the instruments of conquestes.

The fyrst Booke of the Decades of the Ocean, written by Peter Martyr of Angleria Milenoes, counsaylour to the king of Spayne, and Protonotarie Apostolicall to *Ascanius Sphorcia*, Vicount Cardinal, &c.

The reverende and thankful antiquitie was accustomed to esteeme those men as gods, by whose industrie and magnanimitie such landes and regions were discouered, as were unknowen to theyr predecessours. But unto us, hauyng only one God, whom we honour in triplicitie of person, this resteth, that albeit we do not worship that kinde of men with diuine honour, yet do we reuerence them, and worthyly maruelye at theyr noble actes and enterpryses. Unto kynges and princes we geue due obeysaunce, by whose gouernance and furtherance they haue ben aided to perfourme their attempts: we commend both, and for theyr iust desertes worthyly extol them. Wherefore, as concerning the Ilandes of the west Ocean, lately discouered, and of the auctours of the same (whiche thyng you desyre by your letters to knowe) I wyl begyn at the fyrst aucthour thereof, lest I be iniurious to any man. Take it therefore as foloweth. *The rewardes of vertue.* *The Ilandes of the west Ocean.*

Christophorus Colonus (otherwyse called *Columbus*) a gentleman of Italie, borne in the citie of *Genua*, perswaded Fernando and Elizabeth, catholike prynces, that he doubted not to fynde certayne Ilandes of *India*, nere unto our Ocean sea, if they woulde furnyshe hym with shyppes and other thynges apparteynyng: affyrmyng that therby not onely the Christian religion myght be enlarged, but Spayne also enryched by the great plentie of golde, pearles, precious stones, and spices, whiche myght be founde there. At the length three shyppes were appoynted hym at the kinges charges: of the whiche one was a great caracte with deckes, and the other two were lyght [illegible] shyppes without deckes, whiche the [illegible] call [illegible]. [illegible] departed from the [illegible] *Christophorus Colonus.* *India.*

[illegible]

The fyrst voyage of Colonus

calendes of September, in the yeere of Christe. 1492. and set forwarde on his viage, being accompanied with CC.xx. Spanyardes. The fortunate Ilandes (as manye thynke them to be, whiche the Spaniardes call *Canarie*, found but of late dayes) are distaunte from the Ilandes of *Gades* a thousande and two hundreth myles, accordyng to theyr accomptes, for they say they are distant three hundred leagues: whereas suche as are expert sea men, affirme that euery league conteineth foure miles, after theyr supputations. These Ilandes were called fortunate, for the temperate ayre whiche is in them. For neyther the coldnesse of wynter is sharpe vnto them, nor the heate of sommer intollerable. Yet some men are of opinion, that those were in olde tyme called the fortunate Ilandes, whiche the Portugales call *Capo Verde*. *Colonus* therfore sayled fyrst to the Ilandes of *Canariæ*, to the intente there to refreshe his shyppes with freshe water and fuell, before he committed hym selfe to this so laborous a viage. And because I haue heare made mention of the Ilandes of *Canariæ*, it shal not be muche from my purpose, to declare howe of vnknowen they became knowen, and of sauage and wilde, better manured: For by the long course of many yeeres, they were forgotten, and remayned as vnknowen.

The Ilandes of Canarie. Gades, or Calsnals.

A league, what it conteyneth by sea.

The fortunate Ilandes.

Capo Verde.

These seuen Ilandes (therefore) called the *Canaries*, were founde by chaunce by a frenche man, called *Betanchor*, by the permission of queene Katharine, protectrixe of king Iohn her sonne, while he was yet in his nonage, about the yeere of Christe. M.CCCC.V. This *Betanchor* inuaded two of these Ilandes called *Lancelotus* and *Fortisuentura*, which he inhabited & brought to better culture. He being dead, his sonne and heire solde bothe the sayde Ilandes to certayne Spaniardes.

The .vii. Ilandes of Canarie. Betanchor a Frenche man subdued the Ilandes of Canarie. &c.

After this, *Farnandus Peraria* and his wyfe, inuaded *Ferrea* and *Gomera*. The other three were subdued in our time. *Grancanaria*, by *Petrus de Vera*, citizen of the noble citie of *Xericium*, and Michael of *Moxica*, *Palma* and *Tenerifen*, by *Alphonsus Lugo*, at the kings charges. *Gomera* and *Ferrea* were easily subdued: But the matter went harde with *Alphonsus Lugo*. For that naked and wylde nation, fyghtyng only with stones and clubbes, droue his armie to flight at the first assaulte, and slue about foure hundreth of his men: But at the length he ouercame them. And thus all the

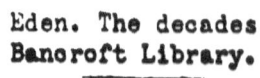

Alphonsus Lugo.

the Ilandes of *Canaria* were added to the dominion of Spayne. From these Ilandes *Colonus* directyng his voyage towarde the west, folowyng the falling of the sunne, but declining somewhat towarde the left hande, sayled on forwarde .xxxiii. dayes continually, hauyng only the fruition of the heauen and the water. Then the Spanyardes whiche were accompanyed with hym, began fyrst to murmure secretely among them selues, and shortly after with wordes of reproche spake euil of *Colonus* theyr gouernour, and consulted with them selues, eyther to rydde hym out of the way, or els to cast hym into the sea: ragyng that they were deceyued of a stranger, an outlandyshe man, a Ligurian, a Genues, and brought into suche daungerous places, that they might neuer returne agayne. And after .xxxiii. dayes were past, they furiously cryed out against him, and threatned him that he shoulde passe no further. But he euer with gentle wordes and large promises, appeased their furie, and prolonged day after day, some tyme desyryng them to beare with hym yet a whyle, and some time putting them in remembraunce that yf they shoulde attempt any thing against him, or otherwyse disobey hym, it would be reputed for treason. Thus after a fewe dayes, with chearefull hartes they espied the lande long looked for. In this fyrst nauigation, he discouered .vi. ilandes, wherof two were exceedyng great: Of whiche, the one he called *Hispaniola*, and the other *Iohanna*. But at that tyme he knewe not perfectly that *Iohanna* (otherwyse called *Cuba*) was an ilande. As they coasted along by the shore of certayne of these ilandes, they hearde Nyghtyngales syng in the thycke wooddes in the moneth of Nouember. They founde also great ryuers of freshe water, and naturall hauens, of capacitie to harbour great nauies of shippes. Saylyng by the coastes of *Iohanna*, from the north poynt to the west, he rode litle lesse then eight hundred miles (for they cal it a hundred and fourescore leagues) supposing that it had ben the continent or fyrme lande, because he coulde neither fynde the landes ende, nor any token of the ende, as farre as he could iudge with his eye: wherfore he determined to turne backe agayne, beyng partly therto [illegible] by the roughnesse of the sea, for the sea bankes of the [illegible] *Iohanna*, by [illegible] [illegible] [illegible], [illegible] [illegible] so muche towarde the north, that the [illegible]

Colonus men rebel agaynst hym.

Fayre wordes and promises.

Hispaniola.
Iohanna.

Nightingales syng in Nouember.

roughly tossed the shyps by reason of the winter. Turning therfore the stemmes of his shyppes towarde the East, he affyrmed that he had found the ilande of *Ophir*, whither Solomons shippes sayled for golde. But the discription of the Cosmographers well considered, it seemeth that both these, and the other ilandes adioynyng, are the ilands of *Antilia*. This ilande he called *Hispaniola*, on whose north syde as he approched neare to the lande, the keele or bottome of the biggest vessell ranne vpon a blynde rocke couered with water, and claue in sunder: but the playnenesse of the rocke was a helpe to them that they were not drowned. Makyng haste therfore with the other two shyps to helpe them, they brought awaye al the men without hurte. Here comming fyrst a land, they sawe certayne men of the Ilande, who perceiuyng an vnknowen nation comming toward them, flocked togeather, and ranne al into the thycke woods, as it had ben hares coursed with grehoundes. Our men pursuing them, tooke onely one woman, whom they brought to the ships: where fylling her with meate and wyne, and appareling her, they let her depart to her companye. Shortly after a greate multitude of them came runnyng to the shore to behold this newe nation, whom they thought to haue discended from heauen. They cast them selues by heapes into the sea, & came swimming to the shyppes, bryngyng gold with them, whiche they chaunged with our men for earthen pottes, drinking glasses, poyntes, pinnes, hawkes bels, looking glasses, & such other trifles. Thus growing to further familiaritie, our men were honorably entertained of the king of that part of the iland, whose name was *Guaccanarilus*: for it hath many kyngs, as when *Eneas* arriued in Italy, he found *Latium* diuided into many kingdoms and prouinces, as *Latium, Mezentium, Turnum*, and *Tarchontem*, which were separated with narowe boundes, as shal more largly appeare hereafter. At the euen tide about the falling of the sonne, when our men went to prayer, and kneeled on their knees after the maner of ye Christians, they dyd the lyke also. And after what maner so euer they sawe them pray to the crosse, they folowed them in al poyntes as wel as they coulde. They shewed much humanitie towards our men, and helped them with their lyghters or smal boates (which they cal *Canoas*) to vnlade their broken shyppe.

The Ilande of Ophir.

The Ilandes of Antilia.

A shypwracke.

The people of the Ilande.

Naked people.

Expert swymmers.

Gold for earth and glasse.

Many kynges.

Religious and humane people.

Canoas.

shyppe, and that with suche celeritie and cherefulnesse, that no frende for frende, or kynseman for kynseman, in such case moued with pitie, coulde do more. Theyr boates are made only of one tree, made holowe with a certaine sharpe stone (for they haue no yron) and are very long and narowe. Many affirme that they haue seene some of them with fortie ores. The wilde and myschevous people called *Canibales*, or *Caribes*, whiche were accustomed to eate mans fleshe (& called of the olde writers, *Anthropophagi*) molest them exceedyngly, inuading their countrey, takyng them captiue, kyllyng & eatyng them. As our men sayled to the ilandes of these meke and humane people, they left the ilands of the *Canibales*, in maner in the middest of theyr viage toward the south. They complayned that theyr ilands were no lesse vexed with the incursions of these manhuntyng *Canibales* when they go forth a rouyng to seeke theyr pray, then are other tame beastes of Lions and Tigers. Such chyldren as they take, they geld to make them fat, as we do cocke chickens and young hogges, and eate them when they are wel fedde: of suche as they eate, they fyrst eate the intralles and extreme partes, as handes, feete, armes, necke, and head. The other most fleshye partes, they pouder for store, as we do pestels of porke, and gammondes of bakon: yet do they absteyne from eatyng of women, and counte it vyle. Therfore suche young women as they take, they kepe for increase, as we do hennes to leye egges: the olde women, they make theyr drudges. They of the ilandes (which we may nowe cal ours) bothe the men and ye women, when they perceiue the *Canibales* commyng, haue none other shyft but onely to flee: for although they vse very sharpe arrowes made of reedes, yet are they of small force to represse ye furie of the *Canibales*: for euen they them selues confesse, that ten of the *Canibales* are able to ouercome a hundred of them if they encountre with them. Theyr meate is a certayne roote, which they cal *Ages*, muche lyke a nauewe roote in fourme and greatnesse, but of sweete tast, much lyke a greene chestnutte. They haue also an other kynde of rootes, which they call *Iucca*, wherof they make bread in lyke maner. They vse *Ages* more often rosted or sodden, then to make bread thereof. But they neuer eate *Iucca*, except it be first sliced and pressed (for it is full of lycoure) and then baked or sodden. But [illegible]

Monoxyla. They haue no iron.

Canibales, or Caribes. Anthropophagi.

The crueltie of the Canibales.

Ages. Rootes in the steede of meate. Iucca. Bread of rootes.

An hearbe of strange nature. marueyled at, that the iuice of this roote is a poyson as strong as *Aconitum*, so that if it be drunke, it causeth present death, and yet the bread made of the masse thereof, is of good taste and holsome, as they all haue proued. They make also another kynde of bread of a certayne pulse, called *Panicum*, muche like vnto wheate, whereof is great plentie in the Dukedome of Millane, Spayne, and *Granatum*. But that of this Countrey is longer by a spanne, somewhat sharpe towarde the ende, and as bygge as a mans arme in ye brawne: the graynes whereof are set in a maruelous order, & are in fourme somewhat lyke a Pease. Whyle they be soure and vnripe, they are whyte, but when they are ripe, they be very blacke, when they are broken, they be whiter then snowe: this kynde of grayne they call *Maizium*. (Maizium.) Golde is of some estimation among them: for some of them hang certayne small peeces thereof at theyr eares and nosethrylles. (Golde in estimation.) A litle beyonde this place, our men went a lande for freshe water, where they chaunced vpon a riuer, whose sande was myxed with muche golde. (Golde in the sandes of riuers.) They founde there no kindes of foure footed beastes, except three kindes of litle conies. These ilandes also nouryshe serpentes, but suche as are without hurt. (Serpentes without venime.) Likewise wilde geese, turtle doues, and duckes, muche greater then ours, and as white as swannes, with heades of purple colour. (Turtle doues. Duckes.) Also Popiniayes, of the whiche some are greene, some yelowe, & some lyke them of *India*, with yelowe rynges about theyr neckes, as Plinie describeth them. (Popiniayes. Plini.) Of these they brought fourtie with them, of most lyuely and dilectable colours, hauyng theyr feathers enterminggled with greene, yelowe, and purple, whiche varietie delyghteth the sense not a litle. Thus muche thought I good to speake of Popiniayes (ryght noble prince) specially to this intent, that albeit the opinion of *Christophorus Colonus* (who affyrmeth these ilandes to be part of *India*) doth not in all poyntes agree with the iudgement of auncient wryters as touchyng the bygnesse of the Sphere and compasse of the Globe, as concernyng the nauigable portion of the same being vnder vs, yet the Popiniayes and many other thynges brought from thence, doo declare that these Ilandes sauour somewhat of *India*, eyther beyng neare vnto it, or els of the same nature: forasmuche as *Aristotle* also, about the ende of his booke *de Cælo & Mundo*, and likewyse *Seneca*, (These Ilandes are part of India. The Indians are Antipodes to the Spaniardes. Aristotle. Seneca.)

with

with diuers other authours not ignoraunt in Cosmographie, do affirme that *India* is no long tracte by sea, distant from Spaine by the west Ocean, for the soyle of these ilandes bryngeth foorth Mastyx, Aloes, and sundry other sweete gummes and spyces, as doth *India*, Cotton also of the Gossampine tree, as in *India* in the countrey of the people called Seres.

India not farre from Spayne. Mastyx. Aloe. Gossampine cotton or bombase. Seres.

The languages of all the nations of these ilandes, may well be wrytten with our Latine letters. For they call heauen *Turei*. A house *Boa*. Golde *Cauni*. A good man, *Taino*. Nothing, *Mayani*. Al other wordes of theyr language, they pronounce as plainly as we do the Latine tongue. In these ilandes they founde no trees knowen vnto them, but Pine apple trees, and Date trees, and those of marueylous heyght, and exceedyng harde, by reason of the great moystnesse and fatnesse of the grounde, with continual and temperate heate of the sunne, whiche endureth so al the whole yere. They playnely affirme the ilande of *Hispaniola* to be the moste fruitefull lande that the heauen compasseth about, as shall more largely appeare hereafter in the particuler description of the same, which we entende to set foorth when we shalbe better instructed. Thus makyng a league of frendshyp with the king, and leauing with hym .xxxviii. men to searche the ilande, he departed to Spayne, takyng with hym tenne of the inhabitauntes to learne the Spanishe tongue, to the intent to vse them afterward for interpretours. *Colonus* therfore at his returne was honourably receiued of the kyng and queene, who caused hym to syt in theyr presence, whiche is a token of great loue and honour among the Spanyardes. He was also made Admiral of the Ocean, and his brother gouernour of the ilande.

The language of these Indians.

Trees & fruites vnknowē to vs.

Fat and moyst grounde. Heate continual & temperate. The fruitefulnesse of Hispaniola.

Toward the seconde voyage he was furnished with .xvii. ships, wherof three were great caractes of a thousande tunne. xii. were of that sort which the Spaniardes cal *Carauelas*, without deckes, and two other of the same sorte somewhat bygger, and more apt to beare deckes, by reason of the greatnesse of theyr mastes. He had also a thousande and two hundred armed footemen well appoynted: among which were many artificers, as smythes, Carpenters, myners, and suche other: certayne horsmen also, well armed: lykewyse mares, sheepe, heyghfers, and suche other of bothe kyndes for encrease: lykewise al kinde of pulse, or grayne,

The seconde voyage of Colonus.

and

Corne & seedes to sowe.

and corne, as wheate, barley, rye, beanes, and pease, and suche other, aswel for foode as to sowe: besyde vines, plantes, and seedes, of suche trees, fruites, and hearbes, as those countreyes lacke, and (not to be forgotten) sundry kyndes of artyllerie and iron tooles, as bowes, arrowes, crossbowes, byllles, hargabusses, brode swoordes, large targettes, pykes, mattockes, shouelles, hammers, nayles, sawes, axes, and suche other. Thus beyng furnished accordyngly, they set forward from the Ilandes of *Gades* (nowe called *Cales*) the seuenth day before the Calendes of October, in the yeere of Christ. 1493. and arriued at the ilandes of *Canarie* at the Calendes of October: Of these ilandes, the last is called *Ferrea*, in whiche there is no other water that may be drunke, but only that is geathered of the deawe, which continually distylleth from one only tree, growyng on the hyghest bancke of the ilande, and falleth into a rounde trenche made with mans hande: we were enfourmed of these thynges within fewe dayes after his departure. What shall succeede, we wyl certifie you hereafter. Thus fare ye well, from the courte, at the Ides of Nouember. 1493.

Tooles and artyllerie.

Water droppyng from a tree continually.

The seconde booke of the first Decade, to *Ascanius Sphorcia*, Vicount Cardinal. &c.

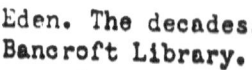

YOu repeate (ryght honourable prince) that you are desyrous to knowe what newes we haue in Spayne from the newe worlde, and that those things haue greatly delyted you, whiche I wrote unto your hyghnesse of the fyrst Nauigation: You shal nowe therefore receiue what hath succeeded. *Methymna Campi*, is a famous towne in high Spayne, in respect from you, and is in that parte of Spayne whiche is called *Castella Vetus*. beyng distant from *Gades* about. xl. myles. Here the courte remayned, when about the. ix. of the Calendes of Apryll, in this yeere of ninetie and foure, there were postes sent to the king and queene, certifying them that there were twelue shyppes come from the newe Ilandes, and arriued at *Gades*: but the gouernour

Methymna Campi. Castella Vetus.

Gades.

of the shyppes sent woorde to the kyng and queene, that he had none other matter to certifie them of by the postes, but only that the Admiral with fiue shyppes, and fourescore and ten men, remayned styll in *Hispaniola* to searche the secretes of the ilande, and that as touchyng other matters, he hym selfe would shortly make relation in theyr presence by woorde of mouth: therefore the day before the Nones of Apryl, he came to the Courte hym selfe. What I learned of hym, and other faythfull and credible men, whiche came with hym from the Admirall, I wil rehearse vnto you, in suche order as they declared the same to me, when I demaunded them: take it therefore as foloweth. The third day of the Ides of October, departyng from *Ferrea*, the laste of the ilandes of *Canariæ*, and from the coastes of Spayne, with a Nauie of seuenteene shippes, they sayled .xxi. dayes before they came to any ilande, inclining of purpose more towarde the left hand then at the fyrst voyage, folowing the north northeast winde, and arriued fyrst at the ilandes of the *Canibales* or *Caribes*, of whiche only the same was knowen to our men. Among these, they chaunced fyrst vpon one, so beset with trees, that they coulde not see so muche as an elle space of bare earth or stonie grounde, this they called *Dominica*, because they found it on the Sunday. They taried here no time, because they saw it to be desart. In the space of these .xxi. dayes, they thynke that they sayled eyght hundred & .xx. leagues, the north northeast wynde was so ful with them, and so freshly folowed the sterne of theyr shyppes. After they had sayled a lytle further, they espied diuers ilandes replenyshed with sundry kindes of trees, from the whiche came fragrant sauours of spyces and sweete Gummes: here they sawe neyther man nor beast, except certayne Lysartes of huge bygnesse, as they reported which went aland to viewe the countrey. This iland they called *Galana* or *Galanta*: from the cape or poynt of this ilande, espying a mountayne a farre of, they sayled thyther. About .xxx. myles from this mountayne, they sawe a ryuer descendyng, which seemed to be a token of some great and large flood. This is the fyrst lande whiche they founde inhabited from the ilandes of *Canaria*, and is an ilande of the *Canibales*, as they learned by the interpretours whiche they tooke with them from *Hispaniola* [illegible]

The Ilande of Ferrea.

Ilandes of the Canibales.

The Ilande of Dominica.

Lysartes.

The Ilande of Galanta.

The Iland of Guadalupea.

Uillages of .xx. .xxx. houses. they founde innumerable villages of .xx. houses, or .xxx. at the most, set rounde about in order, makyng the streete in compasse lyke a market place. And forasmuche as I haue made mention of theyr houses, it shall not be greatly from my purpose to describe

The buildyng of theyr houses. in what manner they are buylded: They are made rounde lyke belles or rounde pauilions. Theyr frame is raysed of exceedyng high trees, set close togeather, and fast rampaired in the grounde, so standyng aslope, and bendyng inwarde, that the toppes of the trees ioyne togeather, and beare one agaynst another, hauyng also within the house certaine strong and short proppes or postes whiche susteyne the trees from fallyng. They couer them with the leaues of date trees, and other trees strongly compact and hardened, wherwith they make them close from winde and weather. At the shorte postes or proppes within the house, they tye

Gossampine cotton. ropes of the cotton of gossampine trees, or other ropes made of certayne long & rough rootes, much lyke unto the shrubbe called *Spartum*, wherof in old tyme they used to make bandes for vines, and gables and ropes for shyppes. These they tye ouerthwarte the house from poste to poste, on these they lay as it were certaine matresses made of the cotton of gossampine trees, whiche growe plentifully in these ilandes. This cotton the Spanyardes

Bombase. Hangyng beddes. cal *Algodon*, and the Italians *Bombasine*: and thus they sleepe in hangyng beddes. At the entrance of one of theyr houses, they sawe two images of wood lyke unto serpentes, whiche they thought had been suche idols as they honour: but they learned afterwarde that they were set there onlye for comelynesse, for they knowe none other god then the sunne and moone, although

Images. they make certaine images of gossampine cotton to ẏ similitude of suche phantasies as they say appeare to them in the nyght. Our men found in theyr houses, al kindes of earthen vessels, not muche unlyke unto ours. They founde also in theyr kytchens,

Fine cookerie. mans fleshe, duckes fleshe, & goose fleshe, al in one pot, and other on the spyts redy to be layde to the fyre. Entring into their inner

Arrowheades of bones. lodgynges, they founde faggottes of the bones of mens armes and legges, whiche they reserue to make heades for theyr arrowes, because they lacke iron, the other bones they cast away when they haue eaten the fleshe. They founde lykewyse the head of a young man fastened to a poste, and yet bleedyng. They haue

in

in some vyllages, one great hall or pallace, about the whiche theyr common houses are placed : to this they resort, as often as they came togeather to playe . When they perceiued the commyng of our men, they fledde. In theyr houses they founde also aboute thirtie children captiues, whiche were reserued to be eaten, but our men tooke them away to vse them for interpreters. Searching more diligently the inner parts of the iland, they founde seuen other ryuers, bygger then this whiche we spake of before, runnyng through the ilande, with fruitefull and pleasaunt bankes, delectable to beholde. This ilande they called *Guadalupea*, for the similitude that it hath to the mount *Guadalupus* in Spayne, where the image of the virgin Marie is religiously honoured, but the inhabitauntes call it *Carucueria*, or *Queraquiera* : It is the cheefe habitation of the *Canibales*. They brought from this iland .vii. Popiniayes, bigger then Phesants, muche dyfferyng from other in colour, hauyng theyr backes, brestes, and bellies of purple colour, and theyr wynges of other variable colours ; in al these ilands is no lesse plentie of Poppyniayes, then with vs of sparrowes or stareylynges. As we bring vp capons and hennes to franke and make them fat, so doo they these bigger kindes of Poppyniayes for the same purpose. After that they had thus searched the ilande, and driuen these *Canibales* to flight (whiche ran away at theyr fyrst approche, as soone as they had espied them) they called their company togeather, and as soone as they had broken ẏ *Canibales* boates or lighters (whiche they cal *Canoas*) they loosed theyr ankers the day before the Ides of Nouember, and departed from *Guadalupea*. *Colonus* the Admiral, for the desyre he had to see his companions, whiche at his fyrst voyage he left the yeere before in *Hispaniola* to search the countrey, let passe many ilandes both on his ryght hande, & left hande, and sayled directly thyther. By the way there appeared from the north a great iland, which the captiues that were taken in *Hispaniola*, called *Madanino*, or *Matinino*, affirmyng it to be inhabited onely with women, to whō the *Canibales* haue accesse at certayne tymes of the yeere, as in olde tyme the *Thracians* had to the *Amazones* in the ilande of *Lesbos* : the men children they sende to theyr fathers, but the women they keepe with them

The mount Guadalupus

Carucueria.

Popiniayes bygger then Phesantes.

The Canibals driue to flygh

Matinino an Ilande of women.

selues. They haue great and strong caues or dennes in the grounde, to the whiche they flee for safegarde if any men resorte vnto them at any other tyme then is appoynted, and there defende them selues with bowes and arrowes, agaynst the violence of suche as attempte to inuade them. They coulde not at this tyme approche to this ilande, by reason of the North northeast wynde, which blewe so vehemently from the same, wheras they nowe folowed the East southeaste. After they departed from *Madanino*, and sayled by the space of .xl. myles, they passed not farre from an other ilande which the captyues sayde to be verye populus, and replenyshed with al thynges necessarie for the life of man. This they called *Mons Serratus*, because it was full of mountaynes. The captyues further declared, that the *Canibales* are woont at some time to goe from theyr owne coastes aboue a thousande myles to hunt for men. The day folowing, they sawe an other ilande, the whiche because it was rounde, they called *Sancta Maria Rotunda*. The next day, they founde an other, whiche they called *S. Martini*, whiche they let passe also, because they had no leasure to tarrye. Lykewyse the thirde daye they espied an other, whose *Diametral* syde, extendyng from the East to the west, they iudged to be a hundred & fyftie myle. They affirme all these ilandes to be maruelous fayre and fruitefull: This last, they called *Sancta Maria Antiqua*. Saylyng forwarde, and leauyng many other ilandes, after they had sayled about fourtie myles, they chaunced vpon an other, much bygger then any of the rest, which thinhabitans call *Ay Ay*, but they named it *Insula crucis*: Here they cast anker to fetche freshe water. The Admiral also commaunded .xxx. men to goe a lande out of his owne shyp, and to search the ilande: Here they founde foure dogges on the shore. The Inhabitants are *Canibales*, and maruelous experte in shooting, as wel women as men, and vse to infect their arrowes with poyson. When they had taried there two dayes, they sawe a farre of a *Canoa*, in the whiche were eight men, and as many women, hauyng with them bowes and arrowes. They fiercely assayled our men without all feare, and hurte some of them with theyr venemous arrowes. Among these there was a certayne woman, to whom the other gaue reuerence, and obeyed as though she were theyr queene. Her sonne wayted vppon her, beyng a yonge man, strongly made,

he Ilandes f Mons Serratus. Huntyng for men.

ancta Maria Rotunda.

anctus Martinus.

ancta Maria Antiqua.

nsula crucis, n Ilande of he Canibales.

The Canibales re expert Archers.

rrowes infected with poyson.

made, of terrible and frownyng countenance, and a Lions face. Our men, leaste they shoulde take the more hurte by beyng wounded a farre of, thought it beste to ioyne with them. Therfore with al speede, settyng forward with their ores the brigandine in whiche they were sette alande, they ouerturned their *Canoa* with a great violence, whiche being ouerwhelmed, they notwithstandyng, as wel the women as the men, swymmyng, caste theyr dartes at our men thicke and threefolde. At the length, geatheryng them selues togeather vpon a rocke couered with the water, they fought manfully vntyll they were ouercome and taken, one beyng slayne, and the queenes sonne sore wounded. When they were brought into the Admirals shippe, they dyd no more put of their fiercenes and cruel countenaunces, then do the Lions of *Lybia* when they perceiue them selues to be bounde in chaynes. There is no man able to beholde them, but he shall feele his bowels grate with a certayne horrour, nature hath endued them with so terrible menacing and cruell aspect. This coniecture I make of mee selfe, & other which oftentymes went with me to see them at *Methymna Campi*: but nowe to returne to the voyage. Proceeding thus further and further, more then fyue hundred myles, fyrste towarde the west southwest, then towarde the southwest, and at the length towarde the west northwest, they entred into a mayne large sea, hauyng in it innumerable ilandes, marueylously dyfferyng one from another, for some of them were very fruitefull, and full of hearbes and trees, other some, very drye, barren, and rough, with high rockye mountaynes of stone, whereof some were of bryght blewe, or asurine colour, and other glysteryng whyte: wherefore they supposed them, by good reason, to be the mynes of mettalles and precious stones: but the roughnesse of the sea, and multitude of ilandes standyng so thycke togeather, hyndered them so, that they coulde cast no anker, lest the bigger vesselles shoulde runne vppon the rockes: therefore they deferred the searchyng of these ilandes vntyll another tyme: they were so manye, and stoode so thycke, that they coulde not number them, yet the smaller vesselles whiche [illegible] entred among them, and numbred fourtie and [illegible] ilandes, but the bygger vessels kept [illegible] for feare of the rockes.

They

A conflict wt the Canibals

The fiercenes & terrible countenance of the Canibales.

Methymna Campi.

Innumerable Ilandes.

The mynes of metals & precious stones.

They call the sea where this multitude of Ilandes are situate, *Archipelagus*. From this tracte procedyng forwarde, in the mydde way there lyeth an Ilande whiche thinhabitantes call *Burichina*, or *Buchena*: but they named it *Insula. S. Iohannis*. Dyuers of them whom we had delyuered from the *Canibales*, sayde that they were borne in this Ilande, affirming it to be verye populous and frutefull, hauing also many faire wooddes and hauens. Ther is deadly hatred and continual battayle betwene them and the *Canibales*. They haue no boates to passe from their owne coastes to the *Canibales*: but if it be their chaunce to ouercome them when they make incursion into theyr countrey to seeke their praye (as it sometyme happeneth, the fortune of warre being uncertayne) they serue them [illegible] like sause, requiting death for death. For one of them mangeleth an other in pieces, and roste them, and eate them euen before their eyes. They taryed not in this Ilande: Yet in the west angle therof, a fewe of them went a lande for freshe water, and founde a great and high house after the maner of their buyldyng, hauing .xii. other of their vulgare cotages placed about the same, but were all lefte desolate, whether it were that they resorted to the mountaynes by reason of the heate which was that tyme of the yeere, and to returne to the playne when the ayre wareth coulder, or els for feare of the *Canibales* whiche make incursion into the Ilande at certayne seasons. In al this Ilande is only one kyng. The south syde hereof extendeth about two hundreth myles. Shortly after, they came to the Ilande of *Hispaniola*, being distance from the firste Ilande of the *Canibales*, fyue hundreth leagues. Here they founde al thinges out of order, and theyr felowes slayne whiche they lefte here at their fyrst voyage. In the begynnyng of *Hispaniola* (hauing in it many regions and kyngdomes as we haue sayde) is the region of *Xamana*, whose kyng is named *Guaccanarillus*. This *Guaccanarillus* ioyned frendship with our men at the fyrst voyage, and made a [illegible] with them: but in the absence of the Admirall, he [illegible] the cause of our mens destruction, although he [illegible], and pretended frendship at the [illegible], [illegible] on yet a litle further, they espied a [illegible] men, in whiche was the brother of *Guaccanarillus*, [illegible] one man wayting on hym. He

The sea called Archipelagus.

Insula. S. Joannes or Burichena.

Death for death

The mountaynes are colder then the playnes.

From Dominica to Hispaniola fyue hundred leagues.

The Spaniardes left in the Ilande are slayne.

Kyng Guaccanarillus rebelleth.

He brought with him [illegible] images of golde, whiche he gaue the Admyrall in the name of his brother, and tolde a tale in his language as concernyng the death of our men, as they proued afterwarde, but at this tyme had no regarde to his communication for lacke of interpretours, whiche were eyther all dead, or escaped and stolne away when they drewe neare the ilandes. But of the ten, seuen dyed by chaunge of ayre and dyet. The inhabitauntes of these ilandes haue ben euer so vsed to lyue at libertie, in play and pastyme, that they can hardly away with the yoke of seruitude, which they attempte to shake of by all meanes they may. And surely yf they had receiued our religion, I woulde thynke theyr lyfe moste happie of all men, yf they myght therewith enioye theyr auncient libertie. A fewe thinges contente them, hauyng no delyte in suche superfluities, for the whiche in other places men take infinite paynes, and commit manye vnlawfull actes, and yet are neuer satisfied, whereas manye haue to muche, and none ynough. But among these symple soules, a fewe clothes serue the naked: weightes and measures are not needefull to suche as can not skyl of craft and deceyte, and haue not the vse of pestiferous money, the seede of innumerable mischeeues: so that yf we shall not be ashamed to confesse the trueth, they seeme to liue in that golden worlde of the whiche olde wryters speake so muche, wherein men lyued symplye and innocentlye without enforcement of lawes, without quarrellyng, iudges, and libelles, content only to satisfie nature, without further vexation for knowledge of thynges to come. Yet these naked people also are tormented with ambition, for ẏ desire they haue to enlarge their dominions: by reason wherof, they kepe war and destroy one another, from the whiche plague I suppose the golden worlde was not free. For euen then also, *Cede, non cedam*, that is, geue place, and I will not geue place, had entred among men. But nowe to returne to the matter from which we haue digressed. The admiral desyrous to know further of ẏ death of his men, sent for *Guaccanerillus* to come to him to his ship, dissimulyng that he knewe any thyng of the matter. After that he came aboorde shyp, salutyng the Admiral and his company, geuing also [illegible] golde to the capitaynes and officers, [illegible] hym to the [illegible]

Two images of golde.

Libertie and idlenesse.

A happie kinde of lyfe.

Superfluitis.

Many haue to much, and none ynough.

The golden worlde.

Naked men troubled with ambition.

Geue place.

The Admiral sendeth for the kyng.

from the *Canibales*, and earnestly be[illegible]yng one of them whom our men called Katherine, he spake gentely unto her. And thus when he had seene and marueyled at the horses, and such other thynges as were in the shyppe, unknowen to them, and had with a good grace and merely asked leaue of the Admiral, he departed. Yet some there were whiche counsayled the Admirall to keepe hym styll, that yf they myght by any meanes proue that he was consentyng to the death of our men, he myght be punyshed accordyngly. But the Admiral consyderyng that it was yet no time to incense the inhabitantes mindes to wrath, dismissed him. The next day folowyng, the kynges brother resortyng to the shyppes, eyther in his owne name or in his brothers, seduced the women. For on the next nyght about mydnyght, this Katherine, aswell to recouer her owne libertie, as also her felowes, being suborned thereto either by the king or his brothers promises, attempted a muche more difficult and daungerous aduenture then dyd *Cloelia* of Rome, whiche beyng in hostage with other maydes to the king *Porcena*, deceiued her keepers, and rode ouer ye riuer *Tiber*, with the other virgins which were pledges with her. For whereas they swamme ouer the riuer on horsbacke, this Katherine with seuen other women, trustyng only to the strength of their owne armes, swam aboue three long miles, and that also at suche time as the sea was somewhat rough: for euen so farre of from the shore lay the shyppes at rode, as nygh as they coulde coniecture. But our men folowing them with the shipboates, by the same light seene on the shore, whereby the women were ledde, tooke three of them, supposing that Katherine with the other foure, went to *Guaccanarillus*: for in the spryng of the mornyng, certaine messengers being sent unto him by the Admirall, had intelligence that he was fledde with al his familie and stuffe, and the women also, whiche thyng ministred further suspection that he was consentyng to the death of our men. Wherefore the Admirall sent forth an armie of three hundred [illegible] which he appoynted one *Melchior* to be captaine, [illegible] *Guaccanarillus*; [illegible]

No horses in the Ilandes.

A tyme for all thynges.

A desperate aduenture of a woman.

Cloelia of Rome.

[illegible]

supposing that it had byn the mouth of some great ryuer. He founde heare also a very commodious and safe hauen, and therfore named it *Portus Regalis*. They say that the enterance of this is so crooked and bending, that after the shyps are once within the same, whether they turne them to the lefte hand, or to the right, they can not perceyue where they came in, untyl they returne to the mouth of the ryuer, although it be there so brode that three of the byggest vessels may sayle togeather on a froont. The sharpe and high hylles on the one syde and on the other, so brake the wynde, that they were uncertaine how to rule theyr sayles. In the myddle gulfe of the ryuer, there is a promontorie or point of the land with a pleasant groue, ful of Popingiayes and other byrdes, which breede therin & sing very sweetly: They perceyued also that two ryuers of no smal largenesse fell into the hauen. Whyle they thus searched the lande betwene both, *Melchior* espied a high house a farre of, where supposing that *Guaccanarillus* had lyen hyd, he made towarde it: and as he was goyng, there met hym a man with a frownyng countenance, and a grymme looke, with a hundred men folowyng hym, armed with bowes and arrowes, and long and sharpe staues lyke iauelynnes, made harde at the endes with fyre, who approching towardes our men, spake out aloud with a terrible voyce, saying that they were *Taini* (that is) noble men, and not *Canibales*: but when our men had geuen them signes of peace, they left both theyr weapons and fiercenesse. Thus geuyng ech of them certayne haukes bels, they tooke it for so great a rewarde, that they desyred to enter bondes of neare frendshyp with us, and feared not immediatly to submit them selues under our power, and resorted to our shyps with their presentes. They that measured the house (beyng made in round fourme) found it to be from syde to syde. xxxii. great paces, compassed about with xxx. other vulgare houses, hauyng in them many beames crosse ouer, & couered with reedes of sundry colours, wrethed & as it were weaued with maruellous art. Whē our men asked some of them where they might find *Guaccanarillus*? They answered, that that region was none of his, but theyr kynges, beyng there present: Yet they sayde they supposed that *Guaccanarillus* was gone from the playne to the mountaynes.

Popyngiayes and byrdes.

Taini.

Haukes belles.

A large house.

Reedes of sundry colours.

Cacicus.

Makyng therefore a brotherly league with this *Cacicus* (that is to say a kyng) they returned to the Admiral, to make relation what they had seene and hearde: wherevpon he sent foorth diuers other Centurians with theyr hundredes, to searche the countrey yet further: among whiche were *Hoiedus* and *Gorualanus*, noble young gentlemen, and of great courage. And as they went towarde the mountaynes to seeke *Guaccanerillus*, diuiding the mountaynes betweene them, one of them founde on the one syde thereof, foure ryuers fallyng from the same mountaynes, and the other founde three on the other syde. In the sandes of al these riuers is founde great plentie of golde, whiche the inhabitauntes of the same ilande whiche were with vs, geathered in this maner: makyng holes in the sande with theyr handes a Cubite deepe, and takyng vp sande with theyr left handes from the bottome of the same, they pycked out graynes of golde with theyr ryght handes without any more art or cunnyng, and so deliuered it to our men, who affirme that many of them thus geathered, were as bygge as tares or fytches. And I mee selfe sawe a masse of rude golde (that is to say, suche as was neuer moulten) lyke vnto suche stones as are founde in the bottomes of ryuers, weighyng niene ounces, whiche *Hoieda* hym selfe founde. Beyng contented with these signes, they returned to the Admirall to certifie hym hereof. For the Admirall had commaunded vnder payne of punyshment, that they shoulde meddle no further then theyr commission: whiche was only, to searche the places with theyr signes. For the fame went that there was a certayne kyng of the mountaynes from whence those ryuers had theyr fall, whom they cal *Cacicus Caunaboa*, that is, the lord of the house of golde, for they cal a house *Boa*, golde, *Cauni*, and a kyng or lorde *Cacicus*, as we haue sayde before. They affirme that there can no where be founde better fyshe, nor of more pleasant taste, or more holsome then in these riuers: also the waters of the same to be moste holsome to drynke. *Melchior* him selfe tolde me, that in the moneth of December, the dayes & nyghtes be of equal length among the *Canibales*: but the sphere or circles of the heauen agreeth not thereunto, albeit that in the same moneth, some byrdes make theyr nestes, and some haue alredye hatched theyr [illegible] of the heate, beyng rather [illegible]

Marginal notes: Hoiedus and Gorualanus. — Golden riuers fallyng from mountaynes. — The manner of gatheryng gold. — Graynes of golde. — A masse of rude gold weyghing ix. ounces. — Caunaboa, kyng of the house of golde. — Holsome water, and plentie of fyshe. — The day and nyght of equall length in December. — Byrdes breede in December.

small then extreme. He tolde me also when I questioned with hym as concerning ẏ eleuation of the pole frō the horizontal line, that al the starres called *Plaustrum* or charles wayne, are hyd vnder the North pole to the *Canibales*. And surely there returned none from thence at this vioage, to whom there is more credit to be geuen, then to this man. But if he had byn skilfull in Astronomie, he shoulde haue sayde that the day was almoste equall with the night: For in no place towarde the stay of the sonne (called *Solsticium*) can the night be equall with the day. And as for them, they neuer came vnder the *Equinoctial*, forasmuch as they had euer the North pole theyr guyde, and euer eleuate in sight aboue the *Horizontal*. Thus haue I briefely written vnto your honour, as muche as I thought sufficient at this tyme, and shall shortly hereafter (by Gods fauoure) wryte vnto you more largely of such matters as shalbe dayly better knowen. For the Admiral hym selfe (whom I vse familierly as my very frende) hath promised me by his letters, that he wyl geue me knowledge of al such thinges as shall chaunce. He hath nowe chosen a strong place where he may build a citie, neare vnto a cōmodious hauen, and hath alredy buylded manẏ houses, and a chapel, in the which (as in a newe worlde heretofore voyde of all religion) God is dayly serued with .xiii. priestes, according to the maner of our churches. When the tyme nowe approched that he promysed to sende to the king and queene, and hauyng prosperous winde for that purpose, sent backe the .xii. Carauelles, whereof we made mention before: which was no smal hynderance and greefe vnto hym, especially consydering the death of his men whom he lefte in the ilande at the fyrst voyage, wherby we are yet ignorant of many places and other secretes, whereof we myght otherwyse haue had farther knowledge: but as tyme shall reueale them agayne, so wyll I aduertyse you of the same. And that you may the better knowe by conference had with the *Apothecaries* and marchaunt strangers *Sirophenicians*, what [illegible] Regions beare, & [illegible] theyr [illegible] of graines, [illegible] that tree whiche they suppose to be the Cinamome tree. [illegible]

The eleuation of the pole.

The starres are called guardens of the pole.

The Equinoctial line.

A chappell and priestes.

Marchantes Sirophenicians.

The Cinamome tree.

selfe, touch them fyrst softly, moouyng them to your lyppes, for although they be not hurtfull, yet for theyr excesse of heate, they are sharpe, and byte the tongue yf they remayne any while thereon: but yf the tongue be blystered by tastyng of them, the same is taken away by drynkyng of water. Of the corne also whereof they make theyr bread, this brynger shall deliuer some graynes to your lordshyp, both whyte and blacke, and therwith also a trunke of the tree of *Aloes*, the whiche yf you cut in peeces, you shall feele a sweete sauour to proceede from the same. Thus fare you hartily well, from the Court of *Methymna Campi*, the thyrde day before the Calendes of May. *Anno Dom.* 1494.

Xiloaloes. or lignum Aloes.

The thyrde booke of the first Decade, to *Lodouike* Cardinall of *Aragonie*, and Neuiewe to the kyng.

You desyre that foolyshe *Phaeton* shoulde agayne rule the chariots of the Sunne, and contende to drawe sweete licours out of the harde flynt, wheras you require me to discribe vnto you the newe worlde, found in the west by the good fortune and gouernaunce of the Catholique princes *Ferdinandus* and Elizabeth, your Uncle and Aunte, shewyng me also the letters of kyng *Frederike* your Uncle, written to me in that behalfe: But syth you haue layde this burden on my backe, in whose power it is to commaunde me to take vppon me more then I am well able, ye both shall receiue this precious stone rudely closed in lead after my manner of workemanshyp. Wherefore, when you shal perceiue the learned sort frendly, the malitious enuiously, and the backbyters furiously, to bende theyr slaunderous dartes agaynst our fayre *Nimphes* of the *Ocean*, you shall freely protest in howe short tyme, and in the myddest of what troubles and calamities you haue enforced me to wryte of the same. Thus fare you wel, from Granata the nineth day before the Calendes of May.

We haue [illegible] before, howe the Admirall [illegible] the ilande of *Hispaniola* with

Hispaniola.

with his whole navie: But nowe we entende further to shewe what he founde as concernyng the nature of this ilande, after that he had better searched the secretes of the same: Lykewyse of the ilande of *Cuba* neare unto it, whiche he supposed to be the fyrme lande. *Hispaniola* therefore (whiche he affirmeth to be *Ophir*, whereof we reade in the thyrde booke of the kynges) is of latitude fyue south degrees, hauyng the north pole eleuate on the north syde .xxvii. degrees, and on the south syde (as they say) .xxii. degrees, it reacheth in length from East to West, seuen hundred and fourescore myles, it is distant from the ilandes of *Gades* (called *Cales*) .xlix. degrees, and more, as some say: the fourme of the ilande resembleth the leafe of a Chestnutte tree.

Ophir, whyther Salomons shippes sayled for Golde.

Upon a hygh hyll on the North syde of the ilande, he buylded a citie, because this place was most apt for that purpose, by reason of a myne of stones whiche was neare unto the same, seruyng well both to buylde with, and also to make Lyme: at the bottome of this hyll, is there a great playne of threescore myles in length, and in breadth somewhere .xii. somewhere .xx. myles where it is brodest, & sixe myles where it is narrowest: through this playne runne diuers fayre ryuers of wholsome waters, but the greatest of them, whiche is nauigable, falleth into the hauen of the citie for the space of halfe a furlong: howe fertile and fruitful this valley is, you may understande by these thynges whiche folowe. On the shore of this ryuer, they haue lymitted and enclosed certayne ground, to make gardens and orchardes, in the whiche al kynde of bygger hearbes, as radishe, letuse, colewortes, borage, & suche other, waxe rype within .xvi. dayes after the seede is sowen, lykewyse Melones, Gourdes, Cucumers, and suche other, within the space of .xxxvi. dayes, these garden hearbes they haue freshe & greene al the whole yeere. Also the rootes of the canes or reedes of the licour whereof suger is made, growe a cubite hygh within the space of .xv. dayes, but the licour is not yet hardened. The lyke they affirme of plantes or shrowdes of young vines, and that they haue the seconde yeere geathered rype and sweete grapes of the same: but by reason of to muche [illegible] they beare [illegible] clusters. Furthermore, a man [illegible]

Isabella.

A token of marueilous fruitefulnesse.

Hearbes greene al the whole yeere.

Suger reedes, Plantes and vines.

[illegible]

of the rype eares of the same the thyrde day before the calendes of Aprill, which was that yeere the vigile of the Resurrection of our Lord. Also, al kyndes of pulse, as beanes, peason, fytches, tares, & such other, are rype twyse in the yeere, as al they whiche come from thence affirme with one voyce, yet the grounde is not vniuersally apte to beare wheate. In the meane tyme whyle these thinges were doing, the Admirall sent out a companye of .xxx. men to searche the Region of *Cipanga*, otherwyse called *Cibana*. This Region is full of mountaynes and rockes: and in the myddle backe of the whole ilande is great plentie of golde. When they that went to searche the region were returned, they reported marueilous thinges as touching the great ryches of this Region. From these mountaynes, descende foure great ryuers, which by the marueilous industrye of nature, diuideth the whole ilande into foure partes, in maner equal, ouer-spreading & wateryng the whole ilande with their braunches. Of these foure ryuers, the one reacheth towarde the Easte, this the inhabitantes call *Iunna*: another towarde the weste, and is called *Attibunicus*: the thirde toward the North, named *Iachem*: the laste reacheth into the South, and is called *Naiba*. The day before the Ides of Marche, the Admirall him selfe, with al his horsemen, and foure hundred footemen, marched directly towarde the South syde of the golden Region. Thus passing ouer the ryuer, the playne, and the mountayne which enuironed the other syde of the playne, he chaunced vppon an other vale, with a ryuer much bygger then the fyrste, & many other meane ryuers running through. When he had also conueighed his armye ouer the ryuer, and passed the seconde vale, which was in no part inferiour to the fyrst, he made a way through the thirde mountaine, where was no passage before, and descended into another vale, whiche was nowe the begynnyng of *Cibana*. Through this also runne many fluddes and ryuers out of every hyll, and in the sandes of them all is founde great plentie of golde. And when he had nowe entred threescore and twelue myles into the golden Region from the citie, he commaunded to buylde a fortresse vppon the toppe of a hyll, [illegible] of a certayne great ryuer, that he [illegible] safelye searche the secretes of the [illegible], this he called the fortresse

The region of Cipanga, or Cibana.

Golde.

The golden region of Cibana.

The vale of Cibana.

fortresse of saint Thomas, the whiche in the meane tyme whyle he was buyldyng, the inhabitauntes beyng desyrous of haukes belles, and other of our thinges, resorted dayly thyther, to whom the Admirall declared, that yf they woulde bryng golde, they shoulde haue whatsoeuer they woulde aske. Forthwith turning theyr backes, and runnyng to the shore of the next riuer, they returned in a shorte tyme, bryngyng with them theyr handes ful of golde. Amongest all other, there came an olde man, bryngyng with him two pibble stones of golde, weyghyng an ounce, desyryng them to geue hym a bell for the same: who when he sawe our men maruayle at the bygnesse therof, he made signes that they were but small and of no value in respecte of some that he had seene, and takyng in his hande foure stones, the least wherof was as bigge as a Walnut, and the biggest as bigge as an Orange, he sayd that there was founde peeces of golde so bygge in his countrey, beyng but halfe a dayes iourney from thence, and that they had no regarde to the geatheryng therof, wherby we perceiued that they passe not muche for golde, inasmuche as it is golde only, but so farre esteeme it, as the hande of the Artificer hath fashioned it in any comely fourme. For who dooth greatly esteeme rough marble, or vnwrought Iuorie? but if they be wrought with the cunning hande of *Phidias* or *Praxiteles*, and shaped to the similitude of ÿ fayre Nimphes or Faires of the sea (called *Nereiades*) or the Fayres of the woodes (called *Hamadriades*) they shal neuer lacke byers. Besyde this olde man, there came also diuers other, bryngyng with them pybble stones of golde, weighing .x. or .xii. drammes, & feared not to confesse, that in ÿ place where they geathered that gold, there were found somtyme stones of golde as bygge as the head of a childe. When he had taried here a few dayes, he sent one *Luxanus*, a noble yong gentleman, with a few armed men, to search al the partes of this region: who at his returne, reported that the inhabitantes shewed him greater thynges then we haue spoken of here before, but he dyd openly declare nothyng therof, whiche they thought was done by the Admirals commaundement. They haue woods ful of certayne spyces, but not such as we commonly vse: these they geather euen as they do golde, spices, [illegible] serue for their [illegible]

Golde for haukes bels.

Graynes and pibble stones of golde.

They passe not for golde, in that it is golde onely but. &c.

Stones of golde as big as the head of a childe.

Spices.

the inhabitauntes of other countreys adioyning to them, for such thynges as they lacke, as dysshes, pottes, stooles, and such other necessaries. As *Luxanus* returned to the Admirall (whiche was about the Ides of Marche) he founde in the woods certaine wilde vines, rype, and of pleasant taste, but the inhabitauntes passe not on them. This region, though it be full of stones and rockes (and is therefore called *Cibana*, whiche is as muche to say as a stone) yet it is wel replenyshed with trees and pastures, yea they constantly affirme, that yf ye grasse of these mountaynes be cutte, it groweth agayne within the space of foure dayes, hygher then wheate. And forasmuche as many showres of rayne doo fall in this region, whereof the ryuers and floodes haue theyr encrease, in euery of the whiche golde is founde myxt with sande in all places, they iudge that the golde is dryuen from the mountaynes, by the vehement course of the streames whiche fall from the same, and runne into the ryuers. The people of this region are geuen to idlenesse and play, for suche as inhabite the mountaynes, syt quakyng for colde in the Wynter season, and had rather to wander vp and downe idelly, then take the paynes to make them apparell, where as they haue woodes full of Gossampine cotton: but suche as dwell in the valles or playnes, feele no colde in Wynter. When the Admirall had thus searched the beginning of the region of *Cibana*, he repayred to *Isabella* (for so he named the citie) where, leauyng the gouernaunce of the Ilande with his deputies, he prepared hym selfe to search further the limittes of the Ilande of *Cuba* or *Iohanna*, whiche he yet doubted to be the firme lande, and distant from *Hispaniola* only .lxx. myles. This dyd he with more speedye expedition, callyng to remembraunce the kynges commaundement, who wylled hym fyrst with al celeritie, to ouerrunne the coastes of the new Ilandes, lest any other prince shoulde in the meane time attempte to inuade the same, for the kyng of Portugale affirmed that it perteyned only to him to discouer these vnknowen landes: but the bishop of Rome, Alexander the sixt, to auoyde the cause of this dissention, graunted to the kyng of Spayne by the auctoritie of his leaden bulles, that no other prince shoulde be so bolde, as to make any vyages to any of these vnknowen regions, lyeng without the [illegible] the North

Wilde vines of pleasaunte taste.

Fruitful mountaynes.

Golde in the sande of ryuers falling from the mountaynes.

Idlenesse and plaie. The mountaynes are colde.

The Ilande of Cuba.

Least any other prince. &c.

Dissention betweene the Portingales and Spaniardes.

to the South a hundred leagues Westwarde, without the paralels of the Ilandes called *Capud Viride*, or *Cabouerde*, whiche we thinke to be those that in olde tyme were called *Hesperides*: these parteyne to the kyng of Portugale, and from these his Pylotes, whiche do yeerely searche newe coastes and regions, directe theyr course to the East, saylyng euer towarde the left hande by the backe of Aphrike, and the seas of the Ethiopians: neyther to this day had the Portugales at any tyme sayled Southwarde or Westwarde from the Ilandes of *Cabouerde*. Preparing therfore three shyppes, he made haste towarde the Ilande of *Iobanna* or *Cuba*, whyther he came in short space, and named the poynt therof, where he fyrste arryued, *Alpha* and *O*, that is, the fyrste and the last: for he supposed that there had ben the ende of our East, because the sonne falleth there, and of the West, because it ryseth there. For it is apparant, that Westwarde, it is the begiuning of *India* beyonde the ryuer of *Ganges*, and Eastwarde, the furthest ende of the same: whiche thyng is not contrary to reason, forasmuche as the Cosmographers haue left the lymittes of *India* beyond *Ganges* undetermined, where as also some were of opinion, that *India* was not farre from the coastes of Spaine, as we haue said before. Within the prospect of the beginnyng of *Cuba*, he founde a commodious hauen in the extreme angle of the Ilande of *Hispaniola*, for in this part the Ilande receiueth a great goulfe: this hauen he named Saint Nicholas porte, beyng scarcely twentie leagues from *Cuba*. As he departed from hence, and sayled Westward by the South syde of *Cuba*, the further that he went, so muche the more the sea seemed to be extended in breadth, and to bende towarde the South. On the South syde of *Cuba*, he founde an Ilande whiche the inhabitauntes call *Iamaica*, this he affirmeth to be longer & brodder then the Ilande of *Seicile*, hauyng in it only one mountaine, which on euery part, beginning from the sea, ryseth by litle and litle into the myddest of the Ilande, [illegible] that such [illegible] [illegible] [illegible] by the shore, [illegible] by the other [illegible]

The Ilandes of Cabouerde or Hesperides.

The Portugales viages.

The ende of the easte and weste.

Note. India not far from Spaine.

Sainte Nicolas porte.

The Ilande of Iamaica.

[illegible]

in many places where he woulde haue aryued, they came armed agaynst hym, and forbode hym with threatnyng wordes: but beyng ouercome, they made a league of frendshyp with hym. Thus departing from *Iamaica* he sayled toward the West, with a prosperous wynde, for the space of threescore and tenne dayes, thynking that he had passed so farre by the compasse of the earth being vnderneath vs, that he had ben neare vnto *Aurea Chersonesus* (nowe called *Malaccha*) in our east India, beyonde the begynnyng of *Persides*: for he playnely beleeued that he had left only two of the twelue houres of the sunne, which were vnknowen to vs, for the olde wryters haue left halfe the course of the sunne vntouched, where as they haue but only discussed that superficial parte of the earth whiche lyeth betweene the Ilandes of *Gades*, and the ryuer of *Ganges*, or at the vttermost, to *Aurea Chersonesus*. In this Nauigation, he chaunced on many furious seas, running with a fall as it had ben the streames of floods, also many whyrlepooles, and shelfes, with many other dangers, and straightes, by reason of the multitude of ilandes whiche lay on euery syde. But not regardyng al these perylles, he determined to procede, vntil he had certaine knowledge whether *Cuba* were an Ilande, or firme lande. Thus he sayled forward, coastyng euer by the shore toward the West for the space of CC. xxii. leagues, that is, about a thousande and three hundred myles, and gaue names to seuen hundred Ilandes by the way, leauyng also on the left hande (as he feared not to report) three thousande here and there. But let vs nowe returne to suche thynges as he founde worthy to be noted in this nauigation. Saylyng therefore by the syde of *Cuba*, and searchyng the nature of the places, he espyed not farre from *Alpha and O* a large hauen of capacitie to harbor many shyppes, whose entraunce is bendyng, beyng inclosed on both sydes with capes or poyntes whiche receiue the water: this hauen is large within, and of exceding deapth. Saylyng by the shore of this porte, he sawe not farre from the [illegible]

The compassing of the earth.

Aurea Chersonesus, or Malaccha.

The secreate of Astronomie.

The riuer of Ganges.

Daungerous straightes by reason of many Ilandes.

A large hauen.

poynt

pounde weight, and two serpentes of eyght foote long apeece: whereat marueylyng, and lookyng about if they could espye any of the inhabitauntes, and that none appeared in syght (for they fledde al to the mountaynes at the commyng of our men) they fel to theyr meate, and ate the fyshe taken with other mens trauayle, but they absteyned from the serpentes, which they affirme to differ nothing from the Crocodiles of Egypt, but only in byggnesse: for (as *Plinie* sayth) Crocodiles haue sometymes ben found of .xviii. cubits long, but of these the biggest were but of eyght foote. Thus being wel refreshed, they entred into the next wood, where they found many of the same kynde of serpentes, hanging vpon boughes of trees, of the whiche, some had theyr mouthes tyed with stringes, and some theyr teeth taken out. And as they searched the places neare vnto the hauen, they sawe about. lxx. men in the top of a hygh rocke, whiche fled as soone as they had espyed our men, who by signes and tokens of peace callyng them agayne, there was one which came neare them, and stoode on the toppe of a rocke, seemyng as though he were yet fearefull: but the Admiral sent one *Didacus* to hym, a man of the same countrey, whom he had at his fyrste voyage taken in the ilande of *Guanabaini*, being neare vnto *Cuba*, wyllyng hym to come neare, and not to be afraide. When he hearde *Didacus* speake to hym in his owne tongue, he came boldly to hym, and shortly after resorted to his company, perswadyng them to come without al feare. After this message was done, there dessended from the rockes to the shyps, about threescore and ten of the inhabitantes, proferring frendship and gentlenesse to our men: whiche the Admiral accepted thankfully, and gaue them diuers rewardes, and that the rather, for that he had intelligence by *Didacus* the interpreter, that they were the kynges fyshers, sent of theyr lorde to take fyshe agaynst a solemne feast whiche he prepared for another kyng. And whereas the Admiralles men had eaten the fyshe whiche they lefte in the fyre, they were the gladder thereof, bycause they had left the serpentes: for there is nothing among theyr [illegible]; [illegible] they esteeme so muche as these serpentes, in [illegible] for common people to eate of them, [illegible] yeare.

Crocodiles of Egipte.

The kinges fishers.

Serpentes [illegible]

as many more the same nyght. Beyng asked why they fyrste rosted the fyshe whiche they entended to beare to theyr kyng: they answeared, that they myght be the fresher and uncorrupted. Thus ioynyng handes for a token of further frendshyp, euerye man resorted to his owne. The Admirall went forwarde as he had appoynted, folowyng the fallyng of the sunne from the beginning of *Cuba*, called *Alpha* and *O*: the shores or sea bankes euen unto this hauen, albeit they be full of trees, yet are they rough with mountaines: of these trees, some were full of blossomes and flowres, and other laden with fruites. Beyonde the hauen, the lande is more fertile and populus, whose inhabitantes are more gentle, and more desyrous of our thynges: for as soone as they had espied our shyppes, they flocked all to the shore, bryngyng with them suche bread as they are accustomed to eate, and gourdes ful of water, offeryng them unto our men, and further, desyryng them to come alande. In al these Ilandes is a certaine kinde of trees as bigge as Elmes, whiche beare Gourdes in the steade of fruites, these they use only for drynkyng pottes, and to fetche water in, but not for meate, for the inner substance of them is sowrer then gall, and the barke as harde as any shell. At the Ides of May, the watchmen lookyng out of the top castle of the shyp, towarde the South, sawe a multitude of Ilandes standyng thycke togeather, being al wel replenished with trees, grasse, and hearbes, and well inhabited: in the shore of the continent, he chaunced into a nauigable riuer, whose water was so hot, that no man might endure to abyde his hande therein anye time. The day folowing, espying a farre of a *Canoa* of fyshermen of the inhabitantes, fearyng lest they shoulde flee at the syght of our men, he commaunded certayne to assayle them priuily with the ship boates: but they fearing nothing, taryed the commyng of our men. Nowe shall you heare a newe kynde of fyshyng. Lyke as we with Greyhoundes do hunt Hares in the playne feeldes, so doo they, as it were with a huntyng fishe, take other fishes: this fyshe was of [illegible] unto us; but the bodye [illegible] a great eele, hauyng on the hynder parte of the [illegible] lyke unto a great bagge or purse: [illegible]

[illegible]

Margin notes:

[illegible]somes & [illegible]tes both [illegible]e tyme.

Trees which beare gourds.

A multitude of Ilandes.

Hotte water.

A straunge kinde of fyshing.

may lye close hid by the keele or bottome of the same, for she may in no case abyde the syght of the ayre. Thus when they espye any great fyshe, or Tortoyse (whereof there is great abundance, bygger then great targettes) they let the corde at length, but when she feeleth her selfe loosed, she inuadeth the fyshe or Tortoyse as swiftly as an arrowe, and where she hath once fastened her holde, she casteth the purse of skynne, whereof we spake before, and by drawyng the same togeather, so graspeleth her pray, that no mans strength is suffycient to vnloose the same, excepte by lytle and lytle drawyng the lyne, she be lyfted somwhat aboue the brymme of the water, for then, as soone as she seeth the brightnesse of the ayre, she letteth goe her holde. The praye therfore beyng nowe drawen nere to the brymme of the water, there leapeth sodenly out of the boate into the sea, so manye fyshers as may suffice to holde fast the praye, vntyll the rest of the companye haue taken it into the boate. Whiche thyng doone, they loose so muche of the corde, that the huntyng fyshe may agayne returne to her place within the water, where by an other corde, they let downe to her a peece of the pray, as we vse to rewarde greyhoundes after they haue kylled theyr game. This fyshe, they cal *Guaicanum*, but our men cal it *Reuersum*. They gaue our men foure Tortoyses taken by this meanes, and those of suche byggenesse, that they almost fylled theyr fyshyng boate: for these fyshes are esteemed among them for delycate meate. Our men recompensed them agayne with other rewardes, and so let them depart. Beyng asked of the compasse of that lande, they aunsweared that it had no ende westwarde. Most instantly they desyred the Admirall to come a lande, or in his name to sende one with them to salute theyr *Cazicus*, (that is) their kyng, affirmyng that he woulde geue our men many presentes, yf they would goe to hym. But the Admirall, lest he shoulde be hindered of the [illegible] whiche he had begunne, refused to goe with them. Then they desyred to knowe his name, and tolde our men lykewise the name of theyr kyng. Thus saylyng on yet further euer towarde the West, within fewe dayes he came nere vnto a certayne [illegible] [illegible], [illegible] [illegible]

Abundance of Tortoyses.

Fisher men.

The fishe Guaicanum.

Humaine people.

A mountayne fruitfull and well inhabited

h.iii.

[illegible], commendyng relygiously [illegible] tours, if this nation descended not from heauen. The kyng of this people, and dyuers other sage men that stoode by him, infourmed hym that that lande was no Ilande. Shortly after, entring into one of the Ilandes beyng on the lefte hande of this lande, they founde no body therin, for they fledde al at the commyng of our men: Yet founde they there foure dogges of marueilous deformed shape, & suche as coulde not barke. This kynde of dogges, they eate as we do goates. Here is great plentie of geese, duckes, and hearons. Betwene these Ilandes and the continent, he entered into so narowe streyghtes, that he coulde scarsely turne backe the shyppes, and these also so shalowe, that the keele of the shyppes somtyme rased on the sandes. The water of these streyghtes, for the space of fourtie myles, was whyte and thycke, lyke vnto mylke, and as though meale had ben sparkeled throughout al that sea. And when they had at the length escaped these straightes, and were nowe come into a mayne and large sea, and had sayled theron for the space of fourescore myles, they espyed an other excedyng hygh mountayne, whyther the Admirall resorted to store his shyppes with freshe water and fuel. Heare among certayne wooddes of Date trees, & pyneapple trees of excedyng height, he founde two natiue sprynges of freshe water. In the meane tyme, whyle the woodde was cuttyng, and the barrelles fyllyng, one of our archers went into the wood to hunt, where he espyed a certayne man with a whyte vesture, so lyke a fryer of the order of saynt Marye of *Mercedis*, that at the fyrste syght he supposed it had ben the Admirals priest, which he brought with hym, beyng a man of the same order: but two other folowed him immediatlye out of the same wooddes. Shortly after, he sawe a farre of a whole company of men clothed in apparel, being about xxx. in number. Then turning his backe, and crying out to his felowes, he made haste to the shyppes with all that he myght dryue. These apparelled men, made sygnes and tokens to hym to tary, [illegible] to be afrayde, but that notwithstandyng he ceassed not to [illegible]. The Admirall beyng aduertysed hereof, and not a [illegible] he had founde a ciuile people, in[illegible] armed men, with commaundement [illegible] they shulde enter fourtie myles into

Dogges of strange shape and [illegible].

White and thicke water.

Woddes of date trees.

Men appareled like white fryers.

Appareled men.

into the lande, untyl they myght fynde eyther those apparelled men, or other inhabitauntes of that countrey. When they had passed ouer the wood, they came into a great playne ful of grasse and hearbes, in whiche appeared no token of any pathway. Here attemptyng to goe through the grasse and hearbes, they were so entangled and bewrapt therein, that they were scarselye able to passe a myle, the grasse beyng there lytle lower then our ripe corne: beyng therefore weeryed, they were enforced to returne agayne, findyng no pathway. The day folowyng he sent foorth .xxv. armed men another way, commaundyng them to make diligent search and inquisition what maner of people inhabited the lande: Who departyng, when they had found, not farre from the sea side, certayne steps of wyld beastes, of the which they suspected some to be of Lions feete, beyng strycken with feare, returturned backe agayne. As they came, they founde a wood in the whiche were many natiue vines, here and there creepyng about hygh trees, with many other trees bearyng aromatical fruites and spyces. Of these vines they brought with them into Spaine many clusters of grapes, very ponderous, and ful of licour: but of the other fruites they brought none, because they putrified by the way in the shyp, & were cast into the sea. They say also that in the landes or medowes of those woodes, they sawe flockes of great Cranes, twyse as bygge as ours. As he went forward, and turned his sayles towarde certayne other mountaynes, he espied two cotages on the shore, in the whiche he sawe only one man, who beyng brought to the shippe, signified with head, fyngers, and by al other signes that he coulde deuise, that the lande whiche lay beyonde those mountaynes was very full of people: and as the Admiral drew neare the shore of the same, there met him certayne *Canoas* hauyng in them many people of the countrey, who made signes and tokens of peace and frendshyp. But here *Didacus* the interpretour, which understoode the language of thinhabitantes of the beginning of *Cuba*, understode not them one whit, whereby they considered that in sundry prouinces of *Cuba*, were sundry languages. He had also intelligence, that in the inlande of this region was a king of great power, & accustomed to weare apparell: he sayde that all the tracte of this shore was drowned with water, and ful of mudde, beset with manye trees,

after

Natiue vines.
Trees bearyng spyces & sweete fruites.

Others languages in the Ilande of Cuba.

Pearles in the fyshes.

after the maner of our maryshes: yet whereas in this place they went alande for freshe water, they founde many of the shel fyshes in the whiche pearles are geathered. But that coulde not cause the Admirall to tracte the tyme there, entending at this viage, only to proue howe many landes & seas he could discouer accordyng to the kinges commaundement. As they yet proceded forwarde, they sawe here and there, al the way along by the shore, a great smoke rysing, untyll they came to an other mountayne foure score myles distant. there was no rocke or hyll that coulde be scene, but the same was all of a smoke. But whether these fyres were made by thinhabitantes for their necessary busynes, or (as we are wont to sette beacons on fyre when we suspecte thapproche of our enimies) thereby to geue warning to theyr neyghbours to be in a redines, & geather togeather, if perhaps our men shoulde attempt any thyng against them, or otherwyse as (semed most lykely) to cal them togeather, as to a wonder, to beholde our shyppes, they knowe yet no certentie. In this tracte, the shores bended somtyme towarde the South, and sometyme towarde the West and west southwest, and the sea was euery where entangled with Ilandes, by reason whereof, the keeles of the shyppes often times rased the sandes for shalownesse of the water: So that the shyppes being very sore brused and appayred, the sayles, cables, and other tackelinges, in maner rotten, and the vytailes (especially the biskette bread) corrupted by takyng water at the ryftes euyll closed, the Admirall was enforced to turne backe agayne: This laste poynte where he touched of *Cuba* (not yet being knowen to be an ilande) he called *Euangelista*. Thus turning his sayles towarde other ilandes lying not farre from the supposed continent, he chaunced into a mayne sea, where was suche a multitude of great Tortoyses, that somtyme they stayed the shyppes: Not long after, he entred into a gulfe of whyte water, lyke unto that wherof we spake before. At the length, fearing the shelfes of the ilandes, he returned to the shore of *Cuba* by the same way whiche he came. Here a multitude of thinhabitantes, as well women as men, resorted to hym with cheerefull countenances, and with feare, bringyng with them popingayes, bread, water, and cunnyes, but especially stocke doues, much bygger then ours, which he af[illegible]meth, in sauour and taste,

The sea entangled with Ilandes.

A multitude of great Tortoyses.

A gulfe of whyte water.

taste, to be muche more pleasaunt then our partryches. Wherefore where as in eating of them he perceiued a certayne sauoure of spyce to proceede from them, he commaunded the croppe to be opened of suche as were newely kylled, and founde the same full of sweete spyces, whiche he argued to be the cause of theyr strange taste: For it standeth with good reason, that the fleshe of beastes, shoulde drawe the nature and qualitie of theyr accustomed nouryshment. As the Admirall harde masse on the shore, there came towarde hym a certayne gouernoure, a man of foure score yeeres of age, and of great grauitie, although he were naked sauing his pryuie partes. He had a great trayne of men wayting on hym. All the whyle the prieste was at masse, he shewed him selfe very humble, and gaue reuerent attendance, with graue and demure countenaunce. When the masse was ended, he presented to the Admirall a baskette of the fruites of his countrey, delyuering the same with his owne handes. When the Admirall had gentelly entertayned him, desyring leaue to speake, he made an oration in the presence of *Didacus* the interpreter, to this effect. I haue byn aduertised (most mighty prince) that you haue of late with great power subdued many lands and Regions, hytherto vnknowen to you, and haue brought no litle feare vppon all the people and inhabitauntes of the same: the whiche your good fortune, you shal beare with lesse insolencie, if you remember that the soules of men haue two iourneyes after they are departed from this body: The one, foule and darke, prepared for suche as are iniurious and cruell to mankynde: the other, pleasaunt and delectable, ordeyned for them which in theyr lyfe tyme loued peace and quietnes. If therfore you acknowledge your selfe to be mortall, and consider that euery man shal receiue condigne rewarde or punyshement for suche thynges as he hath done in this life, you wyl wrongfully hurte no man. When he had saide these wordes and other lyke, which were declared to the Admirall by the interpreter, he marueyling at the iudgement of the naked olde man, aunsweared, that he was glad to heare his opinion as touching the sundry iourneys and rewardes of soules departed from theyr bodyes, supposing that nether he, or any other of thinhabitauntes of those Regions, had had any knowledge therof: declaring further, that the chiefe cause of his

commyng

The humanitie of a reuerende olde gouernour.

An oration of the naked gouernour.

Theyr opinion of the soule of man.

Desyre of gold, founde that which religion coulde not fynde.

Virtus post nummos. &c.

comming thither, was to instruct them in such godly knowledge and true religion: and that he was sent into those countreyes by the Christian kyng of Spayne (his lord and maister) for the same purpose, and specially to subdue and punyshe the *Canibales*, and suche other mischeuous people, and to defend innocentes against the violence of euyl doers, wyllyng hym, and al other suche as imbraced vertue, in no case to be afrayde, but rather to open his mynde vnto hym, yf eyther he, or any other suche quiet men as he was, had susteyned any wrong of theyr neyghbours, and that he woulde see the same reuenged. These comfortable wordes of the Admirall so pleased the olde man, that notwithstandyng his extreme age, he woulde gladly haue gone with the Admiral, as he had done in deede, yf his wyfe and chyldren had not hyndered hym of his purpose: but he marueyled not a lytle, that the Admiral was vnder the dominion of another: and much more, when the interpretour tolde hym of the glorye, magnificence, pompe, great power, and furnimentes of warre of our kinges, and of the multitudes of cities and townes whiche were vnder theyr dominions. Intendyng therefore to haue gone with the Admirall, his wyfe and chyldren fell prostrate at his feete, with teares desyring hym not to forsake them and leaue them desolate: at whose pitiful requestes, the worthy olde man beyng mooued, remayned at home to the comfort of his people and familie, satisfiyng rather them then hym selfe: for not yet ceassyng to woonder, and of heauie countenance because he myght not depart, he demaunded oftentymes yf that lande were not heauen, whiche brought foorth suche a kynde of men? For it is certaine, that among them the lande is as common as the sunne and water, and that Myne and Thyne (the seedes of all myscheefe) haue no place with them. They are content with so lytle, that in so large a countrey they haue rather superfluitie then scarcenesse: so that (as we haue sayde before) they seeme to lyue in the golden worlde without toyle, lyuyng in open gardens, not intrenched with dyches, diuided with hedges, or defended with walles: they deale truely one with another without lawes, without bookes, and without iudges: they take hym for an euyl and myscheuous man, whiche taketh pleasure in doyng hurt to other. And albeit that they delyte not in superfluities, yet make

The lande as common as the sunne and water.

they

they provision for the increase of suche rootes whereof they make theyr bread, as *Maizium, Iucca,* and *Ages,* contented with suche symple dyet, whereby health is preserued, and diseases auoyded. The Amirall therefore departyng from thence, and myndyng to returne agayne shortly after, chaunced to come agayne to the Ilande of *Iamaica,* beyng on the south syde thereof, and coasted all along by the shore of the same from the West to the East, from whose last corner on the East syde, when he sawe towarde the North syde on his left hande certayne hygh mountaynes, he knewe at the length that it was the south syde of the Ilande of *Hispaniola,* whiche he had not yet passed by. Wherefore, at the Calendes of September, entryng into the hauen of the same Ilande, called saint Nicholas hauen, he repayred his shyppes, to the intent that he might agayne waste and spoyle the Ilandes of the *Canibales,* and burne all theyr *Canoas,* that those rauenyng wolues might no longer persecute and deuoure the innocent sheepe: but he was at this tyme hyndered of his purpose, by reason of a disease which he had gotten by to much watching. Thus beyng feeble and weake, he was ledde of the Maryners to the citie of *Isabella,* where, with his two brethren whiche were there, and other of his familiars, he recouered his health in shorte space: yet coulde he not at this tyme assayle the *Canibales,* by reason of sedition that was risen of late among the Spanyardes whiche he had left in *Hispaniola,* whereof we wyll speake more hereafter. Thus fare ye well.

Simple dyet.

Hispaniola.

The Canibales.

Sickenesse of to much Watching.

The fourth booke of the first Decade, to *Lodouike* Cardinal of *Aragonie.*

COlonus the Admiral of the Ocean, returning (as he supposed) from the continent or fyrme lande of East *India,* had aduertisment that his brother *Boilus,* and one *Peter Margarita,* an olde familiar of the kynges, and a noble man, with dyuers other of those to whom he had left the gouernement of the Ilande, were (of corrupted mynde agaynst hym) departed into Spayne. Wherefore, as wel to purge hym selfe of suche crimes,

Easte India.

The Spaniardes rebell in the Admirals absence.

C i as

as they shoulde lay to his charge, as also to make a supply of other men in the place of them whiche were returned, and especiallye to prouide for vyttualles, as wheate, wine, oyle, and suche other, whiche the Spanyardes are accustomed to eate, because they coulde not yet well agree with such meates as they founde in the Ilandes, determined shortly to take his voyage into Spayne: but what he dyd before his departure, I wyll brefely rehearse.

The kynges of the Ilandes which had hytherto lyued quietly, and content with theyr lytle whiche they thought aboundant, wheras they nowe perceiued that our men began to fasten foote within theyr regions, & to beare rule among them, they toke the matter so greeuously, that they thought nothyng els but by what meanes they myght vtterlye destroy them, and for euer abolyshe the memory of theyr name, for that kinde of men (the Spanyardes I meane, which folowed the Admiral in that nauigation) were for the moste part vnruly, regarding nothyng but idlenesse, play, and libertie, and woulde by no meanes absteyne from iniuries, rauishing of the women of the Ilandes before the faces of their husbandes, fathers, and brethren: by which theyr abominable mysdemeanour, they disquieted the myndes of all the inhabitantes, insomuche that wheresoeuer they founde any of our men vnprepared, they slue them with such fercenesse and gladnesse, as though they had offered sacrifice to God. Intendyng therfore to pacifie theyr troubled myndes, and to punyshe them that slue his men before he departed from thence, he sent for the king of that vale, whiche in the booke before we described to be at the foote of the mountaynes of the region of *Cibana*, this kynges name was *Guarionexius*: who, the more straygthly to concyle vnto hym the frendshyp of the Admirall, gaue his syster to wyfe to *Didacus*, a man from his chyldes age brought vp with the Admirall, whom he vsed for his interpreter in the prouinces of *Cuba*. After this, he sent for *Caunaboa*, called the lorde of the house of golde, that is, of the mountaynes of *Cibana*: For this *Caunaboa* he sent one Captayne *Hoieda*, whom the ditionaries of *Caunaboa* had enforced to keepe his holde, besieging for the space of thirtie dayes the fortresse of saint Thomas, in the whiche *Hoieda* with his fyftie souldiers stoode at theyr defence, vntyll the comming of the Admirall. Whyle *Hoieda* remayned with *Caunaboa*, ma-

The kinges of the Ilande rebell.

The Spaniardes misbehauiour.

A iust reuenge.

Captayne Hoieda.

ny

The ambassadours of the kynges of diuers regions were sent to *Caunaboa*, persuadyng hym in no condition to permit the Christians to inhabite the Ilande, except he had rather serue then rule. On the other partie, *Hoieda* aduertised *Caunaboa* to goe to the Admiral, and to make a league of frendshyp with hym: but the ambassadours on the contrary part, threatned hym, that if he woulde so doo, the other kynges woulde inuade his region. But *Hoieda* aunswered them agayne, that whereas they consipired to mayntayne theyr libertie, they should by that meanes be brought to seruitude & destruction, if they entended to resist or kepe warre agaynst the Christians. Thus *Caunaboa* on the one side and the other beyng troubled, as it were a rocke in the sea beaten with contrary floodes, and muche more vexed with the stormes of his gyltie conscience, for that he had priuily slayne .xx. of our men vnder pretence of peace, feared to come to the Admirall: but at the length, hauyng excogitated his deceyte, to haue slayne the Admirall and his companye, vnder the colour of frendshyp, yf oportunitie would so haue serued, he repayred to ye Admiral, with his whole familie, and many other wayting on him, armed after theyr manner. Beyng demaunded why he brought so great a route of men with him, he aunswered, that it was not decent for so great a prince as he was, to goe out of his house without suche a bande of men: but the thyng chaunced muche otherwyse then he looked for, for he fell into the snares whiche he had prepared for other, for whereas by the way he began to repent hym that he came foorth of his house, *Hoieda* with many fayre woordes & promises brought him to the Admiral, at whose commaundement he was immediatly taken and put in prison, so that the soules of our men were not long from theyr bodyes vnreuenged. Thus *Caunaboa* with al his familie beyng taken, the Admirall was determined to runne ouer the Ilande, but he was certified that there was suche famine among the inhabitauntes, that there was alredy fyftie thousande men dead thereof, and that they dyed yet dayly, as it were rotten sheepe, the cause whereof, was wel knowen to be theyr owne obstinacie and frowardnesse: for wheras they sawe that our men entended to choose them a dwellyng place in the Ilande, supposing that they myght haue dryuen them from thence if the vittualles of the Ilande should fayle,

Caunaboa conspireth the Admirals death.

Famine in the Ilande of Hispaniola.

The hunger of golde causeth greate famine.

they determined with them selues, not only to leaue sowyng and plantyng, but also to destroy and plucke vp by the rootes, euery man in his owne region, that whiche they had alredy sowen, of both kyndes of bread, whereof we made mention in the firste booke, but especially among the mountaynes of *Cibana*, otherwyse called *Cipanga*, forasmuche as they had knowledge that the golde whiche aboundeth in that region, was the chiefe cause that deteyned our men in the Iland. In the meane tyme, he sent forth a Captayne with a bande of men, to searche the South syde of the Ilande, who at his returne, reported that throughout all the regions that he trauayled, there was suche scarcenesse of bread, that for the space of. xvi. dayes, he ate nothyng but the rootes of hearbes, and of young date trees, or the fruites of other wylde trees: but *Guarionexius* the kyng of the vale, lying beneath the mountaynes of *Cibana*, whose kyngdome was not so wasted as the other, gaue our men certayne vyttualles. Within a fewe dayes after, both that the iourneys myght be the shorter, and also that our men myght haue more safe places of refuge, if the inhabitauntes shoulde hereafter rebell in lyke manner, he buylded another fortresse (whiche he called the Towre of Conception) betweene the Citie of *Isabella*, and Saint Thomas fortresse, in the marches of the kyngdome of this *Guarionexius*, within the precincte of *Cibana*, vpon the syde of a hyll, hauyng a fayre riuer of holsome water runnyng harde by the same.

The towre of conception.

Thus when the inhabitantes sawe newe buyldinges to be dayly erected, and our shippes lying in the hauen rotten and halfe broken, they began to dispayre of any hope of libertie, and wandred vp and downe with heauie cheare. From the Towre of Conception, searchyng diligentlye the inner partes of the mountaynes of *Cibana*, there was a certayne kyng whiche gaue them a masse of rude golde as bigge as a mans fyst, weighing. xx. ounces: this golde was not founde in the banke of that riuer, but in a heape of drye earth, and was lyke vnto the stone called *Tophus*, whiche is soone resolued into sande. This masse of golde I mee selfe sawe in Castile, in the famous Citie of *Methymna Campi*, where the Court lay al that wynter. I sawe also a great peece of pure *Electrum*, of the which belles, and Apothecaries morters, & many suche other vessells and instrumentes may be made, as were in

olde

made tyme of copper the citie of *Corinthus*. This peece of *Electrum* was of suche weight, that I was not only with both my handes unable to lift it from the grounde, but also not of strength to remoue it eyther one way or other: they affirmed that it weyed more then three hundred pounde weyght, after eyght ounces to the pounde, it was founde in the house of a certayne prynce, and left hym by his predecessours: and albeit that in the dayes of the inhabitauntes yet lyuyng, *Electrum* was no where digged, yet knewe they where the myne thereof was, but our men with muche adoo coulde hardely cause them to shewe them the place, they bore them suche priuie hatred, yet at the length they brought them to the myne, beyng now ruinate and stopped with stones and rubbyshe: it is muche easyer to dygge then is the iron myne, and might be restored agayne, yf myners and other workmen skylful therein were appoynted thereto. Not farre from the towne of Conception, in the same mountaynes, is founde great plentie of Amber, and out of certaine rockes of the same, distilleth a substance of the yelowe colour whiche the Paynters vse. Not farre from these mountaynes are many great woods, in the whiche are none other trees then Brasile, which the Italians cal *Verzino*. But here perhaps (ryght noble prynce) you woulde aske, what shoulde be the cause, that where as the Spanyardes haue brought out of these Ilandes certayne shyppes laden with Brasile, somewhat of Gossampine cotton, a quantitie of Amber, a lytle golde, & some spyces, why they haue not brought suche plentie of golde, and suche other ryche marchaundizes, as the fruitefulnesse of these regions seeme to promyse? To this I aunswere, that when *Colonus* the Admirall was lykewyse demaunded the cause hereof, he made aunswere, that the Spanyardes whiche he tooke with hym into these regions, were geuen rather to sleepe, play, and idlenesse, then to labour, and were more studious of sedition and newes, then desirous of peace and quietnesse: also, that being geuen to licenciousnesse, they rebelled & forsooke him, findyng matter of false accusation against hym, because he went about to represse theyr outragiousnesse: by reason whereof, he was not yet able to breake the power of the inhabitauntes, and freelye to possesse the full dominion of the Ilande, and these hynderaunces to be the cause that hy-

Electrum is a metall naturally mixt of one portion of golde, & an other of siluer, beyng of proportie to beware popsot and was therfore in olde tyme in greater estimation then golde.

The mine of Electrum.

An other kinde of amber is taken out of greate whale fishes.

Orpement or oker.

Wooddes of brasile trees.

Licentiusnes of to much libertie.

therto the gaynes haue scarsely countervayled the charges: albeit, euen this yeere whyle I wrote these thynges at your request, they geathered in two monethes the summe of a thousande and two hundred poundes weyght of gold. But because we entende to speake more largely of these thynges in theyr place, we wyll nowe returne from whence we haue digressed. When the inhabitauntes perceiued that they coulde by no meanes shake the yoke from theyr necks, they made humble supplication to the Admiral, that they myght stande to theyr tribute, and applye them selues to reincrease the fruites of theyr countrey, beyng nowe almost wasted. He graunted them theyr request, and appoynted suche order that euery region shoulde pay theyr tribute, with the commodities of theyr countreys, accordyng to theyr portion, and at suche tyme as they were agreed vpon: but the violent famine did frustrate al these appoyntmentes, for al the trauayles of theyr bodyes, were scarcelye able to suffise to fynde them meate in the woodes, whereby to susteyne theyr lyues, beyng of long tyme contented with rootes and the fruites of wylde trees: yet many of the kynges with theyr people, euen in this extreme necessitie, brought part of theyr tribute, most humblye desyryng the Admiral to haue compassion of their calamities, and to beare with them yet a whyle, vntyl the Ilande were restored to the olde state, promysyng further, that that whiche was nowe wantyng, shoulde then be double recompenced. But fewe of the inhabitauntes of the mountaynes of *Cibaua* kept theyr promise, because they were sorer oppressed with famine then anye of the other. They say that the inhabitantes of these mountaynes dyffer no lesse in language and manners from them whiche dwel in the playnes, then among vs the rusticalles of the countrey, from the gentlemen of the courte: wheras notwithstandyng they lyue as it were both vnder one portion of heauen, and in manythinges much after one fashion, as in nakednesse, and rude simplicitie. But nowe let vs returne to *Cannaboa* the king of the house of golde, beyng in captiuitie. When he perceiued hym selfe to be cast in prison, frettyng and gratyng his teeth, as it had been a Lion of *Libia*, and dayly and nyghtly deuysyng with hym selfe howe he myght be delyuered, beganne to perswade the Admiral, that forasmuche as he had nowe taken vnto his

dominion

Margin notes:

...nd this only ...eathered, and ...ot dygged out ...f the bodye of ...e mine.

The nature of the region disposeth the maner of the people.

Kyng Cannaboa in captiuitie.

[illegible] the region called *Cibana* (whereof he was kyng) it shoulde be expedient to sende thyther a garrison of Christian men, to defende the same from the incursions of his olde enemies and borderers: for he sayde, that it was signified vnto him, that the countrey was wasted and spoyled with suche incursions. By this craftie deuise, he thought to haue brought to passe, that his brother whiche was in that region, and the other his kynsfolkes and frendes with theyr adherentes, shoulde haue taken, eyther by sleyght or force, as many of our men as myght haue redeemed hym. But the Admiral vnderstandyng his craftie meanyng, sent *Hoieda* with suche a companye of men, as myght vanquishe the *Cibanians*, yf they shoulde moue warre agaynst them. Our men had scarcelye entred into the region, but the brother of *Caunaboa* came agaynst them with an armie of fyue thousande naked men, armed after theyr manner, with clubbes, arrowes tipt with bones, and speares made harde at the endes with fyre. He stole vpon our men beyng in one of theyr houses, and encamped rounde about the same on euery syde. This *Cibanian*, as a man not ignorant in the discipline of warre, about the distaunce of a furlong from the house, diuided his armie into fyue battayles, appoyntyng to euery one of them a circuite by equall diuision, and placed the froont of his owne battayle directly agaynst our men. When he had thus set his battayles in good aray, he gaue certayne signes that ye whole armie should marche forwarde in order with equall paces, and with a larome freshly assayle theyr enimies, in such sort that none might escape. But our men iudging it better to encountre with one of the battayles, then to abyde the brunt of the whole armie, gaue onset on the mayne battayle aranged in the playne, because that place was most commodious for the horsmen. When the horsmen therefore had geuen the charge, they ouerthrewe them with the brestes of theyr horses, and slue as many as abode the ende of the fight, the residue beyng stryken with feare, disparcled, and fledde to the mountaynes and rockes: from whence they made a pitifull howlyng to our men, desyryng them to spare them; protestyng that they woulde neuer more rebell, but doo whatsoeuer they woulde commaunde them, yf they woulde suffer them to lyue in theyr owne countrey. Thus the brother of *Caunaboa*

Caunaboa his brother rebelleth.

A conflict betwene the Cibauians and the Spaniards

C iii. beyng

beyng taken, the Admiral licenced the people to resort euerye man to his owne: these thynges thus fortunately atchiued, this region was pacified. Among these mountaynes, the vale whiche *Caunaboa* inhabited, is called *Magona*, and is exceeding fruitful, hauing in it many goodly springes and riuers, in the sande whereof is founde great plentie of golde. The same yeere in the moneth of June, they say there arose such a boystous tempest of winde from the Southwest, as hath not lightly ben hearde of, the violence wherof was such, that it plucked vp by the rootes whatsoeuer great trees were within the reache of the force therof. When this whyrlewynde came to the hauen of the citie, it beat downe to the bottome of the sea three shyppes, whiche lay at anker, and broke the cables in sunder, and that (whiche is the greater maruevle) without any storme or roughnesse of the sea, only turnyng them three or foure tymes about. The inhabitauntes also affyrme, that the same yeere the sea extended it selfe further into the lande, and rose hygher then euer it dyd before by the memorie of man, by the space of a cubit. The people therefore muttered among them selues, that our nation had troubled the elementes, & caused suche portentous signes. These tempestes of the ayre (whiche the Grecians call *Tiphones*, that is, whyrlewyndes) they call *Furacanes*, whiche they say, doo often tymes chaunce in this Ilande: but that neyther they, nor theyr great graundfathers, euer sawe suche violent and furious *Furacanes*, that plucked vp great trees by the rootes, neyther yet such surges and vehement motions on the sea, that so wasted the land: as in deede it may appeare, forasmuche as wheresoeuer the sea bankes are neere to any playne, there are in maner euery where florysshyng medowes reaching euen vnto the shore: but nowe let vs returne to *Caunaboa*. As kyng *Caunaboa* therefore and his brother shoulde haue ben brought into Spayne, they dyed by the way, for very pensiuenesse and anguish of minde. The Admiral, whose shippes were drowned in the foresayd tempest, perceiuing him selfe to be nowe enclosed, commaunded forthwith two other shyppes (whiche the Spaniardes cal *Carauelas*) to be made: for he had with hym all manner of Artificers parteyning thereunto. Whyle these thynges were doyng, he sent foorth *Bartholomeus Colonus* his brother, beyng Lieutenant of the Ilande, with

A greate tempest in the moneth of June.

Whirle windes. Furacanes.

The death of king Caunaboa and his brother.

with an armie of men to searche the golde mynes, beyng distant threescore leagues from the citie of *Isabella*, whiche he went towarde by the conducte of certayne people of the Ilande, before the mynes of *Cipanga* or *Cibana* were knowen. In these mynes they founde certayne deepe pittes, which had ben dygged in old tyme, out of these pyttes, the Admiral (who affirmeth this Ilande of *Hispaniola* to be Ophir, as we sayde before) supposeth that Salomon the kyng of *Hierusalem* had his great ryches of golde, whereof we reade in the olde Testament, and that his shyppes sayled to this Ophir by the gulfe of *Persia*, called *Sinus Persicus*. But whether it be so or not, it lyeth not in me to iudge, but in my opinion it is farre of. As the myners dygged the superficial or uppermost part of the earth of ȳ mynes, durying for the space of sixe myles, & in dyuers places syfted the same on the drye lande, they founde suche plentie of golde, that every hyred labourer could easily finde every day the weight of three drammes. These mynes beyng thus searched & founde, the Lieutenant certifieth the Admirall hereof by his letters, the which when he had receiued, the fifth day of the Ides of Marche, *Anno*. 1495. he entred into his newe shyppes, and tooke his voyage directly to Spayne, to aduertise the kyng of all his affayres, leauyng the whole regiment of the Ilande with his brother the Lieutenant.

The golde mines of Salomon.

Gold in the superficiall partes of the earth.

The fift booke of the fyrst Decade, to *Lodouike* Cardinall of *Aragonie*.

After the Admirals departing into Spaine, his brother the Lieutenaunt buylded a fortresse in the golde mines, as he had commaunded hym: this he called the golden towre, because the labourers founde golde in the earth, and stone wherof they made the walles of the fortresse. He consumed three monethes in makyng the instrumentes wherewith the golde shoulde be geathered, washed, tryed, and moulten: yet was he at this tyme, by reason of wante of vittualles, enforced to leaue al thynges imperfecte, and to goe seeke for meate. Thus as he, with a bande of armed men, had entred threescore myles

The golden tower.

Lacke of vitaples.

further

[illegible] within the lande, the people of the countrey here and there resortyng to hym, gaue hym a certayne portion of theyr bread, in exchaunge for other of our thynges: but he coulde not long tary here, bycause they lacked meate in the fortresse, whyther he hasted with such as he had now gotten. Leauyng therefore in the fortresse a garrison of ten men, with that portion of the Ilande bread whiche yet remayned, leauyng also with them a Hounde to take those kyndes of lytle beastes whiche they call *Vsias*, not muche vnlyke our Conies, he returned to the fortresse of Conception. This also was the moneth wherein the kyng *Guarionexius*, and also *Manicaotexius* borderer vnto hym, shoulde haue brought in theyr tributes. Remaynyng there the whole moneth of June, he exacted the whole tribute of these two kynges, & vytualles necessary for hym and such as he brought with hym, whiche were about foure hundred in number. Shortly after, about the Kalendes of July, there came three Carauels from Spayne, bryngyng with them sundrye kyndes of vyttualles, as wheate, oyle, wine, bakon, & Martelmas beefe, whiche were diuided to euery man accordyng as neede required, some also was lost in the caryage for lacke of good lookyng to. At the aryual of these shyppes, the Lieutenaunt receiued commaundement from the kyng and the Admiral his brother, that he with his men should remoue their habitation to the south syde of the Ilande, because it was nearer to the golde mynes: Also that he shoulde make diligent searche for those kinges whiche had slayne the Christian men, and to sende them with theyr confederates bounde into Spayne. At the next voyage therefore he sent three hundred captiues, with three kynges, and when he had diligently searched the coastes of the south syde, he transported his habitation, and buylded a fortresse there, vpon the toppe of a hyll neare vnto a sure hauen: this fortresse he called saint Dominikes towre. Into this hauen runneth a riuer of wholsome water, replenished with sundry kyndes of good fysshes: they affyrme this ryuer to haue many benefites of nature, for where so euer it runneth, all thynges are exceedyng pleasaunt and fruitefull, hauyng on euery syde groues of Date trees, and diuers other of the Ilande fruites so plentifullye, that as they sayled along by the shore, oftentymes the braunches thereof, laden with flowres and

Vittualles brought from Spayne.

Saint Dominikes towre.

and fruites, hangyng ouer theyr heades, that they might plucke them with theyr handes: also that the fruitfulnes of this grounde, is eyther equall with the soyle of Isabella, or better. In *Isabella* he lefte only certayne sicke men, and shippe wryghtes, whom he had appoynted to make certayne carauels, the residue of his men, he conueighed to the south, to saynt Dominickes towre. After he had buylded this fortresse, leauyng therin a garryson of .xx. men, he with the remanent of his souldiers, prepared them selues to searche the inner partes of the West syde of the Ilande, hytherto knowen onely by name. Therefore about .xxx. leagues, (that is) fourescore and tenne myles from the fortresse, he chaunced on the ryuer *Naiba*, whiche we sayde to desende from the mountaynes of *Cibaua*, ryght towarde the south, by the myddest of the ilande. When he had ouerpassed this ryuer with a companye of armed men diuyded into .xxv. decurions, that is, tenne in a company, with theyr capitaynes, he sent two decurions to the regions of those kynges in whose landes were the great woodds of brasile trees. Inclynyng towarde the lefte hande, they founde the woodes, entred into them, and felled the high and precious trees, which were to that day vntouched. Eche of the decurions filled certayne of the ilande houses with the trunkes of brasile, there to be reserued vntil the shippes came which should cary them away. But the Lieutenaunt directing his iourney towarde the right hande, not farre from the bankes of ye riuer of *Naiba*, founde a certaine kyng whose name was *Beuchius Anacauchoa*, encamped against thinhabitantes of the prouince of *Naiba*, to subdue them vnder his dominion, as he had done many other kings of the ilande, borderers vnto him. The palace of this great king, is called *Xaragua*, & is situate toward the West ende of the ilande, distant from the ryuer of *Naiba* .xxx. leagues. All the prynces which dwell betwene the West ende & his palace, are ditionaries vnto him. All that region from *Naiba*, to the furthest marches of the west, is vtterly without golde, although it be full of mountaynes. When the kyng had espied our men, laying a part his weapons, & geuyng signes of peace, he spake gentelly to them (vncerteyne whether it were of humanitie or feare) and demaunded of them what they woulde haue. The Lieutenaunt answered, That he should

Isabella.

The Riuer of Naiba.

Woodes of Brasile trees.

Mountaynes without golde.

e.v. viii

pay

paye tribute to the Admirall his brother, in the name of the Christian kyng of Spayne. To whom he sayde, Howe can you requyre that of me, whereas neuer a region vnder my dominion bryngeth forth golde? For he had hearde, that there was a strange nation entred into the ilande, whiche made great search for golde: But he supposed that they desyred some other thyng. The lieutenaunt answeared agayne; God forbydde that we shoulde enioyne any man to paye such tribute as he myght not easely forbeare, or such as were not engendered or growing in the region: but we vnderstande that your regions bryng foorth great plentie of Gossampine cotton, and hempe, with such other, wherof we desyre you to geue vs parte. When he heard these woordes, he promysed with cherefull countenaunce, to geue hym as much of these thynges as he woulde requyre. Thus dismissing his army, and sending messengers before, he him selfe accompanied the Lieutenaunt, and brought him to his palace, being distant (as we haue sayde) .xxx. leagues. In al this tracte, they passed through the iurisdiction of other princes, beyng vnder his dominion: Of the whiche, some gaue them hempe, of no lesse goodnes to make tackelinges for shyppes then our wood: Other some brought bread, and some gossamppne cotton. And so euery of them payde trybute with suche commodities as theyr countreys brought foorth. At the length they came to the kinges mansion place of *Xaragua*. Before they entered into the palace, a great multitude of the kynges seruauntes & subiectes resorted to the court, honorably (after their maner) to receyue their kyng *Beuchius Anacauchoa*, with the strangers which he brought with him to see the magnificence of his court. But now shal you heare howe they were intertained. Among other triumphes and syghtes, two are especially to be noted: Fyrst, there mette them a company of .xxx. women, beyng al the kynges wyues and concubines, bearyng in theyr handes branches of date trees, syngyng and daunsyng: they were all naked, sauyng that theyr priuie partes were couered with breeches of gossampine cotton: but the virgins, hauyng theyr heare hangyng downe about their shoulders, tyed about the forehead with a fyllet, were vtterly naked. They affirme that theyr faces, breastes, pappes, handes, and other partes of theyr bodyes, were exceedyng smoothe,

The kynges wyues.

Well fauored women.

H.i.

smothe, and well proportioned, but somwhat inclynyng to a louely browne. They supposed that they had seene those most beutyfull *Dryades*, or the natyue nymphes or fayres of the fountaynes whereof the antiques spake so muche. The braunches of date trees, which they bore in theyr right handes when they daunced, they delyuered to the Lieutenaunt, with lowe curtesy and smylyng countenaunce. Thus enteryng into the kynges house, they founde a delycate supper prepared for them, after theyr maner. When they were well refresshed with meate, the nyght drawyng on, they were brought by the kynges officers, euery man to his lodgyng, accordyng to his degree, in certayne of theyr houses about the pallaice, where they rested them in hangyng beddes, after the maner of the countrey, wherof we haue spoken more largely in an other place. Dryades.

The day folowyng, they broughte our men to their common hall, into the whiche they come togeather as often as they make any notable games or triumphes, as we haue sayde before. Here, after many daunsynges, syngynges, maskinges, runnynges, wrestlynges, and other tryinge of maistryes, sodaynly there appeared in a large plaine neere vnto the hal, two great armies of men of warre, whiche the kyng for his pastyme had caused to be prepared, as the Spaniardes vse the playe with reedes, which they call *Iuga de Canias*. As the armies drewe neere togeather, they assayled the one the other as fiersely, as if mortall enimies with theyr baners spleade, should fight for theyr goodes, theyr landes, theyr lyues, theyr libertie, theyr countrey, theyr wyues & theyr children, so that within the momente of an houre, foure men were slayne, and many wounded. The battayle also shoulde haue contynued longer, yf the kyng had not, at the request of our men, caused them to ceasse. The thyrde day, the Lieutenant counsaylyng the kyng to sowe more plentie of gossampyne vppon the bankes neere vnto the waters syde, that they myght the better paye theyr trybute pryuately, accordyng to the multitude of theyr houses, he prepayred to *Isabella*, to vysite the sycke men whiche he had lefte there, and also to see howe his workes went forwarde. In the tyme of his absence .xxx. of his men were consumed with diuerse diseases. Wherefore beyng sore troubled in his mynde, and in maner at his wyttes ende, A prettie pastyme. Foure men slayne in sport. Prouision for diseased men.

wha.

what he were best to doo, for as muche as he wanted all thinges necessarie, as wel to restore them to health whiche were yet accrased, as also vitaples to mayntayne þ whole multitude, where as there was yet no shyppe come from Spayne: at the length, he determyned to sende abrode the sicke men here and there to sundrye Regyons of the ilande, and to the castelles whiche they had erected in the same. For directly from the citie of Isabella to saynt Dominikes towre, that is, from the north to the south, through the ilande, they had buylded thus many castles. Fyrst, xxxvi. myles distant from Isabella, they buylded the castell of *Sperantia*. From *Sperantia*. xxv. myles, was the castell of saynt Katharine. From saynt Katharines .xx. myles, was saynt James towre. Other .xx. myles from saynt James towre, was a stronger fortresse then any of the other, whiche they called the towre of Conception, which he made the stronger, because it was situat at the rootes of the golden mountaynes of Cibana, in the great and large playne, so fruitefull and well inhabited as we haue before described. He buylded also an other in the mydde waye betwene the towre of Conception, & saynt Dominikes towre, the whiche also was stronger then the towre of Conception, because it was within the lymittes of a great kyng, hauyng under his dominion fiue thousande men, whose chiefe citie and head of the Realme, beyng called *Bonauum*, he wylled that the castell shoulde also be called after the same name. Therefore leauyng the sicke men in these castels, and other of the ilande houses nere unto the same, he hym selfe repayred to saynt Dominikes, exacting trybutes of al the kynges whiche were in his way. When he had taryed there a fewe dayes, there was a rumour spredde, that all the kynges about the borders of the towre of Conception, had conspyred with desperate myndes to rebell agaynst the Spaniardes. When the Lieutenaunt was certified herof, he tooke his iourney towarde them immediately, not beyng discoraged eyther by the length of the waye, or feeblenesse of his souldyers, beyng in maner forewearied with trauayle. As he drewe nere unto them, he had aduertysement that kyng *Guarionexius* was chosen by other prynces to be the Capitayne of this rebellion, and that he was enforsed therto halfe unwyllyng, beyng seduced by persuasions and prouocations: the whiche

The castels and towers of Hispaniola.

The golden mountaynes of Cibana.

The kinges rebell.

whiche is more lykely to be true, for that he had before had experience of the power and policie of our men. They came togeather at a daye appoynted, accompanyed with .xv. thousande men, armed after their manner, once agayne to proue the fortune of warre. Here the Lieutenaunt, consultyng with the Captayne of the fortresse and the other souldiers of whom he had the conducte, determyned to sette upon them unwares in their owne houses, before they coulde prepare theyr army. He sent foorth therefore to euery kyng a Centurion, that is, a captayne of a hundred, which were commaunded upon a sudden to inuade theyr houses in the nyght, and to take them sleepyng, before the people (being scattred here & there) myght assemble togeather. Thus secretly enteryng into their vyllages, not fortified with walles, trenches, or bulwarks, they broke in upon them, toke them, bound them, & led away euery man his prisoner accordyng as they were commaunded. The Lieutenant hym selfe with his hundred men, assayled kyng *Guarionexius* as the worthier personage, whom he tooke prysoner, as did the other captaines theyr kings, and at the same houre appoynted. Fourteene of them were brought the same nyght to the towre of Conception. Shortlye after, when he had put to death two of the kynges whiche were the chiefe autours of this newe reuolte, and had suborned *Guarionexius* & the other kynges to attempt the same, least the people for sorowe of theyr kinges shoulde neglecte or forsake their countrey, whiche thyng myght haue ben great incommoditie to our men, who by thincrease of theyr seedes and fruites were oftentymes ayded, he freely pardoned and dismissed *Guarionexius* and the other kynges, the people in the meane tyme flocking togeather about the towre, to the number of fyue thousande without weapons, with pitiful houling for the deliuerance of their kinges: The ayre thundered, & the earth trembled through the vehemencie of theyr outcry. The Lieutenaunt warned *Guarionexius* and the other kynges, with threatenynges, with rewardes, and with promyses, neuer thereafter to attempt any suche thyng. Then *Guarionexius* made an oration to the people, of ye great power of our men, of theyr clemencie towarde offenders, & liberalitie to suche as remaine faithfull, desyryng them to quiet theyr myndes, and from thenceforth neyther in deede nor thought to interpryse any

An army of xv. thousand Barbarians.

The kinges are taken prisoners.

king Guarionexius is pardoned.

any thyng agaynst the Christians, but to obeye and serue them, excepte they woulde dayly brynge them selues into further calamities. When the oration was fynysshed, they tooke hym vp, and set hym on theyr shoulders, and so caryed hym home to his owne pallace: and by this meanes, this Region was pacifyed for a whyle. But our men, with heauy countenaunce wandered vp and downe, as desolate in a strange countrey, lackyng vittailes, and worne out of apparell, whereas .x. monethes were nowe passed sence the Admirals departure, durynge which tyme, they coulde heare nothyng out of Spayne. The Lieuetenaunt comforted them all that he coulde with fayre wordes and promyses. In the meane tyme, *Beuchius Anacauchoa* (the kyng of the West partes of the Region of *Xaragua* (of whom we spake before) sent messengers to the Lieuetenaunt, to signifye vnto hym, that he had in a redynes the gossampine cotton, and suche other thynges as he wylled hym to prepare for the payment of his trybute. Whereupon the Lieuetenaunt tooke his iourney thyther, and was honorably receiued of the kyng and his syster, somtyme the wyfe of *Caunaboa* the kyng of *Cibana*, bearyng no lesse rule in the gouernaunce of her brothers kyngdome, then he hym selfe: For they affirmed her to be a wyse woman, of good maners, & pleasaunt in company. She earnestly perswaded her brother, by the example of her husband, to loue and obey the Christians. This woman was called *Anacaona*. He founde in the palace of *Beuchius Anacauchoa*. xxxii. kynges, which had brought theyr tributes with them, and abode his commyng. They brought with them also, besyde theyr tribut assigned them, further to demerite ye fauour of our men, great plentie of vitailes, as both kindes of bread, cunnies, and fisshes, alredy dryed, because they shoulde not putrifie: Serpentes also of that kynde which we sayd to be estemed among them as most delicate meat, and lyke vnto Crocodiles sauing in bygnes. These serpentes they cal *Iuannas*, which our men learned (somwhat to late) to haue ben engendred in the ilande: For vnto that day, none of them durst aduenture to tast of them, by reason of theyr horrible deformitie and lothsomnes. Yet the Lieuetenant, being entysed by the pleasantnes of the kynges syster, determined to tast of the serpentes. But when he felte the fleshe therof to be so delycate to his tungue,

Lacke of vytayles.

xxxii. kinges.

Serpentes eaten.

tongue, he fel to it without al feare: the whiche thyng his companions perceiuing, were not behynde hym in greedynesse, insomuch that they had now none other talke, then of the sweetenesse of these serpentes, which they affyrme to be of more pleasaunt taste, then eyther our Phesantes or Partriches: but they lose theyr taste, except they be prepared after a certayne fashion, as doo Peacockes and Phesantes, except they be enterlarded before they be rosted. They prepare them therefore after this manner: Fyrst, taking out theyr bowelles, euen from the throte to the thyghes, they washe and rubbe theyr bodyes very cleane both within & without, then rolling them together on a circle, inuolued after the manner of a sleepyng snake, they thruste them into a pot, of no bigger capacitie then to holde them only, this done, putting a litle water vnto them, with a portion of the Ilande Pepper, they seethe them with a soft fyre of sweete wood, and suche as maketh no great smoke: Of the fatte of them beyng thus sodde, is made an exceedyng pleasant broth or pottage. They say also, that there is no meate to be compared to the egges of these serpentes, which they vse to seethe by them selues: they are good to be eaten as soone as they are sodde, and may also be reserued many dayes after. But hauyng sayde thus much of their enterteynement and dayntie fare, let vs nowe speake of other matters. When the Lieuetenaunt had fylled one of the Ilande houses with the Gossampine cotten which he had receiued for tribute, the kynges promysed furthermore to geue hym as muche of theyr bread as he woulde demaunde: he gaue them hartie thankes, and gently accepted theyr frendly proffer. In the meane tyme, whyle this bread was a geatheryng in sundry regions, to be brought to the pallace of *Beuchius Anacbaucoa* kyng of *Xaragua*, he sent messengers to *Isabella*, for one of the two Carauelles whiche were lately made there, intendyng to send the same againe thither laden with bread. The Maryners glad of these tydynges, sayled about the Ilande, and in shorte space brought the shyppe to the coastes of *Xaragua*. The syster of kyng *Beuchius Anacauchoa*, that wyse and pleasaunt woman *Anacaona* (the wyfe sometyme of *Cannaboa* the kyng of the golden house of the mountaynes of *Cibana*, whose husbande dyed in the way when he shoulde haue ben caryed into Spayne) when

F i she

The dressing of serpentes to be eaten.

Serpentes egges eaten.

Gossopine cotton.

Queene Anacaona.

she hearde say that our shyppe was arriued on the shore of her natiue countrey, perswaded the king her brother, that they both myght goe together to see it: for the place where the shyppe lay, was not paste .xl. myles distant from *Xaragua*. They rested all nyght in the midway, in a certayne vyllage in the which was the

The treasurie of Queene Anacaona.

treasurie or iewel house of *Anacaona*. Her treasure was neither golde, siluer, or pretious stones, but only thynges necessary to be vsed, as chayres, stooles, settels, disshes, potingers, pottes, pannes, basons, treyes, and such other housholde stuffe and instrumentes, workemanly made of a certayne blacke and harde shyning wood, which that excellent learned phisition, Iohn baptist *Elisius*, affirmeth to be Hebene.

Hebene wood.

Whatsoeuer portion of wit nature hath geuen to the inhabitantes of these ilandes, the same doth most appeare in these kynde of workes, in which they shewe great art and cunnyng, but those which this woman had, were made in the iland of *Guanabba*, situate in the mouth of the west syde of *Hispaniola*:

The Ilande of Guanabba.

In these they graue the lyuely images of such phantasies as they suppose they see walke by nyght, which the antiques called *Lemures*: Also the images of men, serpentes, beastes, & what so euer other thing they haue once seene. What woulde you thinke (moste noble prince) that they coulde doo, if they had the vse of Iron and steele? For they only fyrst make these soft in the fyre, & afterwarde make them holowe and carue them with a certayne stone which they fynd in the ryuers.

Cunnyng Artificers.

A stone in the steede of Iron.

Of stooles and chayres, she gaue the Lieutenaunt fourteene, and of vesselles partaynyng to the table and kitchen, shee gaue hym threescore, some of wood, and some of earth, also gossampyne cotton redye spunne, foure great bottomes of exceeding weight. The day folowing, when they came to the sea side, where was an other village of the kynges, the Lieutenaunt commaunded the shyppe boate to be brought to the shore. The kyng also had prepared two Canoas, paynted after theyr maner, one for hym selfe and certayne of his gentelmen, an other for his sister *Anacaona* and her wayting women: but *Anacaona* desyred to be caried in the shippe boate with the Lieutenaunt. When they nowe approched neare vnto the shippe, certayne great peeces of ordinaunce were discharged of purpose, the sea was fylled with thunder, and the ayre with smoke, they trembled and

Gunnes.

and quaked for feare, supposyng that the frame of the worlde had ben in daunger of fallyng, but when they sawe the Lieutenaunt laugh, and looke cheerefully on them, they called agayne theyr spirites, and when they yet drewe nearer to the shyp, and hearde the noyse of the fluites, shawlmes, and drummes, they were wonderfully astonied at the sweete harmonie therof. Entryng into the shyppe, and beholdyng the foreshyp and the sterne, the toppe castel, the maste, the hatches, the cabbens, the keele, and the tacklynges, the brother fyxyng his eyes on the syster, and the syster on the brother, they were both as it were dumme and amazed, and wyste not what to say for to muche woondryng. Whyle beholdyng these thynges, they wandered vp and downe the ship, the Lieutenaunt commaunded the ankers to be loosed, and the sayles to be hoysed vp. Then were they further astonyshed, when they saw so great a mole to mooue as it were by it selfe, without ores, and without the force of man: for there arose from the earth suche a wynde, as a man woulde haue wyshed for of purpose. Yet furthermore, when they perceiued the shippe to mooue sometime forwarde, and sometyme backward, sometyme toward the right hande, and sometyme towarde the lefte, and that with one winde, and in manner at one instant, they were at theyr wyttes ende for to much admiration. These thynges finished, and the shippes laden with bread, and suche other rewardes, they beyng also recompenced with other of our thynges, he dismissed not onely the kyng *Beuchius Anachauchoa* and his syster, but lykewise all theyr seruauntes & women, replenished with ioye & wondering. After this, he hym selfe tooke his iorney by foote with his souldiers to the citie of *Isabella*, where he was aduertised that one *Roldanus Ximenus*, a noughty felowe (whom before, beyng his seruant, he had preferred to be capitayne of the myners and labourers, & after made hym a Judge in causers of controuersie) had vsed hym selfe outragiously, and was maliciously mynded against hym, and further, the cause of much mischiefe in his absence. For kyng *Guarionexius* (who a whyle before was pardoned of his former rebellion, and persuaded the people to obey the Spanyardes) was by his noughtie vsage, and suche other as were confedered with hym, so accensed to reuenge the iniuries whiche they susteyned at his handes, beside the abominable

Musical instrumentes.

Ignorance causeth admiration.

The intemperancie & malice of a seruile wit aduaunced.

F.ii acte

Ciguauians.

acte whiche they, folowing only the lawe of nature, abhorred so much, that he, with his familie, famylyers, and [illegible], of desperate mynde fledde to the mountaines, being distaunt from *Isabella* only tenne leagues westwarde, towarde the north side of the sea. These mountaynes, and also the inhabitauntes of the same, they call by one name, *Ciguaios*. The great king of all the kinges and regions of these mountaynes is called *Maiobanexius*, and his court or pallace is named *Capronus*: the mountaynes are rough, high, and such as no man can passe to the toppes therof, they are also bending, and haue their corners reaching downe to the sea. Betweene both the corners of the mountaynes, is there a greate playne, by the whiche many riuers fall from the mountaynes into the sea, the people are verye fierse and warlike men, hauing theyr original of the Canibales: for when they descend from the mountaynes to the playnes, to keepe warre with theyr borderers, they eate all such as they kil. *Guarionexius* therfore, fleeing to this kyng of these mountaynes, gaue him many presentes of such thinges as are wanting in his countrey, therwith declaring how vilely, villanously, and violently he had ben vsed of our men, with whom he coulde nothyng preuaile, neither by fayre meanes, nor by foule, nother by humilitie, nor by stoutnesse, and that to be the cause of his resortyng, to hym at that tyme, most humbly desyring him to be his defence agaynst thoppressions of suche myschevous people. *Maiobanexius* hereuppon, made hym promisse to ayde and helpe hym against the Christians al that he might. The Lieutenant therefore made haste to the fortresse of Conception, whither, as soone as he was come, he sent for *Roldanus Xeminus*, who with suche as folowed hym, lay in certayne of the Iland villages, xii. myles distant from the fortresse. At his commyng, the Lieutenaunt asked him what al these sturres and tumultes meant: he answered without abashment, Your brother the Admiral hath to doo therewith, and shall aunswere for the same before the kyng, for we perceiue that the kyng hath so put hym in trust, that he hath had no regarde to vs: here we peryshe for hunger, whyle we folowe you, and are dryuen to seeke our vnhappye foode in the desertes: Your brother also assigned me assystaunt with you in gouernyng the Ilande. Wherefore, sith you haue no more respect respecte unto us, we are determined no longer to be under your obedience. When *Roldanus* had spoken these wordes, and suche other, the Lieutenaunt woulde haue layde handes on hym, but he escaped his fyngers, and fledde to the West partes of the region of *Xaragua*, hauyng with hym a trayne of threescore and ten men, whiche were of his confederacie. Here this fylthy synke of rebelles thus conspired, playde theyr vages, and lyued with loose brydles in al kynde of myscheefe, robbyng the people, spoylyng the countrey, and rauishyng both wyues and virgins. Whyle these thynges were doing in the Ilande, the Admiral had eight shippes appoynted hym by the kyng, of the whiche he sent two laden with vyctualles, from *Cales* or *Gades* of Hercules pyllers, directly to the Lieutenaunt his brother. These shyps by chaunce arryued fyrst on that syde of the Ilande where *Roldanus Xeminus* ranged with his companions. *Roldanus* in short tyme had seduced them, promysyng them in the steede of mattockes, wenches pappes: for labour, pleasure: for hunger, abundance: and for wearynesse and watchyng, sleepe and quietnesse. *Guarionexius* in the meane tyme assembled a power of his frendes and confederates, & came oftentymes downe into the playne, and slue as many of the Christian men as he coulde meete conueniently, and also the Ilande men whiche were theyr freendes, wastyng theyr grounde, destroying theyr seedes, and spoylyng their vyllages. But *Roldanus* and his adherentes, albeit they had knowledge that the Admiral woulde shortly come, yet feared they nothyng, because they had seduced the newe men whiche came in the fyrst shyppes. Whyle the Lieutenaunt was thus tossed in the myddest of these stormes, in the meane tyme his brother the Admiral set forwarde from the coastes of Spayne: but not directly to *Hispaniola*, for he turned more towarde the south. In the whiche voyage, what he dyd, what coastes both of the lande and sea he compassed, and what newe regions he discouered, we wyl fyrst declare: for to what ende and conclusion the sayd tumultes and seditions came, we wyl expresse in the ende of the booke folowyng. Thus fare ye well.

Licentiousn in libertie.

Hercules pyllers.

A violent perswasion.

The furie of Guarionexius

The thyrd voyage of Colonus the Admiral.

The syxt booke of the fyrst Decade, to *Lodouike* Cardinal of *Aragonie*.

COlonus the Admirall, the thirde day of the Calendes of Iune, in the yeere of Christe 1498. hoysed vp his sayles in the hauen of the towne *Barramedabas*, not farre distant from *Cales*, and set forwarde on his voyage with eyght shyppes laden with vittualles and other necessaries. He diuerted from his accustomed race, whiche was by the Ilandes of *Canarie*, by reason of certayne frenchmen pyrates and rouers on the sea, whiche lay in the ryght way to meete with hym. In the way from *Cales* to the Ilandes of *Canarie*, about fourescore and tenne myles towarde the left hande, is the Ilande of *Madera*, more southwarde then the citie of *Ciuile* by foure degrees, for the Pole Artike is eleuate to *Ciuile*.xxxvi.degrees, but to this Ilande (as the Mariners say) only. xxxii. He sayled therefore fyrst to *Madera*, and sendyng from thence directly to *Hispaniola* the residue of the shippes laden with vittualles and other necessaries, he him selfe with one shyppe with deckes, and two Marchant Carauelles, coasted towarde the South to come to the Equinoctial lyne, and so foorth to folowe the tracte of the same towarde the West, to the intent to search the natures of suche places as he coulde finde vnder or neare vnto the same, leauing *Hispaniola* on the north side on his ryght hande. In the middle of this race, lye xiii. Ilandes of the Portugales, whiche were in olde tyme called *Hesperides*, and are nowe called *Caput Viride*, or *Cabouerde*, these are situate in the sea, ryght ouer agaynst the inner partes of Ethiope, Westwarde two dayes saylyng. One of these the Portugales call *Bonauista*. With the Snayles, or rather the Tortoyses of this Ilande, many leprous men are healed and cleansed of theyr leprosie. Departing sodainly from thence, by reason of the contagiousnesse of the ayre, he sayled. CCCClxxx myles towarde the West southwest, whiche is in the middest betweene the West and the South. There was he so vexed with maladies and heate (for it was the moneth of Iune) that his shyps were almost set on fyre [illegible] hoopes of his barrelles cracked and brake, and the fresh wa[illegible] [illegible]: the men also complayned that they were not able

...nche men
...ates.

...e iland of
...adera.

...ailing of
...e leper.

...ontagious
[illegible]

be

to abide that extremitie of heate. There the north pole was eleuate onely. v. degrees from the Horizontall. For the space of .viii. dayes, in the which he suffered these extremites, onely the fyrst day was fayre, but al the other, clowdy and rayny, yet neuertheles feruent hotte: Wherefore it oftentymes repented hym not a litle, that euer he tooke that way. Being tossed in these dangers and vexations eyght continuall dayes, at the lengthe an Eastsoutheast wynde arose, and gaue a prosperous blaste to his sayles. Whiche wynde folowing directly towarde the west, he founde the starres ouer that paralell placed in other order, and an other kynde of ayre, as the Admirall hym selfe tolde me. And they al affirme, that within three dayes saylyng, they founde most temperate and pleasaunt ayre. The Admiral also affirmeth, that from the clime of the great heate and vnholsome ayre, he euer ascended vp the backe of the sea, as it were vp a hygh mountayne towarde heauen, yet in all this tyme, coulde he not once see any land: But at the length, the day before the Calendes of Iuly, the watchman lookyng foorth of the toppe castel of the greatest shippe, cried out aloude for ioy that he espied three exceding hygh mountaynes, exhorting his felowes to be of good cheere, and to put away al pensiuenes: for they were very heauy and sorowfull, as well for the greefe which they susteyned by reason of the intollerable heate, as also that their freshe water fayled them, whiche ranne out at the ryftes of the barels, caused by extreme heate, as we haue sayd. Thus being wel comforted, they drew to the land, but at theyr fyrst approch they could not aryue, by reason of the shalownes of the sea neere the shore: Yet loking out of theyr shyppes, they myght well perceiue that the Region was inhabyted, and wel cultured, for they sawe very fayre gardens, and pleasaunt medowes: from the trees and herbes wherof, when the mornyng deawes beganne to ryse, there proceaded manye sweete sauours. Twentie myles distant from hence, they chaunced into a hauen, very apte to harborowe shyppes, but it had no ryuer running into it. Saylyng on yet somwhat further, he founde at the length a commodious hauen, wherin he might repayre his shyppes, and make prouision of freshe water and fuel. *Arenalis* calleth this land *Puta*. They founde no houses neere vnto the hauen, but innumerable sheppes of certeyn wilde beastes

The iland of Puta.

beastes feete, of the whiche they founde one dead, muche lyke a goate. The day folowyng, they sawe a Canoa commyng a farre of, hauyng in it foure and twentie young men of goodly corporature and high stature, al armed with targets, bowes, & arrowes: the heare of theyr heades was long and playne, and cutte on the forehead much after the maner of the Spanyardes, their priuie partes were couered with fylletes of gossampine cotton, of sundry colours enterlaced, & were beside al ouer naked. Here the Admiral, considering with him selfe the corporature of this people, and nature of the lande, he beleeued the same to be so muche the nearer heauen, then other regions of the same paralel, and further remooued from the grosse vapours of the vales, and marysshes, howe muche the hyghest toppes of the byggest mountaynes are distant from the deepe vales. For he earnestly affirmeth, that in al that nauigation, he neuer went out of the paralels of Ethiope: So great difference is there betweene the nature of thinhabitauntes, and of the soyles of diuers regions, al vnder one clime or paralel, as is to see betweene the people and regions beyng in the fyrme lande of Ethiope, and them of the Ilandes vnder the same clime, hauyng the pole starre eleuate in ye same degree. For the Ethiopians are all blacke, hauing theyr heare curled, more like wool then heare: but these people of the Iland of *Puta*, (beyng as I haue sayde vnder the clyme of Ethiope) are white, with long heare, and of yelow colour. Wherefore it is apparant, the cause of this so great difference, to be rather by the disposition of the earth, then constitution of heauen. For we knowe, that snowe falleth on the mountaynes of the Equinoctial, or burnt lyne, and the same to endure there continuallye: we knowe lykewyse, that the inhabitauntes of the regions farre distant from that lyne towarde the north, are molested with great heate. The Admirall, that he myght alure the young men to hym with gentlenesse, shewed them lookyng glasses, fayre and bryght vessels of copper, haukes belles, and suche other thynges vnknowen to them. But the more they were called, so muche the more they suspected craft and deceypte, and fledde backewarde: Yet dyd they with great admiration beholde our men and theyr thynges, but styll hauyng theyr ores in theyr handes redy to flee. When the Admirall sawe that he coulde by

...ple of comly corporature, long heare, re the Equinoctial.

...e higher, the ...der.

by no meanes allure them by gyftes, he thought to prove what he coulde do with musicall instrumentes, and therefore commaunded that they whiche were in the greatest shyp, should play on theyr drummes and shawlmes. But the young men supposing this to be a token of battayle, left theyr ores, & in the twinclyng of an eye had theyr arrowes in theyr bowes, and theyr targets on their armes: and thus directing theyr arrowes towarde our men, stoode in expectation to knowe what this noyse might meane. Our men likewyse preparyng theyr bowes and arrowes, approched towarde them by litle and litle. But they departing from the Admirals shyppe, and trusting to the dexteritie of theyr ores, came so neare one of the lesse shyppes, that one of them plucked the cloke from the gouernour of the shyppe, and as wel as they coulde by signes, required hym to come alande, promisyng fayth that they woulde commune with him of peace. But when they sawe him goe to the Admirals shyp, whyther he went to aske leave that he might commune with them, suspecting hereby some further decept, they leapt immediatlye into the Canoa, and fledde as swyft as the wynde, so that to conclude, they could by no meanes be allured to familiaritie: Wherfore the Admiral thought it not conuenient to bestowe any long time there at this voyage. No great space from this Ilande, euer towarde the West, the Admiral sayth he found so outragious a fal of water, runnyng with suche a violence from the East to the West, that it was nothyng inferior to a myghtie streame fallyng from hygh mountaynes. He also confessed, that synce the fyrst day that euer he knewe what the sea meant, he was neuer in suche feare. Proceedyng yet somewhat further in this daungerous voyage, he founde certayne gulfes of eyght myles, as it had ben the entraunce of some great hauen, into the whiche the sayde violent streames dyd fall. These gulfes or streyghtes he called *Os Draconis*, that is, the Dragons mouth: and the Ilande directly oueragaynst the same, he called *Margarita*. Out of these straightes, issued no lesse force of freshe water, whiche encounteryng with the salte, dyd stryve to passe forth, so that betwene both the waters, was no small conflycte. But saylyng into the gulfe, at the length he founde the [illegible]. The Admirall

hym

Musicall instrumentes.

The violent course of the water from the East to the West.

The gulfe called Os Draconis.

hym selfe, and they which were his companions in this vyoage, beyng men of good credit, and perceauing my dilygence in searchyng for these matters, tolde me yet of a greater thyng, that is, that for the space of .xxvi. leagues, amountyng to a hundreth and foure myles, he sayled euer by freshe water, insomuch that the further he proceaded, especially towarde the west, he affirmed the water to be the fresher. After this, he came to a highe mountayne inhabited onely with Monkeyes or Marmasits, on that part towarde the East: For that syde was rowgh with rockye and stony mountaynes, and therefore not inhabited with men. Yet they that went a lande to searche the countrey, founde nere vnto the sea, many fayre fieldes, well tylled and sowen, but no people, nor yet houses or cotages: Parhappes they were gone further into the countrey, to sowe theyr corne, and applye theyr husbandry, as wee often see our husbandemen to leaue theyr stations and villages for the same purpose. In the west syde of that mountayne, they espyed a large playne, whither they made hast, and cast anker in the brode ryuer. As soone as the inhabitantes had knowledge that a straunge nation was arryued in theyr coastes, they came flockyng without all feare to see our men. We vnderstode by theyr sygnes and poyntynges, that this Region was called *Paria*, and that it was very large: in so muche that the further it reacheth towarde the weste, to be so muche the better inhabited and replenished with people. The Admiral therfore, takyng into his shippe foure of the men of that lande, searched the west partes of the same. By the temperatenes of the ayer, the pleasauntnes of the grounde, and the multitude of people which they sawe daily more & more as they sayled, they coniectured that these thynges portended some great matter: as in deede their opininon failed them not, as we will further declare in his place. The sonne not yet rysen, but beginnyng euen nowe to ryse, being one day allured by the pleasauntnes of the place, and sweete sauours whiche breathed from the lande to the shyppes, they went a lande: Here they founde a greater multytude of people, then in any other place. As our men approched towarde them, there came certeine messengers from their *Cacici*, that is, the kinges of the countrey, to desyre the Admirall in the name of theyr princes to come to theyr palaces with-

A sea of fresh water.

Marmasets. Monkeyes.

The fayre and large region of Paria.

[illegible] people.

without feare, and that they and al theyrs shoulde bee at his commaundement. When the Admirall had thanked them, and made his excuse for that tyme, there came innumerable people with theyr boates to the shyppes, hauyng for the most parte cheynes about theyr neckes, garlandes on theyr headdes, and braselettes on theyr armes of pearles of India, and that so commonlye, that our women in playes and tryumphes, haue not greater plentie of stones of glasse and crystall in theyr garlands, crownes, girdels, and suche other tyrementes. Beyng asked where they gathered them, they poynted to the next shore by the sea bankes. They signified also, by certeyne scornefull iestures whiche they made with theyr mouthes and handes, that they nothyng esteemed pearles. Takyng also baskettes in their handes, they made signes that the same myght be fylled with them in shorte space. But because the corne wherwith his shyppes were laten to be caryed into *Hispaniola*, had taken hurt by reason of the salt water, he determined to deferre this marte to a more conuenient tyme: Yet he sent to land two of the shyp boates laden with men, to thintent to fetch some garlands of pearles for exchaunge of our thynges, and also somwhat to searche the nature of the Region, and disposition of the people. They enterteyned our men gentelly, and came flocking to them by heapes, as it had ben to beholde some strange monsters. Fyrst there came to meete our men, two men of grauitie, whom the multitude folowed. One of these was well in age, and the other but young. They thinke it was the father, with his sonne whiche should succeede hym. When the one had saluted and embrased the other, they brought our men into a certeyne rounde house, neere vnto the whiche was a great courte. Hyther were brought many chayers and stooles made of a certeyne blacke wood, and very cunningly wrought. After that our men and theyr Princes were sette, theyr [illegible] came in laden, some with [illegible] delycate [illegible] with wyne: But theyr meat [illegible] and [illegible], and utterly [illegible]. They [illegible] wyne [illegible] white, not made of grapes, [illegible] and very pleasaunt [illegible] the [illegible] [illegible] made of [illegible]

Chayers and stooles of Ebene.

Whyte men nere the Equinoctiall.

was a great company both of men and women, but they stoode disseuered the one from the other. They are whyte, euen as our men are, sauing suche as are much conuersant in the sunne. They are also very gentle, and full of humanitie towarde strangers. They couer theyr priuie partes with gossampine cotton, wrought with sundry colours, and are besyde all naked. There was fewe, or none, that had not eyther a coller, a chayne, or a bracelet of golde and pearles, and many had all. Beyng asked where they had that golde, they poynted to certayne mountaynes, seemyng with theyr countenaunce to disswade our men from goyng thither: For putting theyr armes in theyr mouthes, and grynnyng as though they bytte the same, styll poyntyng to the mountaynes, they seemed to insinuate that men were eaten there: but whether they meant by the Canibales, or wylde beastes, our men coulde not wel perceiue. They tooke it exceedyng greeuouslye, that they coulde neyther understande our men, nor our men them. When they whiche were sent to lande, were returned to the shyppes about three of the clocke at after noone the same day, bryngyng with them certayne garlandes, and collers of pearles, they loosed theyr ankers to departe, myndyng to come agayne shortlye, when all thynges were set in good order in *Hispaniola*: but he was preuented by another, whiche defeated him of the rewarde of his trauayle.

Shalownesse of the sea.

He was also hyndered at this time by reason of the shalownesse of the sea, & violent course of the water, which with continuall tossyng, bruised the greatest shyppe as often as any great gale of wind arose. To auoyde the daungers of suche shalowe places and shelfes, he euer sent one of the smallest Carauelles before to trye the way with soundyng, and the byggest shyppes folowed behynde.

The use of Carauels or Brigandines.

The regions beyng in the large prouince of *Paria*, for the space of CC.xxx. myles, are called of the inhabitantes, *Cumana*, and *Manacapana*: from these regions distant .lx. leagues, is there an other region called *Curiana*. When he had thus passed ouer this long tract of sea, supposing styl that it had ben an Ilande, & doubtyng that he myght passe by the West to the North directly to *Hispaniola*, he chaunced into a ryuer of .xxx. cubites depth, and of suche bredth as hath not lyghtly ben hearde of. For he affyrmeth it to be .xxviii. leagues. A lytle further towarde the West,

A ryuer of maruelous depth and bredth.

West, yet somewhat more southwarde, as the bendyng of the shore requyred, he entered into a sea full of herbes or weedes. The seede of the herbes whiche swymme on the water, are muche lyke the berryes of the tree called *Lentiscus*, whiche beareth the sweete gumme called *Mastix*: they growe so thycke, that they somtyme in maner stayed the shyppes. The Admiral reported, that here there is not one daye throughout all the yeere much longer or shorter then an other, and that the North pole is here eleuate onely fyue degrees as at *Paria*, in whose tracte all these coastes lye. He also declared certayne thinges as concernyng the varietie of the north pole: the whiche because they seeme contrarye to thopinyons of all the Astronomers, I wyll touche them but with a drye foote, as sayth the prouerbe. But it is well knowen (most noble prince) that whiche we call the pole starre, or north starre (called of the Italians *Tramontana*) is not the very poynt of the pole Artyke, uppon the whiche the axes or extremities of heauens are turned about. The whiche thing may well be proued, if when the starres fyrst appeare, you beholde the pole starre through any narowe hole: For so, applying your instrument therto in the mornyng, somwhat before the daye spring haue blemisshed theyr light, yf then you looke through the same hole, you shall perceiue it to be moued from the place where you sawe it fyrst. But howe it commeth to passe, that at the begynnyng of the euenyng twilight it is eleuate in that Region only fyue degrees in the moneth of June, and in the mornyng twylyght to be eleuate .xv. degrees by the same quadrant, I doo not understande, nor yet doo the reasons whiche he bryngeth, in any poynt satysfye me. For he sayth, that he hereby coniectured, that the earth is not perfectly rounde: but that when it was created, there was a certayne heape raysed theron, muche hygher then the other partes of the same. So that (as he sayth) it is not rounde after the forme of an apple or a bal (as other thinke) but rather lyke a peare as it hangeth on the tree, and that *Paria* is the Region which possesseth the [illegible] or hyghest part therof nearest unto heauen: In so muche that he earnestly contendeth, the earthly Paradyse to be [illegible] in the toppes of those three hylles, whiche we sayde before, that the watchman sawe out of the toppe castel of [illegible]

The eleuation of the Pole at Paria.

Note a secrete as concernyng the Pole starre.

An experience.

A marueylous secrete.

the shyppe, and that the outragious streames of the freshe waters whiche so violentlye isshue out of the sayde gulfes, and stryue so with the salt water, fall headlong from the toppes of the saide mountaynes: But of this matter, it shall suffyce to haue sayde thus muche. Let vs nowe therefore returne to the hystorie from whiche we haue digressed. When he perceiued him selfe to be thus intrapped in so great a gulfe beyonde his expectation, so that he had nowe no hope to fynde any passage towarde the north, wherby he myght sayle directly to *Hispaniola*, he was enforced to turne backe the same way by the whiche he came, and directed his vyoage to *Hispaniola* by the north of that lande lyinge towarde the East. They whiche afterwarde searched this lande more curyouslye, wyll it to be parte of the continent or firme lande of India, and not of *Cuba* as the Admiral supposed: For there are many whiche affirme that they haue sayled round about *Cuba*. But whether it be so or not, or whether enuying the good fortune of this man, they seeke occasyon of quarelyng agaynst hym, I can not iudge: But tyme shall speake, whiche in tyme appoynted, reuealeth both truth and falshod. But whether *Paria* be continent or not, the Admirall doth not muche contende, but he supposeth it to be continent: He also affirmeth that *Paria* is more southwarde then *Hispaniola*, by eyght hundred fourescore and two myles. At the length he came to *Hispaniola* (to see his souldiers which he left with his brethren) the thyrd day of the calendes of September, in the yeere. 1498. but (as often times chaunceth in humane thynges) among his so many prosperous, pleasaunt, and luckye affayres, fortune myngled some seedes of wormewood, and corrupted his pure corne with the malicious weedes of cockle.

Time reuealeth al thynges.

The seuenth booke of the fyrst decade, to the same *Lodowike* Cardinal. &c.

When the Admiral was now come to the Ilande of *Hispaniola*, he founde all thynges confounded and out of order. For *Roldanus* (of whom we spake before) refused in his absence to obey his brother, trustinge to the multitude of such as were confedered with hym,

The Spaniardes rebell in the Admiralles absence.

hym, and not onely behaued hym selfe proudely agaynst the Admiralles brother and Lieuetenant, sometyme his maister, but also sent letters to his reproche to the kyng of Spayne, therin accusyng both the brethren, laying heynous matters to theyr charges. But the Admirall agayne sent messengers to the kyng, whiche myght informe hym of theyr rebellyon, instantly desyring his grace to sende hym a newe supplye of men, wherby he might suppresse theyr lecentiousnes, and punish them for theyr mischeuous actes. They accused the Admirall and his brother to be uniust men, cruel enimies, and shedders of the Spanyshe blood, declaryng that uppon euery lyght occasyon they woulde racke them, hang them, and head them, and that they tooke pleasure therin, and that they departed from them, as from cruell tyrantes and wylde beastes reioycyng in blood, also the kynges enimies: affyrmyng lykewyse, that they wel perceiued theyr entent to be none other then to usurpe thempire of the Ilandes, whiche thyng (they sayde) they suspected by a thousande coniectures, and especially in that they woulde permit none to resorte to the golde mynes, but only suche as were theyr familiers. The Admirall on the contrary part, when he desyred ayde of the kyng to infring theyr insolencie, auouched that al those his accusers, which had deuised suche lyes agaynst hym, were noughtie felowes, abhominable knaues and vilains, theeues and baudes, ruffians, adulterers, & rauishers of women, false periured vagaboundes, and such as had ben eyther conuict in prysons, or fledde for feare of iudgement: so escaping punishment, but not leauing vice, wherin they styll contynued, and brought the same with them to the iland, lyuing there in like maner as before, in thefte, lechery, & all kyndes of mischeefe, and so gyuen to Idlenes and sleepe, that wheras they were brought thyther for myners, labourers, & scullyans, they would not now goe one furlong from theyr houses, except they were borne on mens backes, lyke unto them whiche in olde time were called *Ediles Curules*. For, to this office they put the miserable Iland men, whom they handled most cruelly. For least theyr handes should discontinue from the sheddyng of bloode, and the better to trye theyr strength and manhod, they used now & then for theyr pastyme, to stryue among them selues, and proue who coulde most cleanely [illegible]

The Spaniardes accuse the Admiral.

The Admirals answere.

These [illegible] the [illegible] of the temples.

> A cruel & deuillyshe pastyme.

with his swoorde at one stroke stryke of the head of an innocent: soo that he whiche coulde with moste agilitie make the head of one of these poore wretches to flee quyte and cleane from the bodye to the grounde at one stroke, he was the best man, and counted most honorable. These thynges, and many suche other, the one of them layd to the others charge before the kyng. While these thinges were doynge, the Admirall sent his brother the Lieuetenaunt with an army of fourescore and tenne footemen, and a fewe horsemen (with three thousande of the Ilande men, whiche were mortall enemyes to the Ciguauians) to meete the people of *Ciguaua*, with Kyng *Guarionexius* theyr graunde capitayne, who had doone muche myscheefe to our men, and suche as fauoured them. Therefore when the Lieutenaunt had conducted his army to the bankes of a certeyne great ryuer runnyng by the playne, whiche we sayde before to lye betwene the corners of the mountaynes of *Ciguaua* and the sea, he founde two scoutes of his enemies lurkyng in certeyne busshes, whereof the one, castyng hym selfe headlong into the sea, escaped, and by the mouth of the ryuer swamme ouer to his companions: the other being taken, declared that in the woodde on the other syde the ryuer, there lay in campe sixe thousande Ciguauians redy, vnwares to assaile our men passing bye. Wherefore the Lieutenaunt fyndyng a shalowe place where he might passe ouer, he with his whole army entred into the ryuer, the which thing when the Ciguauians had espyed, they came runnyng out of the wooddes with a terrible crye, and most horrible aspect, much like vnto the people called *Agathyrsi*, of whom the poet Virgil speaketh: For they were all paynted and spotted with sundry colours, and especiall with blacke and red, which they make of certeyne fruites norysshed for the same purpose in theyr gardens, with the iuyce whereof they paynt them selues from the forhead, euen to the knees, hauyng theyr heare (whiche by art they make long and

> Heare made long & blacke by arte.

blacke, if nature deny it them) wreathed and rolled after a thousande fasshions, a man would thinke them to be deuylles incarnate newly broke out of hell, they are so like vnto helhoundes. As our men waded ouer the ryuer, they shotte at them, and hurled dartes so thycke, that it almost tooke the lyght of the sonne from our men: insomuche that if they had not borne of the forst therof thereof with theyr targettes, the matter had gone wrong with them. Yet at the length, manye beyng wounded, they passed over the ryver: which thyng when the enimies sawe, they fledde, whom our men pursuyng, slue some in the chase, but not manye, by reason of theyr swyftnesse of foote. Thus beyng in the woodes, they shotte at our men more safely, for they beyng accustomed to the woodes, and naked without anye lette, passed through the bushes and shrubbes, as it had ben wylde bores or Hartes, whereas our men were hyndered by reason of theyr apparell, targets, long iauelins, & ignoraunce of the place. Wherfore, when he had rested there al that nyght in vayne, and the day folowyng he sawe no stirring in the woodes, he went (by the counsel and conducte of the other Ilande men whiche were in his army) immediatly frō thence to the mountaynes, in the whiche kyng *Maiobanexius* had his cheefe mansion place, in the village called *Capronum*, by the which name also the kyngs palace was called, beyng in the same village. Thus marchyng forwarde with his armie, about twelue myles of, he encamped in the village of another kyng, whiche the inhabitauntes had forsaken for feare of our men: Yet makyng diligent searche, they found two, by whom they had knowledge that there was tenne kinges with *Maiobanexius* in his palace of *Capronum*, with an armie of eight thousand Ciguauians. At the Lieutenauntes fyrst approch, he durst not geue them battayle, vntyll he had somewhat better searched the region: yet dyd he in the meane tyme skyrmyshe with them twyse. The next nyght about mydnyght, he sent forth scouttes, and with them guides of the Ilande men whiche knewe the countrey: Whom the Ciguauians espying frō the mountaines, prepared them selues to the battayle, with a terrible crye or alarum after their maner, but yet durst not come out of the woods, supposyng that the Lieutenaunt with his mayne army had ben [illegible]. The day folowyng, when he brought his army to the place where they encamped, [illegible] out of the woodes, they twyse attempted [illegible] our men with a mayne force, [illegible] they [illegible] them with theyr [illegible] [illegible]

Kyng Maiobanexius.

An army of eight thousand Ciguauians.

most lyke belde. Of them whiche were taken, he sent one, and with hym another of the Ilande men, which was of his part, to *Maiobanexius*, with commaundement in this effect, The Lieutenaunt brought not hyther his army (O *Maiobanexius*) to kepe warre either agaynst you, or your people, for he greatly desyreth your frendshyp: but his intent is, that *Guarionexius*, who hath perswaded you to be his ayde against him, to the great destruction of your people, and undoyng of your countrey, may haue due correction, as well for his disobedience towarde hym, as also for raysyng tumultes among the people: Wherefore he requireth you, and exhorteth you to deliuer *Guarionexius* into his handes, the whiche thing yf you shal perfourme, the Admirall his brother wyll not only gladly admypt you to his frendshyp, but also enlarge and defende your dominion. And yf herein you refuse to accomplyshe his request, it wyll folowe, that you shal shortlye repente you thereof: For your kyngdome shalbe wasted with swerde and fyre, and you shall abyde the fortune of warre, whereof you haue had experience with fauour, as you shall further knowe heareafter to your payne, yf with stubbernesse you prouoke him to shewe the uttermoste of his power. When the messenger had thus doone his errant, *Maiobanexius* answered, that *Guarionexius* was a good man, indued with many vertues as all men knewe, and therfore he thought him worthy his ayde, especially in as much as he fled to him for succoure, and that he had made hym suche promise, whom also he had proued to be his faithfull frend: againe, that they were naughty men, violent, and cruell, desiring other mens goodes, and such as spared not to shed innocentes blood: in fine, that he would not haue to doo with suche myscheuous men, nor yet enter into frendshyppe with them. When these thynges came to the Lieutenauntes eare, he commaunded the village to be burnt where he hym selfe encamped, with manye other villages there about: and when he drewe nere to the place where *Maiobanexius* lay, he sent messengers to him agayne, to common the matter with him, and to wyll hym to send some one of his moste faythfull frendes to entreate with hym of peace. Whereuppon the kyng sent unto hym one of his cheefe gentelmen, and with hym two other to wayte on hym. When he came to the Lieutenauntes presence,

Kyng Guarionexius.

Naturall hatred of vyce.

sence, he frendly requyred hym to perswade his lord and maister in his name, and earnestly to admonishe hym, not to suffer his florishyng kyngdome to be spoyled, or hym selfe to abyde the hasarde of warre for *Guarionexius* sake: and further to exhorte hym to delyuer hym, excepte he woulde procure the destruction both of hym selfe, his people, and his countrey. When the messenger was returned, *Maiobanexius* assembled the people, declaring vnto them what was doone: but they cryed out on him to deliuer *Guarionexius*, and began to curse the daye that euer they had receaued hym, thus to disturbe theyr quietnesse. *Maiobanexius* answered them, that *Guarionexius* was a good man, & had well deserued of him, geuing him many princely presentes, and had also taught both his wife and him to sing and daunce, which thing he did not little esteeme, and was therfore fully resolued in no case to forsake him, or agaynst al humanitie to betray hys frende, which fled to him for succoure, but rather to abide al extremities with him, then to minister occasion of obloquie to slaunderers, to reporte that he had betraied his ghest, whom he toke into his house with warranties. Thus dimissing the people, sighing and with sorowfull hartes, he called *Guarionexius* before him, promising him agayne, that he would be partaker of his fortune while life lasted: in so much that he thought it not best to send any further worde to the Lieuetenaunt, but appoynted him whom before he sent to him, to keepe the way with a garrison of men, to thintent, that yf any messengers should be sent from the Lieuetenaunt, to slay them by the way, and admit none to communication, or further entreatie of peace. In the meane time, the Lieutenaunt sent two, wherof the one was a captiue Ciguauian, and the other an Ilande man, of them which were frendes to our men: and they were both taken and slaine. The Lieutenaunt folowed them only with ten footemen & foure horsemen, finding his messengers dead in the way, he was further prouoked to wrath, and determined more extremely to deale with *Maiobanexius*, & therfore went forward incontinently with his whole army to his chiefe pallace of *Capronum*, where he yet lay in campe. At his approche, al ẏ kinges fled, euery man his way, & forsoke theyr [illegible] *Maiobanexius*, [illegible] with al his famylye, [illegible]. Some of the Ciguauians sought for

The Lieuetenaunts gentelnesse toward Maiobanexius.

A rare faithfulnesse in a barbarous kyng.

The Lieuetenauntes messengers are slayne.

Guarionexius to slay hym, for that he was the cause of all these troubles: but his feete saued his lyfe, for he fledde in tyme to the mountaines, where he lurked in maner alone among the desolate rockes. Wheras now the Lieuetenauntes souldiers were forewearyed with long warre, with watching, laboure, and hunger (for it was nowe three monethes sence the warres began) many desyred leaue to departe to the towne of Conception, where they had graneges, & exercised tillage. He gaue them their passeportes with alowance of vittaples, and so that onely thyrtie remayned with hym. These three monethes warre, they contynued very paynefull and myserablye: So that durynge al that tyme, they had none other meate but only *Cazibi*, that is, such rootes wherof they make theyr bread, and that but seldome to theyr fyll: also *Vsias*, that is, lyttle beastes lyke Conyes, if by chaunce nowe and then they tooke some with theyr houndes. Their drinke was none other then water, such as they founde, sometyme sweete, and sometyme muddy sauerynge of the maryshes. Emong these delicates, that lyttle sleepe that they had, was euer for the most parte abrode vnder the firmament, and that not without watchemen, and in continual remoouing, as the nature of warre requireth. With these fewe therfore, the Lieuetenaunt determined to searche the mountaynes, dennes, and caues, if he coulde in any place fynde the steppes of *Maiobanexius* or *Guarionexius*. In the meane tyme certayne of his men (whom hunger enforced to goe a hunting, to proue if they coulde take any conies) chaunced vppon two of *Maiobanexius* familyers, which were sent to certaine villages of his, to make prouision of bread. These he enforced to declare where theyr lorde lay hid, & vsed the same also for guides, to bring our men to the place. Twelue of our men tooke this enterpryse in hand, paynting them selues after the maner of the Ciguauians: So that by this stratageme or policie, they came sodenly vppon *Maiobanexius*, and tooke hym prisoner, with his wyfe, children, & family, and conueighed them to the towne of Conception to the Lieuetenaunt. Within a fewe dayes after, hunger compelled *Guarionexius* to come out of the dennes, whom certaine of the people fearing the Lieuetenaunt, betrayed to our hunters. The Lieuetenaunt being certified hereof, sent foorth a bande of foote men, commaunding them to lye in ambushe vntyll

The Spaniardes are painfull in the warres.

A desperate aduenture with thirtie men.

A policie.

tyll suche tyme as *Guarionexius* went from the playnes to the mountaynes, and then sodenly to entrappe hym. They went as they were commaunded, tooke hym, and broughte hym away with them, and by this meanes were al the regions neare about pacified and quieted. A certayne noble woman of neare kynred to *Maiobanexius*, and wyfe to another kyng, whose dominion was yet untouched, folowed hym in all these aduersities. They affirme this woman to be the fayrest and most beautifull, that euer nature brought foorth in the Ilande: Whom, when the king her husbande, who loued her most ardently (as her beautie deserued) hearde say that she was taken prysoner, he wandered up and downe the desartes lyke a man out of his wytte, not knowyng what to doo or say. But at the length, he came to the Lieutenaunt, promisyng most faythfullye, that he woulde submit him selfe and al that he coulde make, under his power, so that he woulde restore hym his wyfe. The Lieutenaunt accepted the condition, & restored him his wife, with certaine other rulers and gentlemen which he had taken prysoners before: charging them, and byndyng them with an othe, to be euer redy at his commaundement. Shortly after, this king of his owne free motion, came agayne to the Lieutenaunt, bryngyng with him fyue thousande men without weapons, sauyng only suche instrumentes as they use in tyllage of theyr grounde. He brought with hym also seedes to sowe, wherwith at his owne charge, he caused such plentie of theyr corne and fruites to growe in sundry places of the larg uale, wherof we spake before, that shortly after, were seene many fayre and fruitfull feeldes that came therof: and for his gentelnesse being rewarded of the Lieuetenaunte with certayne of our thynges, he departed ioyfullye. When the report hereof came to the Ciguauians, it moued the myndes of the kynges to hope of clemencie, whereuppon they came together to the Lieuetenaunt with humble submission and faithfull promyse, euer after to be under his obedience, desyryng hym to restore unto them theyr kyng with his familie. At theyr request, the kynges wyfe and his housholde was set at libertie, but the king kept styl as a prysoner. These thynges dyd the Lieutenaunt in the Ilande, not yet knowyng what his aduersaries and accusers had layde to his charge before the kyng of

A beautifull woman.

The kynges submit them selues to the Lieuetenaunt.

Spaine who being disquieted with theyr quarelinges and accusations, and especially for that by reason of theyr dissention, of so greate abundance of golde and other thynges, there was as yet but lyttle brought into Spayne, appoynted a newe gouernour, which shoulde see a redresse in theie thynges: and eyther to punyshe such as were fautie, or els to sende them to him. What was founde agaynst the Admirall and his brother, or agaynst his aduersaries which accused hym, I do not well knowe. But this I am sure of, that both the brethren are taken, brought, and caste in prison, with theyr goodes confiscate. But as soone as the king understode that they were brought bounde to Cales, he sent messengers in poste, with commaundement that they should be loosed and come freely to his presence: wherby he declared that he toke their troubles greeuously. It is also said, that the new gouernour sent letters to the kyng, written with the Admiralles hand in straunge and unknowen syfferinges, to his brother the Lieuetenaunt being absent, wyllyng hym to be in a redynes with a power of armed men to come and ayd hym, if the Gouernour should proffer hym any violence, Wherof the gouernour hauing knowledge (as he sayth) beyng also aduertised that the Lieuetenaunt was gone to his brother before the men whiche he had prepared were in a redines, apprehended them both unwares, before the multitude came togeather. What wyl folowe, tyme, the most true and prudent Iudge wyll declare. Thus fare ye well.

A newe gouernour of the Ilands.

¶ The eygth booke of the fyrst Decade, to Cardinall *Lodouike*.

The Ocean sea heretofore unknowen.

The great, ryche, and plentifull Ocean sea, heretofore unknowen, and nowe founde by *Christophorus Colonus* the Admirall, by the autoritie & furtherance of the Catholyke king, I haue presented unto your honour (ryght noble Prince) like a golden chayne unworkmanly wrought: but you shal now receiue a precious iewell to be appendaunt therto. Therefore among such as were pylotes or gouernours under the admyrall, and had diligently marked the courses & differences of the windes, many

many had lycences graunted them of the kyng to seeke further at theyr owne charges, vpon condition to pay hym faythfully his portion, which is the fyfte part. But because amonge all other, one *Petrus Alphonsus*, called *Nignus* by his surname, sayled towarde the south with more prosperous fortune then any of the other, I thinke it best first to speake somewhat of his voyage. He therfore with only one shyp, well furnished at his owne charges, after that he had his passeporte, with commaundement in no case to cast anker past fyftye leagues distant from anye place where the Admirall had touched, sayled fyrst to *Paria*, where the Admiral founde both the men and women so laden with cheines, garlandes, and braselettes of pearles, as we haue sayde before. Coastyng therfore along by the same shore, accordyng to the kings commaundement (yet leauing behynd hym the regions of *Cumana* and *Manacapana*) he came to the regions which thinhabitantes therof cal *Curiana*, where he found a hauen (as he saith) much lyke the port of *Gades* or *Cales*: into the which enteryng, he sawe a farre of certayne houses one the shore, and perceyued, when he drewe neere, that it was a village of only eyght houses. Proceading yet further for the space of three myles, he espied an other village well replenyshed with people, where there met hym fyftye naked men on a company, hauing with them a certayne ruler, who desyred Alphonsus to come to theyr coastes. He brought with hym at thys tyme, many haukes belles, pynnes, nedels, braselettes, cheynes, garlandes, and rynges, with counterfet stones and glasses, and such other tryfelles, the which within the moment of an houre, he had exchaunged for fyfteene ounces of theyr pearles, which they wore aboute theyr neckes and armes. Then they yet more ernestly desyred hym to sayle to theyr coastes, promysyng hym that he shoulde there haue as many pearles as he woulde desyre. He condiscended to theyr request: and the day folowing, came to the place where they appoynted hym: Lying there at anker, a great multitude of people resorted to hym, instantly requyring hym to come alande. But when he considered the innumerable multitude of people which was there assembled, and he had only .xxxiii. men in his company, he durst not commit hym selfe to theyr handes, but gaue them to vnderstande by signes and tokens, that they shoulde

The nauigation of Petrus Alphonsus.

Pearles for tryfles.

Great plentie of pearles.

came to the ship with their *Canoas*: for their boates (which the ... call *Canoas*) are made only of one whole peece of wood as in the ..., yet more rude, and not so artificially as theyrs are: these they call *Gallitas*. These swarmed therfore to the shyp as faste as they might, bryngyng with them greate plenty of pearles (which they cal *Tenoras*) exchanging the same for our marchaundies. We founde this people to be of gentyll nature, simple, and innocent, being conuersant with them in theyr houses, ... the space of xx. dayes. Theyr houses are made of wood, couered with the leaues of date trees. Their meate for the moste parte, is the shelfyshes in the which the pearles are engendered, wherof their sea costes are full. They haue also greate plenty of wyld beastes, as hartes, wyld bores, and connies like vnto hares, both in colour ... bignesse, stocke doues also, and turtle doues: lykewyse geese and duckes, which they norishe in theyr houses as we doo. Peacockes flee aboute in maner in euery wood and groue, but they are not distinct with sundry colours as ours are: for the cockes are like vnto the hennes. These people of *Cur...na* are craftie hunters, and exceding cunning archers, so that they will not lyghtly misse any ...easte or byrde that they shoote at. Our men consumed certayne dayes heare very plesauntely: duryng which time, whosoeuer brought them a peacocke, had for the same foure pinnes: he that brought a pheasaunte, had two, and for a stocke doue, or turtle doue, one, and for a goose, a smale looking glasse, or a litle stone of glasse. Thus they bought and solde with profering and byddyng, denying and refusing, as it had byn in a greate market. When pinnes were profered them, they asked what they shoulde do with them, beyng naked. But our men satisfied them with a craftie answere, declaring by tokens that they were very necessary, to picke theyr teeth, and to pull thornes out of theyr fleshe. But aboue all thynges, haukes belles were most esteemed among them, for theyr sound and faire colour, and woulde therfore geue much for one of them. Our men, lodging in their houses, heard in the nyght season horrible noyses and roringes of wild beastes in the woodes, whiche are full of exceding great and hygh trees of sundrye kindes: but the beastes of these woodes, are not noysome ..., for the people of the countrey goo dayly a huntyng ... naked,

Shel fyshes in which pearles are engendred.

Theyr manner of bargaynyng.

The vse of pynnes.

Haukes belles in great estimation.

Roaring of wild beastes.

naked, with theyr bowes and arrowes, yet hath it not ben harde of, that any man hath ben slayne of any wylde beast. As many hartes or wylde bores as our men woulde desyre them to bryng, they woulde kyll in the woodes with their arrowes, and not to fayle to bryng them. They lacke kyne, goates and sheepe. Theyr bread is made of rootes, as is theyrs of the Ilands. This nation, hath blacke heare, grosse and somwhat curled, yet long also. They keepe theyr teeth very whyte, and for that purpose use to cary a certaine herbe betwene theyr lyppes for the most part of the day, and to washe theyr mouthes when they cast it away. The women doo all theyr busynes at home in theyr howses, and haue also the cure of tyllage of the grounde: but the men apply them selues to the warres and huntyng, to playe, syngyng and dauncyng. They haue sundry kyndes of water pottes, iugges, and drinkyng cuppes made of earth in other places about them, and brought thyther for exchaung of other thynges: For they use fayres and markettes for the same purpose, and are greatly desyrous of such thynges, as are not brought forth or made in theyr countrey, as nature hath geuen a disposytion to al men, to desyre and be delyted with newe and strang thynges. Many of them had hangyng at theyr pearles the images of certeine beastes and birdes, very artifitiously made of golde, but not pure: these also are brought them from other places for exchang of other thynges. The golde wherof they are made, is natiue, and of much lyke finenes to that wherof the florens are coyned. The men of this countrey, inclose theyr priuie members in a gourde, cutte after the fashiō of a coddepice, or els couer the same with the shell of a tortoyse, tyed about theyr loynes with laces of gossampine cotton: In other places of that tract, they thrust the synew within the sheeth therof, and bynde the skinne fast with a string. The great wylde beastes wherof we spake before, and many other thynges which are not found in any of the Ilandes, testifie that this region is parte of ẏ continet or firme lande. But the chiefest coniecture wherby they argue the same, is, that by the coastes of that lande, from *Paria* towarde the west, they sayled about three .M. myles, fyndyng no signe or token of any ende. These people of *Curiana* (whiche some call *Curtana*) being demaunded where they had such plentie of golde, signified that it was

Hartes and wylde bores.

Cunnyng artificers.

Base golde.

Tokens of the continent or firme lande.

The golden region of Canchieta.

was brought them from a region called *Canchieta*, or *Cauchieta*, beyng distant from them sixe sunnes, that is, sixe dayes iourney westwarde: and that theyr images of golde were made in the same region. Whereupon our men directed theyr voyage thyther immediatly, and aryued there at the Kalendes of Nouember, in the yeere of Christe a thousande and fyue hundred. The people of the countrey resorted to them without feare, bryngyng with them of the golde whiche we sayde to be natiue in that region. This people had also collers of pearles about theyr neckes, which were brought them from *Curiana* for exchaunge of theyr marchandises. None of them woulde exchaunge anye of those thynges whiche they had out of other countreys: as neyther the Curians golde, nor the Canchietans pearles: yet among the Canchietans they founde but lytle golde redy geathered. They toke with them from thence certayne very fayre Marmasets or Munkeyes, and many Popyngayes of sundrye colours. In the moneth of Nouember, the ayre was there most temperate, and nothyng colde. The guardens of the north pole were out of syght to both these people, they are so neare the Equinoctial. Of the degrees of the pole, they can geue none other accompte. These people are wel disposed men, of honest conditions, and nothyng suspitious, for almost al the nyght long they resorted to the shyppe with theyr boates, and went aboorde shyppe without feare, as dyd the Curians. They call pearles, *Corixas*. They are somewhat ielous, for when anye straungers come among them, they euer place theyr women behynde them. In this region of *Canchieta*, the gossampine trees growe of them selues commonly in many places, as doo with vs elmes, wyllowes, and sallowes: and therefore they vse to make breeches of cotton, wherewith they couer theyr priuie partes in many other regions thereabout. When they had yet sayled on forwarde by the same coastes, there came forth against them about two thousande men, armed after theyr manner, forbyddyng them to come alande. These people were so rude and sauage, that our men coulde by no meanes allure them to familiaritie. Our men therefore, contented only with theyr pearles, returned backe ye same way they came, where they remained with the Curians continually for the space of .xx. dayes, & fylled theyr

The Equinoctial line.

Gossampine trees.

bellies

bellies wel with good meate. And here it seemeth to me not farre from my purpose, to declare what chaunced vnto them in theyr returne when they came now within the sight of the coast of *Paria*. They happened therfore in the way, at *Os Draconis*, and the gulfes of *Paria* (wherof we spake before) to meete with a nauy of xviii. Canoas of Canibales, which went a rouing to hunt for men: who assoone as they had espied our men, assailed their ship fiercely, & without feare enclosed ye same, disturbing our men on euery side with their arrowes: but our men so feared them with theyr gunnes, that they fled immediatly, whō our men folowing with the shyp boate, tooke one of theyr Canoas, and in it only one Canibal (for the other had escaped) and with him another man bounde, who with teares runnyng downe his cheekes, and with gesture of his handes, eyes, and head, signified that sixe of his companions had ben cruelly cut in peeces, and eaten of that mischeuous nation. and that he shoulde haue ben likewyse handled the day folowyng: wherefore they gaue hym power ouer the Canibal, to do with him what he would. Then with the Canibals owne clubbe, he layde on hym al that he might dryue with hande and foote, grinding and fretting as it had ben a wyld bore, thinkyng that he had not yet sufficiently reuenged the death of his companions, when he had beaten out his braynes and guttes. When he was demaunded after what sort the Canibales were woont to inuade other countreys, he answered, that they euer vsed to carye with them in theyr Canoas, a great multitude of clubbes, the whiche, wheresoeuer they do lande, they pytch in the grounde, and encampe them selues within the compasse of the same, to lye the more safely in the nyght season. In *Curiana* they founde the head of a captayne of the Canibales, nayled ouer the doore of a certayne gouernour for a token of victorye, as it had ben the standerde or helmet taken from the enimie in battayle. In these coastes of *Paria* is a region called *Haraia*, in the which great plentie of salt is geathered after a strange sorte: for the sea beyng there tossed with the power of the wyndes, dryueth the salte waters into a large playne by the sea syde, where, afterwarde when the sea waxeth calme, and the sunne begynneth to shine, the water is congealed into most pure and whyte salte, wherewith innumerable shyppes myght be laden, yf men dyd resorte

Canibales in the gulfes of Paria.

Death for death.

Howe the Canibales fortifie their campe.

Haraia.

resorte thether for the same before there fale any rayne: For the rayne melteth it, and causeth it to synke into the sande, and so by the pores of the earth, to returne to the place from whence it was dryuen. Other say, that the playne is not fylled from the sea, but of certeine sprynges whose water is more sharpe and salt then the water of the sea. Thinhabitantes do greatlye esteeme this bay of salt, whiche they vse, not only for theyr owne commoditie, but also woorking the same into a square forme lyke vnto brickes, they sell it to strangers for exchaunge of other thynges whiche they lacke. In this Region, they stretche and drye the dead bodies of theyr kinges and noble men, laying the same vpon a certayne frame of woodde, muche lyke vnto a hurdle or gredyren, with a gentell fyre vnder the same, by lyttle and lyttle consumyng the fleshe, and kepyng the skynne hole with the bones inclosed therein. These dryed carcases, they haue in great reuerence, and honour them for theyr housholde and famylier gods. They say that in this place they sawe a man, & in an other place a woman, thus dryed and reserued. When they departed from *Cutiana*, the .viii. day of the Ides of February, to returne to Spayne, they had threescore and .xvi poundes weight (after .viii. vnces to the pounde) of pearles, which they bought for exchange of our thinges, amounting to the value of fyue shillinges. Departing therfore, they consumed threescore dayes in theyr iourney (although it were shorter then from *Hispaniola*) by reason of the continuall course of the sea in the west, which dyd not only greatly stey the shippe, but also somtymes dryue it backe. But at the length they came home so laden with pearles, that they were with euery maryner, in maner as common as chaffe. But the master of the shyppe, *Petrus Alphonsus*, being accused of his companyons that he had stowlen a great multitude of precious pearles, and defrauded the kyng of his portion which was the fifth parte, was taken of *Fernando de Vega*, a man of great lerning and experience, & gouernour of *Gallecia*, where they aryued, and was there kept in pryson a long tyme. But he styll denyeth that euer he deteyned any part of the pearles. Many of these pearles were as bygge as hasell nuttes, and as oriente (as we call it) as they be of the East partes. Yet not of so great pryce, by reason that the holes therof are not so perfecte. When I my selfe

Sprynges of salt water.

The bodyes of princes dryed and reserued.

Orient pearles as bygge as hasel nuts.

selfe was present with the right honorable duke of *Methyna*, and was bydde to dynner with him, in the citie of Ciuile, they brought to hym aboue a hundred and twentie ounces of pearles to be solde, whiche surely dyd greatly delyte me with their fayrenes and brighenes. Some say, that *Alphonsus* had not these pearles in *Curiana*, being distant from *Os Draconis* more then a hundred & twentie leagues, but that they had them in the regions of *Cumana* and *Manacapana*, nere vnto *Os Draconis* and the ilande of *Margarita*: for they deny that there is any pearles founde in *Curiana*. But sith the matter is yet in controuersie, we wyl passe to other matters. Thus muche you haue, whereby you may coniecture, what commoditie in tyme to come may bee looked for from these newe landes of the west Ocean, whereas at the fyrst discouering, they shewe suche tokens of great ryches. Thus fare ye well.

The Ilande of Margarita.

The .ix. booke of the fyrst Decade to Cardinal *Lodouike*.

The nauigation of Vincentius, and Aries Pinzonus.

V*incentiagnes Pinzonus*, & also *Aries Pinzonus*, his neuiew by his brother syde, whiche accompanyed the Admiral *Colonus* in his fyrst vyage, & were by him appoynted to be maisters of two of the small shippes which the Spaniardes call *Carauelas*, being moued by the great ryches & amplitude of the new landes, furnysshed of theyr owne charges foure Carauels, in the hauen of theyr owne countrey, which the Spanyardes cal *Palos*, bordering on the west Ocean. Hauing therfore the kings licence & passeport to depart, they loosed from the hauen, about the Calendes of December in the yeere. 1499. This hauen of *Palos*, is threescore & twelue myles distant from *Gades*, commonly called *Cales*, and .lxiiii. myles from Ciuile. All thinhabitantes of this towne, not one excepted, are greatly geuē to searching of the sea, and continually exercised in sayling. They also directed their viage fyrst to the ilande of Canarie by the ilandes of *Hesperides*, now called *Cabouerde*, which some cal *Gorgodas Meducias*. Sayling therfore directly toward the south from that ilande of *Hesperides* which the Portugales (beyng possessers of the same) cal *Sancti Iacobi*,

The Ilandes of Canarie, Cabouerde.

S. James Ilande.

Iacobi, and departing from thence at the Ides of Ianuary, they folowed the southwest wynde, beyng in the myddest betwene the south and the west. When they supposed that they had sayled about thre hundreth leagues by the same wynde, they say that they lost the syght of the Northe starre: and were shortely after tossed with excedyng tempestes bothe of wynde and sea, and vexed with intollerable heate: Yet sayled they on further (not without great daunger) for the space of two hundred & fortie leagues, folowing yet the same wynd by the lost pole. Wherfore, whether habitable regions be vnder the Equinoctiall lyne or not, let these men and the oulde wryters, aswel Philosophers as poetes and cosmographers discusse. For these mē affirme it to be habitable, and merueloūsly replenished with people: and they, that it is vnhabitable by reason of the sonne beames depending perpendicularly or directlye ouer the same. Yet were there many of the olde wryters, whiche attempted to proue it habitable. These maryners beinge demaunded, if they saw the south pole, they answered that they knew no starre there like vnto this pole, that might be decerned about the poynt: but that they sawe an other order of starres, and a certeyne thicke myst rysyng from the horizontall lyne, whiche greatly hyndered theyr syght. They contende also, that there is a great heape or rysyng in the myddest of the earth, whiche taketh away the syght of the south pole, vntyll they haue vtterly passed ouer the same: but they verely beleeue that they sawe other images of starres, muche differing from the situation of the starres of our hemisphere, or halfe circle of heauen. Howe so euer the matter be, as they informe vs, we certifie you. At the length, the seuenth day of the calendes of Februarye, the espied lande a farre of, and seeing the water of the sea to be trobelous, sounding with theyr plummet, they found it to be .xvi. fathames depe. Going a lande, and taryinge there for the space of two dayes, they departed, bycause they sawe no people stering, although they founde certeyne steppes of men by the sea syde. Thus grauing on the trees & the stones nere vnto the shore, the kynges name and theyrs, and the tyme of theyr commyng thether, they departed. Not farre from this station, folowyng the fyer on the lande by nyght, they founde a nation lying vnder the

The north pole out of sight.

Habitable regions vnder the Equinoctial lyne.

the open fyrmament, after the maner of warre. Our men thought it not best to trouble them untyll the mornyng. Therefore, at the rysyng of the sonne, fortie of our men well armed, wente towarde them: agaynst whom came forth. xxxii. of them, with bowes, slynges and dartes, euen redy to fyght. The other companye folowed them, armed after the same maner. Our men affirme that they were of hygher stature then eyther the Almaynes or Pannonians. They beheld our men with frownyng & threatenyng countenaunce: but our men thought it not good to fal to bickering with them, uncertayne whether it were for feare, or bycause they would not dryue them to flighe. Wherfore they went about to allure them by faire meanes & rewardes: but they refused all kynde of gentelnes, and stoode euer in a redines to fight, declaring the same by signes and tokens. Thus our men resorted to theyr shyppes, and they to the place from whence they came, without any further busines. The same nyght about mydnyght, they fledde, & left the place voyde where they lay in the campe. Our men suppose them to be a vagabund and wandering nation, lyke unto the Scythians, without houses or certeyne dwelling places, lyuing only with the fruites of the earth, hauing theyr wyues and chyldren folowing them. Suche as measured their footesteppes in the sande, affirme with great othes, that one of theyr fecte is almost as long as two feete of our men of the meane sorte. Sayling on yet further, they founde an other riuer, but not of deapth sufficient to beare the Carauels: they sent therefore the foure shippe boates to lande, full of armed men to search the countrey. They espyed uppon a hygh hyll nere unto the sea syde, a greate multitude of people, to whom our company sent foorth one man with certeyne of our thynges to allure them to exchange. And when he had cast a haukes bell towarde them, they cast downe a wedge of golde a cubit longe: the which as he stouped to take up, they sodenly inclosed hym, and caryed hym away, But he was shortly after rescued by his companions, to some of their paynes: for they slue eyght of our men, & wounded many a farre of, with theyr arrowes, and dartes made of wood, hardened at the endes with fyre. After this they encompassed our shippe boates within the ryuer, and came rashly within the reache of our men, laying holde on the boates

syde,

People of high stature.

A vagabounde nation.

Giantes.

Desperate boldnesse. sydes, where they were thrust through, and hewen in peeces as it had ben sheepe, by reason they were naked. Yet woulde they not for al this geue ouer, but tooke from our men one of their boates, hauing no men in it: for the gouernour thereof being slayne with an arowe, the other fledde and escaped. And thus they lefte this fierce and warlyke people, saylyng towarde the northwest, along by the same coastes, with sorowfull hartes for the death of theyr companyons. When they had sayled about .xl. leagues, they chaunced into a sea of suche freshe water, that they fylled theyr barelles and hoggesheades therewith. Searching the cause hereof, they vnderstoode that a vehement course of riuers discended with great violence from the toppes of certayne great hylles. They say also that there lyeth within the sea, manye fortunate and fruitful Ilandes, and well inhabited, and that thinhabitantes of this tracte are men of meeke nature, and suche as doo not refuse straungers, yet lyttle profytable to them, because they haue no marchandyes for their purpose, as golde, or precious stones. for lacke whereof, they brought from thence thyrtie captiues to sell for slaues. Thinhabitantes call this region *Mariatambal*. The region of the east part of that ryuer, is called *Camomorus*, and that of the west part *Paricora*, in the midlande whereof, thinhabitantes signifyed that there is great plentie of golde: For, folowing this riuer directly towarde the North (as the bending of the shore requyred) they recouered agayne the syght of the north pole. All the coaste of this tracte, partetpneth to *Paria*, the which (as we sayd before) was fyrst found by *Colonus* hym selfe, and hath in maner in euery place great abundaunce of pearles. They say that these coastes are adioynyng vnto, and all one with *Os Draconis*, and also borderyng vppon the regions of *Cumana, Manacapana, Curiana, Cauchi[illegible]a*, and *Cuchibach*[illegible]: Wherfore they thought it to be part of the [illegible] lande of India, beyonde the riuer of *Ganges*. For the great & large compasse thereof, doth not permit that it shoulde be an ilande, albeit the whole earth vncouered with water, largely taken, may be called an Ilande. From the poynt of that land where they lost the sight of the north pole, saylyng by a continuall tracte about three hundred leagues towar[illegible] west syde of *Paria*, they say that (almost in the [illegible] way) they chaunced into a riuer called *Mara*[illegible]*um*,

Marginal notes: A sea of freshe water. — Many fruitful Ilandes. — Humane people. — Regions of Paria. — Gold & pearles.

[illegible]

which they affirme to be of suche exceadyng breadth, that it might seeme incredible, yf the antiquities dyd not make mention of the lyke. Beyng demaunded of me yf it were not salt water where it diuided the lande, they answeared that the water therof was very freshe and sweete, and that the further it ranne, to be so muche the fresher: also ful of Ilandes and wholsome fyshe: they dare auouche the breadth therof to be more then thirtie leagues. Yet yf we wel weigh and consyder the largenesse and widenesse of *Boriostomea* and *Spiriostomea*, the mouthes of the famous riuer of *Ister* (nowe called *Danubius*) and howe farre they violate or corrupt the salt water with their freshnesse, we shal ceasse to marueyle, although this other riuer be greater: for who can diminish the power of nature, but that it may make this bigger then the other, and another bygger then this? And I suppose this to be the ryuer whereof *Colonus* the Admirall made mention in the description of his voyage in these coastes. But we shal hereafter haue further knowledge hereof: let vs nowe therefore returne to the commodities of these regions. They found in many Ilandes about *Paria*, great woodes of Brasile trees, and brought away with them three thousande poundes weyght thereof. They say that the Brasile of *Hispaniola*, is muche better then this to dye cloth with a more fayre and durable colour. From hence, folowing the winds (which the Spaniards cal *Northuest*, and the Italians *Graeco*) they passed by many Ilandes very fruiteful, yet left desolate and wasted by reason of the crueltie of the Canibales: for they went alande in many places, they founde the ruines of many destroyed houses: yet in some places they founde men, but those exceedyng fearefull, fleeyng to the mountaynes, rockes, and woodes at the syght of euery straunger or shyppe, & wanderyng without houses or certayne abydyng places, for feare of the Caniballes layinge wayte and huntyng after them. Here they found those great trees whiche of them selues in dyuers places bryng forth that fruite or spice, which the Apothecaries cal *Cassia Phistula*, and that of no lesse goodnesse, then that which the phisitians minister to suche as be diseased with the ague, but it was not rype at theyr beyng there. They affirme that there are trees of suche bygnesse, that .xvi. men ioynyng handes togeather, and standyng in compasse, can scarcely embrace some of them.

The commodities of the regions & Ilandes about Paria.
Brasile.

Canibales.

Trees of Cassia fistula.

A monstrous beast.

Among these trees is founde that monstrous beaste with a snowte lyke a foxe, a tayle lyke a marmasette, eares lyke a bat, handes lyke a man, and feete lyke an ape, bearyng her whelpes aboute with her in an outwarde bellye much lyke vnto a great bagge or purse. The deade carkas of this beaste, you sawe with me, and turned it ouer and ouer with your owne handes, marueylyng at that new belly, and wonderful prouision of nature. They say it is knowen by experience, that she neuer letteth her whelpes goo out of that purse, except it be ether to play, or to sucke, vntyll suche tyme that they be able to gette theyr lyuyng by them selues. They tooke thys beaste with her whelpes: But the whelpes dyed shortely after in the shyppes. Yet the damme liued certaine monethes: but at the length, not being able to abide so great alteration of ayre, and change of meate, she dyed also in the way. But of this beaste, we haue saide enough. Let vs now therfore returne to the auctours of these thinges. These two *Tinzoni*, the vncle and the neuiew, susteyned many greate troubles & horrible tempestes and perilles in this nauigation. For when they had nowe sailed by the coastes of *Paria* about syxe hundred leagues, & (as they supposed) beyond the citie of *Cathay*. and the costes of East India beyond the riuer of Ganges, there rose sodenly so fierce a tempest in the moneth of July, that of the four Carauels which they had with them, two were drowned euen before theyr eyes: and the thyrd lying at anker, with lyke sodennes caried out of theyr syght through the violence of the tempest: the fourth also lying at anker, was so shaken and broosed, that all the seames therof were almost losed: Yet came they to land out of this last shyp, but vtterly despayryng of the shyp. Wherfore consultyng with them selues what was best to bee doone in so extreeme a case, and how to prouyde them a safe dwellyng place in those Regions, beyng out of all hope how to depart from thense, they determyned to slay all the inhabytauntes of the countrey nere about them, least they with the other should conspyre together to kyll them; but theyr fortune was better. For the Carauel which the tempest had caried away, was come to them agayne. This had in it .l. men, [illegible] [illegible]

Extreme remedie in a desperate case.

[illegible] and

and thus being [illegible] with tempestes [illegible] they returned to theyr natiue countrey of *Palos*, to theyr wyues and chyldren, the day before the Calendes of December, with the losse of many of theyr deere frendes & neighbours. They brought with them Cinamome and ginger: but not very good, because they were not there fully seasoned with the heate of the sonne, before they brought them from thence. They brought also certayne pretious stones, which *Baptista Elysius* that excellent philosopher, and your lordshyppes physition, affirmeth to be true Topases. After these mens returne, other of theyr neighbours being moued therto by a certaine emulation, to proue yf theyr fortune wold be any better, lyke men of good corage, beyng nothing discomforted by the hard fortune of their neighboures, knowing that it often times chaunceth, that that which is one mans vndoing, is an other mans making, attempted a newe voiage toward the south by ý coastes of *Paria*, folowyng the steps of *Colonus* the Admiral, who had fyrste discouered the same. They also brought with them great plentie of *Cassia fistula*, and founde that precious medicine called of the Spaniards *Animæ album*, whose perfume is of most excellent effect to heale the reumes, murres, and heauines of the head. As touching this vyage, as yet I know no other newes that I thought woorthy to certifie you of, wherfore, I wyl nowe make an ende of this booke, because you put me so often in remembrance of your departure: Yet to accomplyshe the Decade, I wyl declare somewhat of the superstitions of *Hispaniola*. You shall nowe therfore vnderstand the illusions wherewith the people of the Ilande haue ben seduced after the errours of the olde gentilitie, and wandered in the ignoraunce and blyndnesse of humane nature, corrupted by the disobedience of our fyrst parentes, whiche hath remayned in all nations vpon the face of the earth, except where it hath pleased GOD by the lyght of his spirite by his woorde, to poure vpon his electe the grace of renouation, by the lyght whereof the natural darknesse receiueth some clearenesse as in a glasse, vntil imperfection shalbe abolished. Our men therfore were long in the Ilande of *Hispaniola*, before they knewe that the people therof honoured any other thyng then the lyghtes of heauen, or had any other religion: but [illegible]

Cinamome and Ginger.

Topases.

Men of noble courage.

Another voyage.

Animæ album

The superstitions of Hispaniola.

The errours of the olde gentilitie.

with them, and by understandyng their language, drewe to a further familiaritie, they had knowledge that they used diuers rites and superstitions: I haue therefore geathered these fewe thinges followyng, out of a booke wrytten by one *Ramonus* an Heremite, whom *Colonus* had left with certayne kynges of the Ilande to instruct them in the Christian fayth. And because in manner their whole religion is none other thyng then idolatrie, I wil begyn at theyr idolles. It is therefore apparant by the images whiche they honour openly and commonly, that there appeare unto them in the nyght seasons, certayne phantasies and illusions of euil spirites, seducing them into many fonde and foolish errours: for they make certayne images of Gossampine cotton, folded or wreathed after theyr manner, and hard stopped within. These images they make syttyng, muche lyke unto the pyctures of spirites and deuyls which our paynters are accustomed to paynt upon walles: but forasmuche as I mee selfe sent you foure of these images, you may better presently signifie unto the kyng your uncle, what manner of thynges they are, and howe like unto paynted deuylles, then I can expresse the same by wrytyng. These images, the inhabitantes call *Zemes*, whereof the leaste, made to the lykenesse of young deuyls, they bynde to their foreheades when they goe to the warres agaynst theyr enimies, and for that purpose haue they these stringes hangyng at them which you see. Of these, they beleeue to obteyne rayne, yf rayne be lackyng, lykewyse fayre weather: for they thynke that these *Zemes* are the mediatours and messengers of the great god, whom they acknowledge to be only one, eternal, without ende, omnipotent, and invisible. Thus euery kyng hath his particuler *Zemes*, whiche he honoureth. They cal the eternall god by these two names, *Iocauna* and *Guamaonocon*, as theyr predecessours taught them, affyrmyng that he hath a father called by these fiue names: that is, *Attabeira, Mamona, Guacarapita, Liella, Guimazoa*. Nowe shal you heare what they fable on the earth as touchyng the original of man. There is in the Ilande, a region called *Caunana*, where they fayne that mankynde came fyrst out of two caues of a mountayne: and that the byggest sort of men came [illegible] the biggest caue, [illegible]
[illegible] they call

Cauta.

Illuminatrie [illegible]

Idolatrie and idolles.

Illusions of euil spirites.

Images of gossampine cotton.

Young deuyls.

Caua. The greater caue, they name *Cazibaxagua*, and the lesse, *Amaiauna*. They say, that before it was lawfull for men to come foorth of the caue, the mouth of the caue was kepte and watched nyghtly by a man whose name was *Machochael*: this *Machochael*, departyng somewhat farre from the caue, to the intent to see what things were abrode, was sodenly taken of the sunne, (whose syght he was forbidden) & was turned into a stone. They fayne the lyke of diuers other, that whereas they went foorth in the nyght season a fyshyng so farre from the caue, that they could not returne before the rysyng of the sunne (the whiche it was not lawful for them to beholde) they were transfourmed into Myrobalane trees, which of them selues grow plentifully in the Ilande. They say furthermore, that a certayne ruler called *Vagoniona*, sent one foorth of the caue to goe a fyshyng, who by like chaunce was turned into a Nyghtingale, because the sunne was rysen before he came agayne to the caue: and that yeerely about the same time that he was turned into a byrde, he doth in the nyght with a mournyng song bewayle his mysfortune, and call for the helpe of his maister *Vagoniona*. And this they thynke to be the cause why that byrd syngeth in the nyght season. But *Vagoniona*, beyng sore troubled in his mind for the losse of his familiar frend whom he loued so entirely, leauyng the men in the caue, brought foorth only the women with theyr suckyng chyldren, leauyng the women in one of the Ilands of that tracte, called *Mathinino*, and caryed the chyldren away with hym: which poore wretches oppressed with famine, fayned and remayned on the banke of a certayne ryuer, where they were turned into frogges, and cryed *toa, toa*, that is, *mamma, mamma*, as chyldren are woont to crye for the mothers pappe. And hereof they say it commeth that frogges use to crye so pitifully in the spryng tyme of the yeere: And that men were scattered abrode in the caues of *Hispaniola* without the company of women. They say also, that where as *Vagoniona* hymselfe was accustomed to wander in diuers places, and yet by a speciall grace neuer transfourmed, descended to a [illegible] in the bottome of the sea, [illegible]

Fables muche lyke Ouides transformations.

The Nyghtyngale.

The Ilande of Mathinino.

Children turned into Frogs.

A speciall grace.

great estimation amonge the kynges, as goodly [illegible], and most holy reliques. But nowe (moste noble prynce) you shall heare a more pleasaunt fable. There is a certayne caue called *Iouanaboina*, in the territorie of a certayne kyng whose name is *Machinnech*: This caue they honour more religiously then dyd the Grekes in tyme paste, *Corinth*, *Cyrrha*, or *Nysa*, and haue adourned it with pyctures of a thousand fashions. In thentrance of this caue they haue two grauen *Zemes*, wherof the one is called *Binthaitel*, and the other *Marohu*. Beyng demaunded why they had this caue in so great reuerence, they answered earnestly, because the sunne and the moone came fyrst out of the same to geue lyght to the worlde: they haue religious concourse to these caues, as we are accustomed to goe on Pylgrimage to Rome, or Vaticane, Compostella, or Hierusalem, as most holy & head places of our religion. They are also subiect to another kynde of superstition: for they thynke that dead folkes walke in the night, and eate the fruite called *Guannaba*, unknowen unto us, & somewhat like unto a Quinse: affyrmyng also that they are conuersant with lyuyng people, euen in theyr beddes, and to deceiue women in takyng upon them the shape of men, shewyng them selues as though they woulde haue to do with them: but when the matter commeth to actual deede, sodaynely to vanishe away. If any do suspect that a dead body lyeth by him, whē he feeleth any strange thyng in the bed, they say he shalbe out of doubt by feelyng of the belly thereof: affyrmyng that the spirites of dead men may take upon them al the members of mans body, sauyng only the nauel. If therfore by the lacke of ŷ nauel he do perceaue that a dead body lyeth by him, the feelyng is immediatly resolued. They beleue verily, that in the nyght, and ofentimes in their iourneys, and especially in common and high wayes, [illegible] with the lyuyng: Agaynst whom, if any man [illegible] out of feare, the fantasie [illegible] [illegible]

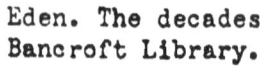

Margin notes:

Holy reliques.

A holy caue.

The original of the sunne and moone.

Walkyng spirites.

A remedie agaynst walkyng spirites.

[illegible] the same before the memorie of man, [illegible] in rymes and songues, whiche it was lawful for none to learne, but only the kynges sonnes, who commit suche same to memorie, because they had neuer any knowledge of letters. These they syng before the people on certayne solemne and festiuall dayes, as most religious ceremonies: whyle in the meane tyme they play on a certaine instrument made of one whole peece of wood, somewhat holowe lyke a tymbrel. Theyr priestes and diuines (whom they cal *Boitios*) instructe them in these superstitions. These priestes are also phisitions, deuysing a thousande craftes and subtilties howe to deceiue the symple people whiche haue them in great reuerence: for they perswade them that the *Zemes* vse to speake with them familiarlye, and tel them of thinges to come. And yf any haue ben sycke, and are recouered, they make them beleue that they obteyned theyr health of the *Zemes*. These *Boitii* bynde them selues to muche fastyng, and outwarde cleanlynesse, and pourgynges, especially when they take vpon them the cure of any prince, for then they drynke the powder of a certaine herbe by whose qualitie they are driuen into a furie, at whiche time (as they say) they learne many thinges by reuelation of the *Zemes*. Then puttyng secretely in theyr mouthes, eyther a stone, or a bone, or a peece of fleshe, they come to the sicke person, commaundyng al to depart out of that place, except one or two, whom it shal please the sycke man to appoynt: this done, they goe about hym three or foure tymes, greatly deformyng theyr faces, lyps, and nosethrils with sundry fylthy gestures, blowing, breathyng, and suckyng the forehead, temples, and necke of the patient, whereby (they say) they drawe the euyl ayre from him, and sucke the disease out of his vaynes: then rubbyng hym about the shoulders, thighes, and legges, and drawyng downe theyr handes close by his feete, holdyng them yet fast togeather, they runne to the [illegible]

Priestes and diuines.

Phisitions.

Ignorance is norished with superstition.

A powder of maruelous effect.

A strange maner of curyng.

Angry goddes.

taken [illegible] from you. But yf he attempte yet further to deceiue the patient, he persuadeth hym that his *Zemes* is angry, eyther because he [illegible] chappell, or not honoured him religiously, or not dedicated vnto hym a groue or gerden. And if it so chaunce that the sycke person dye, his kynsfolkes, by witchcrafte, enforce the dead to confesse whether he dyed by naturall destenye, or by the negligēce of the *Boitius*, in that he had not fasted as he shoulde haue done, or not ministred a conuenient medicine for the disease: so that if this physicion be founde fautie, they take reuenge of hym. Of these stones or bones whiche these *Boitii* cary in theyr mouthes, yf the women can come by them, they keepe them religiously, beleeuyng them to be greatly effectuall to helpe women trauaylyng with chylde, and therefore honour them as they do theyr *Zemes*. For diuers of the inhabitantes honour *Zemes* of diuers fashions: some make them of wood, as they were admonyshed by certayne visions appearing vnto them in the woods: Other, whiche haue receiued aunswere of them among the rockes, make them of stone and marble. Some they make of rootes, to the similitude of suche as appeare to them when they are gatheryng the rootes called *Ages*, whereof they make theyr bread, as we haue sayd before. These *Zemes* they beleue to sende plentie & fruitfulnes of those rootes, as the antiquitie beleued such fayries or spirites as they called *Dryades*, *Hamadryades*, *Satyros*, *Panes*, and *Nereides*, to haue the cure & prouidence of the [illegible] woodes, springes, and fountaines, assigning to euery [illegible] [illegible] [illegible] of this [illegible] *Zemes* [illegible] the same to [illegible] theyr [illegible]. [illegible] as often as the [illegible] theyr *Zemes* [illegible] [illegible]

They make the dead to speake.

Fayries or spirites of the gentiles, much like to the papistes.

The powder of the herbe Cohoba.

[illegible]

hedd, as one that came newe out of sleape: and thus lookyng vp toward heauen, fyrst he fumbleth certaine confounded wordes with hym selfe, then certayne of the nobilitie or cheefe gentlemen that are about him (for none of the common people are admitted to these mysteries) with loude voyces geue tokens of reioycing that he is returned to them from the speach of the *Zemes*, demaundyng of hym what he hath seene. Then he openyng his mouth, doateth that the *Zemes* spake to hym durynge the tyme of his traunce, declaryng that he had reuelations either concerning victorie or destruction, famine or plentie, health or sickenesse, or whatsoeuer happeneth fyrst on his tongue. Nowe (most noble Prince) what neede you hereafter to marueyle of the spirite of *Apollo* so shakyng his Sibylles with extreme furie: you had thought that the superstitious antiquitie had peryshed. But nowe wheras I haue declared thus muche of the *Zemes* in generall, I thought it not good to let passe what is sayde of them in particuler. They say therefore that a certayne kyng called *Guamaretus*, had a *Zemes* whose name was *Corocbotum*, who (they say) was oftentimes woont to descend from the hyghest place of the house where *Guamaretus* kept hym fast bound. They affirme, that the cause of this his breakyng of his bandes and departure, was eyther to hyde hym selfe, or to goe seeke for meate, or els for the acte of generation: and that sometymes beyng offended that the kyng *Guamaretus* had ben negligent and slacke in honouring hym, he was woont to lye hyd for certayne dayes. They say also, that in the kynges village there are sometyme chyldren borne hauyng two crownes, whiche they suppose to be the children of *Corocbotum* the *Zemes*. They fayne likewyse, that *Guamaretus* being ouercome of his enemies in battayle, and his village with the pallace consumed with fyre, *Corocbotus* brake his bondes, and was afterwarde founde a furlong of, safe and without hurte. He hath also [illegible] *Epileguanita*, made of wood, in shape lyke [illegible]: who also is sayde, [illegible] where he is honou[illegible] perceiue hym to be [illegible] to seeke hym, [illegible] fyndyng hym [illegible]

Secrete mysteries.

Reuelations.

The spirite of Apollo.
The Sibylles.

Children with two crownes.

Wanderyng images.

[illegible]. But they [illegible], that since the commyng of the Christian men into the Ilande, he fled [illegible] altogether, and could neuer [illegible] be founde, whereby they diuined the destruction of theyr countrey. They honoured an other *Zemes* in the lykenes of a woman, on whom wayted two other lyke men, as they were ministers to her. One of these, executed thoffice of a mediatour to the other *Zemes*, which are vnder the power and commaundement of this woman, to raise wyndes, cloudes, and rayne. The other is also at her commaundement a messenger to the other *Zemes*, which are ioyned with her in gouernaunce, to geather togeather the waters which fall from the hygh hylles to the valleies, that beyng loosed, they may with force burste out into greate floodes, and ouerflowe the countrey, yf the people do not geue due honoure to her Image. There remayneth yet one thing worthy to be noted, wherwith we will make an end of this booke. It is a thing well knowen, and yet freshe in memory among the inhabitantes of the Iland, that there was sometime two kings (of the which one was the father of *Guarionexius*, of whom we made mention before) which were woont to absteyne fyue daies togeather continualy from meate & drinke, to know somewhat of their *Zemes* of thinges to come, and that for this fasting beyng acceptable to their *Zemes*, they receyued answere of them, that within few yeeres there shoulde come to the Ilande a nation of men couered with apparell, which should destroy al the customes and cerimonies of the Iland, and eyther slay al theyr children, or bring them into seruitude. The common sort of the people vnderstode this oracle to be ment of the Canibales, & therfore when they had any knowledge of theyr commyng, they euer fled, and were fully determined neuer [illegible] the battayle with them. But when they sawe that the [illegible] [illegible]

A woman Zemes of great power.

Mediatours.

A marueylous [illegible] of the deuyll.

haue seene [illegible] many thynges, because you [illegible] that to [illegible] rowne you take your iorney towarde your [illegible], bryngyng home the queene your aunt, whom you [illegible] at the [illegible] of kyng Frederike your uncle. Wherfore I byd you farewell for this time, desyryng you to remember your *Martyr*, whom you haue compelled in the name of the kyng your uncle, to geather these fewe thynges out of a large feelde of hystories.

The tenth and last booke of the fyrst Decade, as a conclusion of the former bookes: wrytten to *Inacus Lopez Mendocius*, Countie of *Tendilla*, & viceroy of *Granata*.

AFter the fyrst begynning and newe attempte, when *Colonus* had taken vpon hym the enterpryse to searche the Ocean sea, I was earnestly moued and required by the letters of certaine of my frendes and noble men of Rome, to wryte suche thinges as shoulde happen. For they whispered with great admiration, that where as there were many newe landes founde, and nations which liued naked and after the lawe of nature, they coulde heare no certentie therof, beyng greatly desyrous of ȳ same. In this meane tyme [illegible] *Ascanius* (his brother *Lodouike* being cast out of Millane by the frenchmen) [illegible] auctoritie [illegible] to haue my pen in hand. To whom I wrote the [illegible] bookes of this decade, beside many other of my [illegible] commentaries whiche you shal see shortly: [illegible] then [illegible] *Ascanius* [illegible] [illegible]

Millane in the handes of the frenche men.

[illegible] epystell [illegible] which I wrote to *Ascanius*: For they [illegible] acknowledged that they had the copye of al that I wrytte to cardinall *Asfanius*. And albeit that euen then I was sicke (as you knowe) yet tooke I the burden [illegible], and applyed my selfe to wrytyng. I haue therfore chosen these fewe thynges, out of a greate heape of such as seemed to me most worthy to be noted among the large wrytynges of the autthoures and searchers of the same. Wherfore, forasmuch as you haue endeuored to wrest out of my handes the whole example of all my woorkes, to adde the same to the innumerable volumes of your lybrarie, I thought it good nowe to make a breefe rehersall of those thynges which were done from that yeare of a thousande and fiue hundred, euen vnto this yeare which is the tenth from that: For I entend to wryte more largely of these thynges hereafter, if god graunt me lyfe. I had wrytten a whole booke by it selfe of the superstycions of the people of the ilande, supposyng therwyth to haue accomplyshed the whole Decade consistyng of ten bookes. But I haue added this to the tenth as a perpendycular lyne, and as it were a backe guide or rereward to the other: so that you may knytte the fyrst tenth to the nynth, & impute this to occupye the place of the tenth to fyll vp the Decade. This [illegible] I appoynted, lest I shoulde be compelled often tymes to wryte ouer the whole worke, or sende you the same defaced with blottes and interlynyng. But nowe let vs come to our purpose. The shyppe [illegible] and marriners [illegible] durying these ten yeares [illegible] *Colonus*, [illegible] *Paria*, which they [illegible] east India, [illegible]

The historye for wrytyng, conteyneth the actes of ten yeeres.

[illegible]

[illegible] East India.

long staues lyke iauelens, made hard at the ende with fire. They founde many beastes, both crepyng and foure footed, much dyffeyng from ours, varyable and of sundrye shapes innumerable: yet not hurtfull, except Lions, Tigers, and Crocodiles. This I meane in sundry regions of that greate lande of *Paria*, but not in the ilandes: no not so muche as one, for all the beastes of the ilandes, are meeke and without hurte, except men, which (as wee haue sayde) are in many ilandes deuourers of mans fleshe. There are also dyuers kyndes of foules. And in many places battes of such bygnes, that they are equall with turtle doues. These battes, haue oftentymes assalted men in the night in theyr sleepe, and so bytten them with theyr venemous teeth, that they haue ben therby almost dryuen to madnes, in so much that they haue ben compelled to flee from such places, as from rauenous Harpies. In an other place, where certaine of them slept in the night season on the sands by the sea syde, a monster commyng out of the sea, came vpon one of them secretelye, and caryed hym away by the myddest out of the syght of his felowes, to whom he cryed in vayne for helpe, vntyl the beast leapt into the sea with her pray. It was the kynges pleasure that they shoulde remayne in these landes, and buylde townes and fortresses: whereunto they were so well wyllyng, that diuers profered them selues to take vpon them the subduyng of the lande, makyng great suite to the kyng that they myght be appoynted thereto. The coast of this tracte is exceedyng great and large, and the regions and landes thereof extende marueylous farre, so that they affirme the continent of these regions with the Ilandes about the same, to be thryse as bygge as al Europe, beside those landes that the Portugales haue founde southwarde, whiche are also exceedyng large. Therfore doubtlesse Spayne hath deserued great prayse in these our dayes, in that it hath made knowen vnto vs so many thousandes of *Antipodes* whiche lay hid before, and vnknowen to our forefathers: and hath thereby ministred so large matter to wryte of, to suche learned wyttes as are desyrous to set foorth knowledge to the commoditie of men: to whom I opened a way when I geathered these things rudelye togeather as you see: the whiche, neuerthelesse I truste you wil take in good part, aswell for that I can not amplifie my

A man deuoured of a monster of the sea.

Note the largenesse of the new Ilandes.

Antipodes.

my rudenesse with better defence, as also that I neuer toke penne in hande to wryte lyke an hystoriographer, but only by epistles scribeled in haste, to satisfie them, from whose commaundementes I myght not drawe backe my foote. But nowe I haue digressed ynough, let vs nowe therefore returne to *Hispaniola*. Our men haue founde by experience, that the bread of the Ilande is of smal strength to suche as haue ben vsed to our bread made of wheate, and that theyr strengthes were muche decayed by vsyng of the same: wherefore the kyng hath of late commaunded that wheate shoulde be sowen there in diuers places, and at sundry tymes of the yeere: It groweth into holow reedes, with fewe eares, but those very bygge and fruitefull. They fynde the lyke softnesse and delicatenesse to be in hearbes, whiche growe there to the height of corne. Neat or cattel, become of bygger stature, and exceedyng fat, but theyr fleshe is more vnsauerie, and theyr bones (as they say) eyther without marow, or the same to be very waterysshe: but of hogges and swyne, they affirme the contrary, that they are more wholsome, and of better taste, by reason of certayne wylde fruites whiche they eate, beyng of much better nourishment then maste. There is almost none other kynde of fleshe commonly solde in the market. The multitude of hogges are exceedyngly encreased, and become wylde as soone as they are out of the swyneheardes keepyng. They haue suche plentie of beastes and foules, that they shal hereafter haue no neede to haue any brought from other places. The increase of al beastes grow bigger then the broode they came of, by reason of the ranknes of the pasture, although theyr feedyng be only of grasse, without eyther barley or other grayne. But we haue sayd ynough of *Hispaniola*. They haue nowe founde that *Cuba* (which of long tyme they thought to haue ben firme lande, for the great length thereof) is an Ilande: yet is it no marueyle that the inhabitantes them selues tolde our men when they searched the length thereof, that it was without ende. For this nation beyng naked, and content with a lytle, and with the limites of theyr owne countrey, is not greatly curious to knowe what theyr neyghbours doo, or the largenesse of theyr dominion, nor yet knowe they yf there were any other thyng vnder heauen, besyde that whiche they walked on with theyr feete. *Cuba* is frome the [illegible]

The nature of the place, alteeth the formes and qualities of thynges.

Plentie of beastes and fouls.

Cuba is an Ilande.

into the West, muche longer then *Hispaniola*, and in breadth from the North to the South, muche lesse then they supposed at the fyrst: for it is very narowe in respect of the length, and is for the most part very fruitefull and pleasaunt. Eastwarde, not farre from *Hispaniola*, there lyeth an Ilande lesse then *Hispaniola* more then by the halfe, whiche our men called *Sancti Iohannis*, beyng in manner square, in this they founde exceedyng ryche golde mynes: but beyng nowe occupyed in the golde mynes of *Hispaniola*, they haue not yet sent labourers into the Ilande. But the plentie and reuenue of golde of al other regions, geue place to *Hispaniola*, where they geue them selues in manner to none other thyng then to geather golde, of whiche worke this order is appointed. To euery such wittie and skilful man as is put in trust to be a surueyour or ouerseer of these workes, there is assigned one or more kings of the Ilande, with their subiects. These kings accordyng to theyr league, come with theyr people at certayne tymes of the yeere, and resort euery of them to the golde myne to the whiche he is assigned, where they haue al manner of dyg- ging or mining tooles delyuered them, and euery king with his men, haue a certayne rewarde alowed them for theyr labour. For when they depart from the mynes to sowyng of corne, and other tyllage (whereunto they are addict at certaine other tymes, lest theyr foode shoulde faile them.) they receiue for their labour, one a ierkin, or a dublet, another a shyrt, another a cloke or a capp: for they nowe take pleasure in these thyngs, and goe no more naked as they were woont to doo. And thus they use the helpe and labour of the inhabitauntes, both for the tyllage of theyr grounde, and in theyr golde mynes, as though they were theyr seruantes or bondemen. They beare this yoke of seruitude with an euyll wyl, but yet they beare it: they cal these hyred labourers, *Anaborias*: yet the kyng dooth not suffer that they shoulde be used as bondemen, and only at his pleasure, they are set at libertie, or appoynted to worke. At suche tyme as they are called togeather of theyr kynges to worke (as souldiers or pyoners are assembled of theyr centurions) many of them steale away to the mountaynes and woodes, where they lye lurkyng, beyng content for that tyme to lyue with wylde fruites, rather then take the paynes to labour. They are docible and apte to learne, and haue

The discription of Cuba.

The Ilande of Burichena, or S. Iohannis. Golde mynes.

Tyllage.

They abhorre labour.

They are docible.

haue in a maner vtterly forgotten theyr olde superstitions. They beleue godly, and beare well in memory such thynges as they haue learned of our fayth. Theyr kynges chyldren are brought vp with the chiefest of our men, and are instructed in letters and good maners. When they are growen to mans age, they sende them home to theyr countreyes to be example to other, and especially to gouerne the people, yf theyr fathers be dead, that they may the better set forth the Christian religion, and keepe theyr subiectes in loue and obedience. By reason wherof, they come now by faire meanes & gentel persuasions, to the mines which lye in two regions of the Ilande, about thyrtie myles dystaunt from the cytie of *Dominica*, wherof the on is called *Sancti Christophori*: and the other beyng distant aboute fourscore and tenne myles, is called *Cibana*, not farre from the cheefe hauen called *Portus Regalis*. These regions are very large, in the which in many places here and there, are founde somtyme euen in the vpper crust of the earth, and somtyme among the stones, certayne rounde pieces or plates of golde, sometime of smale quantytie, and in some places of great wayght: in so much that there hath byn founde rounde pieces of three hundred pounde weyght, and one of three thousande, three hundred and tenne pounde weyght, the whiche (as you harde) was sent whole to the kyng in that shyp in the which the gouernour *Boadilla* was commyng home into Spaine, the shyp with all the men beyng drowned by the way, by reason it was ouer laden with the weyght of gold & multitude of men, albeit, there were mo then a thousande persons which sawe and handeled the piece of gold. And wheras here I speake of a pounde, I do not meane the common pounde, but the summe of the ducate of golde, with the coyne called *Triens*, which is the third part of a pounde, which they call *Pesus*. The summe of the weight hereof, the Spanyardes call *Castelanum Aureum*. All the gold that is digged in the mountaines of *Cibana* and *Portus Regalis*, is caried to the towne of Conception, where shoppes with al thinges apperteyning therto are furnished to fine it, melte it, and caste it into wedges. That done, they take the kynges parte therof, which is the fyfte parte, and so restore to euery man his owne which he gatte with his labour. But the golde which is founde in Sainct Christophers mynes and

The kynges chyldren.

The two cheefe golde mynes of Hispaniola.

A costly shypwracke.

Pesus.

The fynyng and distributing of golde.

and the regions there about, is caryed to the shoppes which are in the vyllage called *Bonauentura*. In these two shops, is moulten yeerely aboue three hundred thousand poundes wayghte of golde. If any man be knowen deceptfullye to keepe backe any portion of golde, whereof he hath not made the kynges officers priuie, he forfeyteth the same for a fyne. There chaunceth among them oftentymes many contentions and controuersies, the whiche unlesse the magistrates of the Ilande do fynyshe, the case is remoued by appellation to the hygh counsayle of the court, from whose sentence it is not lawfull to appeale in al the dominions of Castyle. But let vs nowe returne to the newe landes, from whence we haue digressed. They are innumerable, diuers, and exceedyng fortunate. Wherefore the Spanyardes in these our dayes, and theyr noble enterpryses, do not geue place eyther to the factes of *Saturnus*, or *Hercules*, or anye other of the auncient prynces of famous memory, which were canonized among the goddes, called *Heroes*, for theyr searchyng of newe landes and regions, and bryngyng the same to better culture and ciuilitie. Oh God, howe large & farre shal our posteritie see the Christian religion extended? howe large a campe haue they now to wander in, whiche by the true nobilitie that is in them, or mooued by vertue, wyll attempt eyther to deserue lyke prayse among men, or reputation of well doyng before God? What I conceiue in my mynde of these thynges, I am not able to expresse with penne or tongue. I wil now therfore so make an end of this perpendiculer conclusion of the whole Decade, as myndyng hereafter to search and geather euery thyng particulerly, that I may at further leysure wryte the same more at large. For *Colonus* the Admiral, with foure ships, and a hundred, threescore, and ten men, appoynted by the kyng, discouered in the yeere of Christe. 1520. the lande ouer agaynst the West corner of *Cuba*, distant from the same about a hundred and thirtie leagues: in the myddest of whiche tracte, lyeth an Ilande called *Guanassa*. From hence he directed his voyage backwarde towarde the East, by the shore of that coast, supposyng that he shoulde haue founde the coastes of *Paria*, but it chaunced otherwise. It is sayde also that *Vincentius Agnes* (of whom we haue spoken before) and one *Iohannis Diaz* (with diuers other, of whose voyages I haue as yet no certayne knowledge)

Thre hundreth thousand weight of gold molten yeerly in Hispaniola.

The newe landes.

Enlargyng of the Christian religion.

The original of true nobilitie.

The Ilande of Guanassa.

The voyage of Iohannes Diaz.

I i

knowledge) have overcome these causes: but yf God graunt me lyfe, I wyll to knowe the trueth hereof, and to advertise you of the same. Thus fare ye well.

The ende of the fyrst Decade.

The fyrst booke of the seconde Decade, to *Leo* Bishop of Rome, the tenth of that name, of the supposed continent or firme lande.

Since the tyme that *Galeatius Butrigarius* of *Bononie*, and *Iohannes Cursius* of Florence (most holy father) came to the Catholique kyng of Spayne, the one of your holinesse ambassage, and the other for the affayres of his common wealth, I was ever for the moste parte in theyr companye, and for theyr vertues and wysedome had them in great reverence. And whereas they were greatlye geven to studie, and continuall revoluing of divers auctours, they chaunced upon certayne bookes, negligently let slyppe out of my handes, entreatyng of the large landes and regions hytherto lying hyd, and almost West *Antipodes*, founde of late by the Spanyardes. Yet being allured and delyted with the newnesse and straungenesse of the matter, although rudely adourned, they commended the same, therewith earnestly desyryng me in theyr owne names, and requiring me in the name of your holynesse, to adde hereunto al such thynges as were founde after that tyme, and to geve them a copie therof, to sende to your holynesse, that you myght thereby understande, both howe great commodities is chaunced to the progenie of mankynde, as also encrease of the militant congregation in these our dayes, by the fortunate enterpryses of the kynges of Spayne. For lyke as rased and unpaynted tables, are apte to receave what formes soo ever are fyrst drawen theron by the hande of the paynter, even so these naked and simple people, doo soone receave the customes of our religion, and by conversation with our men, shake of theyr feerse and native barbarous-

West Antipodes.

The encrease of the Christian congregation.

barbarousnesse. I haue thought it good therfore to satisfie the request of these wyse men, especially vsyng thauthoritie of your name, wherunto not to haue obeyed, I shoulde esteme my selfe to haue committed a heynous offence. Wherfore I wyll nowe briefly reheatse in order, what hyd coastes the Spanyardes ouerran, who were thauthours therof, where they rested, what further hope they brought, and finallye what greate thynges those tractes of landes do promyse in time to come. In the declaration of my decade of the ocean, which is nowe prynted and dyspersed throughout Chrystendome vnwares to me, I described howe *Christophorus Colonus* founde those ilandes wherof wee haue spoken, and that turnyng from thence towarde the left hande southward, he chaunced into greate regions of landes, and large seas, dystant from the Equinoctiall lyne, onely from fyue degrees to tenne: where he founde brode ryuers and exceedyng hygh mountaynes couered with snowe, and harde by the sea bankes, where were manye commodious and quyet hauens. But *Colonus* being now departed out of this lyfe, the kyng beganne to take care, how those lands might be inhabited with Christian men, to thincrease of our fayth: Wherupon he gaue lycence by his letters patentes to al such as would take the matter in hand, and especially to two, wherof *Diego Nicuesa* was one, & the other was *Alphonsus Fogeda*. Wherfore about the Ides of December, *Alphonsus* departing fyrst with three hundred souldiers from the ilande of *Hispaniola* (in the which we sayd the Spaniardes had builded a cytie, & planted theyr habitation) & saylyng in maner ful south, he came to one of the hauens founde before, which *Colonus* named *Portus carthaginis*, both because of the iland standyng agaynste the course of the streame, and also that by reason of the largenesse of the place and bendyng sydes, it is much lyke to the hauen of Spayne called *Carthago*. The inhabytantes call the Ilande *Codego*, as the Spanyardes cal the Ilande of theyr hauen *Scombria*. This region is called of the inhabitantes *Caramairi*, in the whiche they affyrme both the men and women to bee of goodly stature, but naked. The men haue theyr heare cutte rounde by theyr eares, but the women weare it long, both the men and women are very good archers. Our men founde certayne trees in this prouince, which beare great plenty of sweete

It apples,

Ilandes distant from the Equinoctiall, from fyue degrees to ten.

The death of Colonus.

A generall licence.

The nauigation of Alphonsus Fogeda.

The region of Caramairi.

Apples whiche turne into wormes.

A tree whose shadowe is hurtful.

apples, but hurtful, for they turne into wormes when they are eaten. Especially the shadowe of the tree is contagious, for such as sleepe under it any tyme, haue theyr heades swolne, and lose their sight: but if they sleepe but a while, theyr sight commeth agayne after a fewe dayes. This porte is distant foure hundred, fyftie, & sixe myles from that port of *Hispaniola* whiche the Spanyardes call *Beata*, in the whiche also they furnishe them selues when they prepare anye voyage to seeke other newe landes. When *Fogeda* had entred into the hauen, he enuaded, slue, and spoyled the people, whom he founde naked and scattered: for they were geuen him for a pray by the kynges letters patentes, because they had ben before tyme cruell agaynst the Christians, and coulde neuer be allured to permytte them quietlye to come within theyr dominions. Here they founde golde, but in no great quantitie, nor yet that pure: they make of it certayne brest plates and brooches whiche they weare for comelynesse. But *Fogeda* not content with these spoyles, usyng certayne captiues, which he had taken before, for guydes, entred into a vyllage twelue myles dystant from the sea syde further into the lande, into the which they were fled when he fyrst enuaded. Here he found a naked people, but apte to warre: for they were armed with targettes, shieldes, long swoordes made of wood, and bowes with arrowes typt with bone, or hardened with fyre. As soone as they had espyed our men, they with theyr ghestes whō they had receiued, assayled them with desperate myndes, beyng therto more earnestly prouoked, beholdyng the calamitie of these whiche fled unto them, by the violence done to theyr women and chyldren, in the spoyle and slaughter. In this conflyct our men had the ouerthrowe: in the which, one *Iohannes de Lacossa* (being in auctoritie next unto *Fogeda* the captayne, and also the fyrste that geathered gold in the sandes of *Vraba*) was slayne with fiftie souldiers: for these people infecte their arrowes with the deadlye poyson of a certayne herbe. The other with theyr captayne *Fogeda* beyng discomfited, fledde to the shyppes. Whyle they remayned thus in the hauen of *Caribago*, sorowful and pensiue for the losse of theyr companions, the other captayne *Diego Nicuesa*, (whom they left in *Hispaniola*, preparyng hym selfe towarde the voyage in the hauen *Beata*) came to them with fyue shyppes,

Warlike people.

Arrowes infected with poyson.

The nauigation of Diego Nicuesa.

and

and seven hundred fourescore and syxteene men. For the greater number of souldyers folowed *Nicuesa*, bothe because free lybertye was geuen them to choose which of the capytaynes them lyst, and also that by reason of his age, he was of greater auctoritie: But esspeciallye because the rumoure was that *Beragua* being by the kynges commission appoynted to *Nicuesa*, was rycher in golde then *Vraba* assygned to *Alphonsus Fogeda*. Therfore, at the arryual of *Nicuesa*, they consulted what was best to be doone: and determyned fyrste to reuenge the deathe of theyr felowes. Wheruppon, settyng theyr battayle in araye, they marched in the nyght towarde them whiche slue *Cossa* with his companyons. Thus stealyng on them bnwares in the laste watche of the nyght, and encompassyng the vyllage where they lay, consystyng of a hundred houses and more, hauyng also in it thryse as many of theyr neyghbours as of them selues, they set it on fyre, with dilygent watche that none myght escape. And thus in short tyme they brought them and theyr houses to asshes, and made them paye the raunsome of blood with blood: for of a great multitude of men and women, they spared only syre chyldren, all other beyng destroyed with fyre or swoorde, except fewe whiche escaped priuily, they learned by these reserued chyldren, that *Cossa* and his felowes were cut in peeces, and eaten of them that slue them. By reason whereof, they suppose that these people of *Camairi* tooke theyr original of the *Caribes*, otherwyse called *Canibales*. Here they founde some golde among the asshes. For the hunger of golde dyd no lesse incourage our men to aduenture these peryls and labours, then dyd the possessyng of the landes. These thinges thus finished, and the death of *Cossa* and his felowes reuenged, they returned to the hauen. After this, *Fogida* whiche came fyrst, fyrst lykewyse departyng with his armie to seeke *Vraba*, committed to his gouernaunce, sayled by an Ilande called *Fortis*, lyinge in the mydway betweene *Vraba* and the hauen of *Carthago*: into the whiche descendyng, he founde it to be an Ilande of the Canibales, bryngyng with hym from thence two men and seuen women, for the residue escaped. Here he founde in the cotages of them that fledde, a hundreth, foure-score, and tenne drammes of golde, caste and wrought in dy-uers fasshions. Departyng therefore from hence, he came to the

The regions of Vraba and Beragua.

The Spanyardes reuenge the death of theyr companions.

A great slaughter.

Canibales.

The hunger of golde.

The Ilande Fortis.

Wrought golde.

[illegible] coastes of *Vraba*, whiche the inhabitantes call *Caribana*, from whence the Caribes or Canibales of the Ilandes are sayd to haue theyr name and originall. Here he began to builde a fortresse, and a vyllage neere vnto the same, therein intendyng to place theyr fyrst habitation. Shortly after, beyng instructed by certayne captyues, that there was about twelue myles further within the lande, a certayne vyllage called *Tirufi*, hauyng in it a ryche golde myne, he determined to destroy the village, to the which when he came, he founde the inhabitantes redy to defende theyr ryght, and that so stoutlye, that encounteryng with them, he was repulsed with shame and domage: for these people also vse bowes and venemous arrowes. Within a fewe dayes after, beyng enforced for lacke of vittualles to inuade another village, he hym selfe was strycken in the thygh with an arrowe. Some of his felowes say, that he was thus wounded of one of the inhabitauntes whose wyfe he had ledde away captiue before. They say also that he had fyrst frendlye communed with *Fogeda* for redeeming of his wife, and had appoynted a day to bring a portion of golde for her raunsome, and that he came at the day assigned, not laden with golde, but armed with bowes and arrowes, with eyght other confederate with hym, which had ben before partakers of the iniuries done to them fyrst at the hauen of *Carebago*, and afterward at the burnyng of the vyllage, in reuenge wherof, they had desperately consecrated them selues to death. But the matter beyng knowen, the captayne of this conspiracie was slayne of *Fogeda* his companions, and his wyfe delyuered fro captiuitie. *Fogeda* also through the maliciousnesse of the venime, consumed and was dryed vp by lytle and lytle. Whyle these thinges chaunced thus, they espied *Nicuesa* the other captayne, to whom *Beragua* the region of the West syde of *Vraba* was assigned to inhabite.

Nicuesa.

He gaue [illegible] to his sayles to take his vyage towarde *Beragua*, the day after that *Fogeda* departed out of the hauen of *Carebago*. He with his armie [illegible] brought with hym, sayled next along by the shore, [illegible] he came to the goulfe [illegible] vyages name is *Cerete*. Here he founde theyr language to be [illegible] *Hispaniola*, [illegible] hauen of *Carebago* [illegible]

The goulfe Cerete.

[illegible]

departyng from *Coiba*, went to the prouince or Lieutenaunteshyp of *Fogeda* his companion. Within a fewe dayes after, he hym selfe entryng into one of those marchaunt shyppes whiche the Spanyardes call *Carauelas*, commaunded that the bigger vessels should folow farre behinde. He tooke with hym two smal shyppes commonly called Bergandines or Brigandines. I haue thought it good in al the discourse of these bookes, to vse the common names of thinges, because I had rather be playne then curious, especially forasmuche as there do dayly aryse many newe thynges vnknowen to the antiquitie, whereof they haue left no true names. After the departure of *Nicuesa*, there came a shyppe from *Hispaniola* to *Fogeda*, the captayne wherof, was one *Barnardino de Calauera*, who had stolne the same from *Hispaniola* with threescore men, without leaue or aduice of the Admiral and the other gouernours. With the vyttualles which this shyppe brought, they refreshed them selues, and somewhat recouered theyr strengthes, muche weakened for lacke of meate. *Fogeda* his companions whyspered and muttered agaynst hym dayly more and more, that he fedde them foorth with vayne hope: for he had tolde them that he left *Ancisus* in *Hispaniola* (whom he chose by the kinges commission to be a iudge in causes, because he was learned in the law) to come shortly after him with a shyp laden with vyttualles, and that he marueyled that he was not come many dayes synce. And herein he sayd nothing but trueth: for when he departed, he left *Ancisus* halfe redye to folowe hym. But his felowes supposyng that al that he had sayde of *Ancisus* had ben fayned, some of them determined priuily to steale away the two Brigandines from *Fogeda*, and to returne to *Hispaniola*. But *Fogeda* hauyng knowledge hereof, preuented theyr deuices: for leauyng ÿ custodie of the fortresse with a certayne noble gentleman called *Francisco Pizarro*, he him selfe thus wounded, with a fewe other in his companye, entred into the shyppe wherof we spake before, and sayled directly to *Hispaniola*, both to heale the wounde of his thygh, if any remedie myght be founde, and also to knowe what was the cause of *Ancisus* tarying: leauyng hope with his felowes (which were nowe brought from three hundred to threescore, partly by famine, and partly by warre) that he woulde [illegible]

Barnardino de Calauera.

Fogeda returneth to Hispaniola.

Famine.

also committed to *Pizarro* and his companions, that it shoulde not be imputed to them for treason, to depart from thence yf he came not agayne at the day appoynted, with vyttuales, and a newe supplye of men. These .xx. dayes beyng nowe past, wheras they coulde yet heare nothyng of *Fogeda*, and were dayly more and more oppressed with sharpe hunger, they entred into the two Brigandines which were left, and departed from that land. And as they were nowe saylyng on the mayne sea towarde *Hispaniola*, a tempest sodaynely arysyng, swalowed one of the Brigandines with all that were therein. Some of theyr felowes af-

A Brigandine drowned with the stroke of a fyshe.

fyrme, that they playnely sawe a fyshe of huge greatnesse, swimmyng about the Brigandine (for those seas bryng foorth great monsters) and that with a stroke of her tayle, she broke the rudder of the shyppe in peeces, whiche faylyng, the Brigandine beyng dryuen about by force of the tempest, was drowned not farre from the Ilande called *Fortis*, lying betwene the coastes of the hauen *Carthago* and *Vraba*. As they of the other Brigandine would haue landed in the Ilande, they were dryuen backe with the bowes and arrowes of the fierce barbarians. Proceedyng therefore on theyr voyage, they mette by chaunce with *Ancisus*, be-

The region of [illegible].

twixte the hauen of *Carthago*, and the region of *Cuchibacoa* in the mouth of the riuer whiche the Spanyardes called *Boium gatti*, that is, the house of the catte, because they sawe a catte fyrste in that place: *Boium*, in the tongue of *Hispaniola*, is a house. *Ancisus* came with a shyppe laden with al thynges necessarie, both for meate, and drynke, and apparell, bryngyng also with hym an another Brigandine. This is he for whose commyng the capitayne *Fogeda* looked for so long. He loosed anker from *Hispaniola* in the Ides of September [illegible] the fourth day after his departure, he sawe certayne hygh mountaynes, the whiche for the aboundance of snowe whiche lyeth there continually in the toppes therof, the Spanyardes called *Sierra Neuada*, when *Colonus* the fyrst fynder of those regions [illegible]. The [illegible] day he [illegible] *Os Draconis* [illegible] *Ancisus* [illegible] *Fogeda* [illegible] *Hispaniola* [illegible] *Ancisus* [illegible]

[illegible]

Sierra Neuada.

Os Draconis.

he woulde graunt them that with his fauour they myght eyther goe agayne to *Hispaniola*, or that he hym selfe woulde bryng them to *Nicuesa*: and that they woulde for his gentlenesse declared towarde them in this behalfe, rewarde hym with two thousande poundes of golde: for they were ryche in golde, but poore in bread. But *Ancisus* assented to neyther of theyr requestes, affyrmyng that he myght by no meanes goe any other way, then to *Vraba* the prouince assigned to *Fogeda*. Whereupon, by theyr conduct, he tooke his voyage directly towarde *Vraba*. But nowe let it not seeme tedious to your holynesse, to heare of one thyng worthy to be remembred, whiche chaunced to this Lieutenant *Ancisus* as he came thyther: for he also cast anker in the coastes of the region of *Caramairi*, whiche we sayde to be famous, by reason of the hauen of *Carthage*, and of the goodly stature, strength, and beautie both of men and women beyng in the same. Here he sent certayne to goe alande on the shore both to fetch fresh water, & also to repayre the ship boate which was sore brused. In this meane tyme, a great multitude of the people of the countrey, armed after theyr manner, came about our men, as they were occupyed about theyr busynesse, and stoode in a redynesse to fyght, for the space of three dayes continually, duryng whiche time, neyther durst they set vpon our men, nor our men assayle them. Thus both parties keepyng theyr aray, stoode styll three whole dayes, the one gasyng on the other. Yet al this while our men applyed theyr worke, placyng the shypwryghtes in the myddest of theyr armie. As they stoode thus amased, two of our company went to fyll theyr water pottes at the mouth of the ryuer neere vnto them both, where sodenly there came foorth agaynst them a capitayne of the barbarians with tenne armed men, whiche inclosed them, and with terrible countenaunce bent theyr arrowes agaynst them, but shot them not of. One of our men fledde, but the other remayned, callyng his felowe agayne, and rebukyng hym for his fearefulnesse. Then he spake to the barbarians in theyr owne language, whiche he had learned beyng conuersant with the captiues that were caryed from thense long before. They marueylyng to heare a straunger speake in theyr mother tongue, put of theyr fearcenesse, and lyke frendes demaunded of them, demaundyng who were the capitaynes of the straungers

Ryche in golde, and poore in bread.

were arryued in theyr lande. He aunswered that they were strangers passing by, and that he marueyled why they wolde attempt to driue them from theyr coastes, and disturbe their shyppe: arguyng them of follie and crueltie, and further threatnyng their ruine and destruction, excepte they woulde vse them selues more frendely towarde them. For he aduertised them that there woulde shortlye come into theyr lande armed men, in number like vnto the sandes of the sea, and that to theyr vtter destruction, not only yf they resysted them not, but also except they receiued them, and entertayned them honourably. In the meane time, *Ancisus* was enfourmed that his men were detayned: wherfore suspectyng some deceypte, he brought foorth all his target men, for feare of theyr venemous arrowes: and settyng them in battel araye, he marched forwarde towarde them whiche stayed his men. But he whiche communed with the barbarians, geuyng hym a signe with his hande to procede no further, he stayed, and callyng to hym the other, he knewe that all was safe: for the barbarians profered hym peace, because they were not they whom they suspected them to haue ben, meanyng by *Fogeda & Nicuesa*, who had spoyled the vyllage standyng there by the sea syde, and caryed away many captiues, and also burnt another vyllage further within the lande. And therfore (as they sayde) the cause of theyr commyng togyther, was to reuenge those iniuries, yf by any meanes they coulde, yet that they woulde not exercise theyr weapons agaynst the innocent: for they sayd, it was vngodly to fyght agaynst any, not beyng prouoked. Layeng apart therfore theyr bowes and arrowes, they entertayned our men gentelly, and gaue them great plentie of salted fyshe, and bread of theyr countrey, and filled theyr vessels with syder made of their countrey fruites and seedes, not inferior to wine in goodnesse. Thus *Ancisus* hauing entred into frendship, and made a league of peace with thinhabitauntes of *Caramairi*, which were before sore prouoked by other capitaynes, he launched from the lande, and directed his course to *Vraba* by the [illegible]

[illegible]

The vse of targets agaynst venemous arrowes.

The barbarians haue respect to iustice.

Salted fyshe.

Wine of fruites and seedes.

[illegible]

made of targettes, swordes, iavelyns, and suche other weapons for the warres, but all this with evill speede, and in an evill houre: for as they were even nowe entryng into the haven, the governour of the shyppe whiche sate at the helme, stroke the shyppe upon the sandes, where it was so fast enclosed and beaten with the waves of the sea, that it opened in the myddest, and all lost that was therein, a thyng surelye miserable to beholde: for of all the vyttualles that they had, they saved only twelve barrelles of meale, with a fewe cheeses, and a lytle bysket bread, for al the beastes were drowned, and they them selves escaped hardly and halfe naked, by helpe of the Brigandine and ship boate, carying with them only a fewe weapons. Thus they fell from one calamitie into another, beyng nowe more carefull for theyr lyves then for golde. Yet beyng brought alyve and in health to that lande whiche they so greatly desyred, they coulde do no lesse, then to provide for the susteynyng of theyr bodyes, because they coulde not lyve only by ayre: and whereas theyr owne fayled, they must nedes lyve by other mens. Yet among these so many adversities, one good chaunce offered it selfe unto them: for they founde, not farre from the sea syde, a grove of Date trees, among the which, and also among the reede and weedes of the marisshes, they chased a multitude of wylde bores, with whose fleshe they fed them selves well certayne dayes. These they say to be lesse then ours, and with so short tayles that they thought they had ben cut of. They differ also from ours in theyr feete: for theyr hinder feete are whole undivided, and also without any hoofe. But they affirme that they have proved by experience, theyr fleshe to be of better taste and more wholsome then ours. During this time, they fed also of Dates, and the buddes of young Date trees, which they eate likewise in Civile and *Granata*, where they call them *Palmitos*, of the leaves wherof they make beesomes in Rome. Sometymes also they eate of the apples of that region, whiche have the taste of [illegible], and have also stones in them, and are but lytle [illegible] I suppose [illegible] whereof I [illegible] *Alexandria in Egypte*, in the moneth of Apryll, [illegible] beyng [illegible] in [illegible]

Ancisus shyppe wracke.

A grove of date trees.

Wylde bores.

[illegible]

Apples of a straunge kynde.

[illegible]

Cedars of [illegible]

as doth the orenge tree. These apples are good to be eaten, and haue a certayne sweetenesse myxte with a gentyll sharpnesse, as haue the fruites called *Sorbes*. Thinhabytantes plant these trees in theyr orchyardes and gardens, and norysshe them with greate diligence as we do cheries, peaches, and quinses. This tree in leaues, heyght, and trunke, is very lyke vnto the tree that beareth the fruyte called *Zizipha*, which the Apothecaries call *Iuiuba*. But whereas nowe the wylde boxes began to fayle them, they were agayne enforced to consulte and prouyde for the tyme to come: Whervppon with theyr whole armye, they entered further into the lande. The Canibales of this prouynce, are most expert archers. *Ancisus* had in his companye, a hundred men.

Men of desperate boldenesse.

They mette by the way with only three men of thinhabitantes, naked, and armed with bowes & venomous arowes, who without all feare, assayled our men fyercelly, wounded manye, and slue manye, and when they emptyed theyr quiuers, fledde as swyftely as the wynde: For (as we haue sayde) they are excedyng swyfte of foote by reason of theyr loose gooing from theyr chyldes age, they affyrme that they lette slyp no arrowe out of theyr bowes in vayne. Our men therfore returned the same way that they came, muche more vnfortunate then they were before, and consulted among them selues to leaue the lande, especially because the inhabytantes had ouerthrowne the fortresse which *Fogeda* buylded, and had burnt thyrtie houses of the vyllage, as soone as *Pizarrus* and his company lefte of *Fogeda*, and forsaken the land. By this occasion therfore, being dryuen to seeke further, they had intelligence that the west syde of that goulfe of *Vraba*, was more fruitfull & better to inhabite.

The goulfe of Vraba.

Wherfore, they sent the one halfe of theyr men thither with the brigantine, and left the other where to the sea syde on the east parte. This goulfe, is fourteene myles in breadth, and howe muche the further it entereth into the firme lande, it is so muche the narrower. Into the goulfe of *Vraba*, there fall many ryuers, but one (as they saye) more famous then the ryuer of *Nilus* in Egypte. This ryuer is called *Dariena*, vpon the bankes wherof, being very fruitfull of trees and grasse, [illegible] habitation. [illegible]

The golden ryuer of Darien.

[illegible]

therof, fyrst sent away theyr chyldren and weakest sort of theyr people with theyr baggage and houshould stuffe, and assembled all suche togeather both men and women, as were meete for the warres. Thus beyng armed with weapons and desperate myndes, they stoode in a redynesse to fyght, and taryed the comming of our men vpon a lytle hyll, as it were to take the aduauntage of the grounde: our men iudged them to be about fiue hundred in number. Then *Ancisus* the captayne of our men, and Lieuetenaunt in the steede of *Fogeda*, settyng his men in order of battayle aray, and with his whole company kneelyng on his knees, they all made humble prayers to GOD for the victorie, and a vowe to the image of the blessed virgin whiche is honoured in Ciuile, by the name of *Sancta Maria Antiqua*, promysyng to sende her many golden gyftes, and a straunger of that countrey: also, to name the vyllage *Sancta Maria Antiqua* after her name: lykewyse to erecte a temple called by the same name, or at the least to dedicate the king of that prouince his pallace to that vse, if it should please her to assist them in this dangerous enterpryse. This done, al the souldiers toke an oth, that no man should turne his backe to his enimie. Then ye captayne commaundyng them to be in a redynesse with theyr targets and iauelyns, and the trumpetter to blowe the battayle, they fiercely assayled theyr enimies with a larome: but the naked barbarians, not long able to abyde the force of our men, were put to flight, with theyr kyng and captayne *Cemaccus*. Our men entred into the vyllage, where they founde plentie of meate, such as the people of the countrey vse, sufficient to asswage theyr present hunger, as bread made of rootes, with certayne fruites vnlyke vnto ours, whiche they reserue for store, as we doo Chestnuttes. Of these people, the men are vtterly naked, but the women, from the nauel downewarde are couered with a fyne cloth made of gossampine cotton. This region is vtterly without any sharpenesse of wynter: for the mouth of this ryuer of *Darien*, is onlye eyght degrees distant from the *Equinoctiall* lyne, so that the common sorte of our men, scarcely perceyue any dyfference in length betweene the day and nyght all the whole yeere: but because they are ignorant in astronomie, they can perceyue no small dyfference. [illegible]

The souldiers make an othe.

The barbarians are dryuen to flyght.

The riuer of Darien, but viii. degrees from the Equinoctial lyne.

what from theyr opinion, forasmuche as the dyfference can not be great. The day after that they arryued at the lande, they sayled along by the ryuer, where they founde a great thycket of reedes, continuyng for the space of a myle in length, supposing (as it chaunced in deede) that the borderers thereabout whiche had fled, had eyther lyen lurkyng there, or els to haue hid theyr stuffe among those reedes: Whereupon, armyng them selues with theyr targets, for feare of the people lying in ambushe, they searched the thycket diligently, and founde it without men, but replenyshed with housholde stuffe and golde. They founde also a great multitude of shetes, made of the silke or cotton of the gossampine tree: lykewyse diuers kyndes of vessels & tooles made of wood, and many of earth: also many brest plates of golde, and ouches wrought after theyr manner, to the summe of a hundred & two pound weight: for they also take pleasure in the beautie of golde, and worke it very artificially, although it be not the price of thynges among them as with vs. They haue it out of other regions, for exchaunge of such thynges as theyr countrey bryngeth forth: for such regions as haue plentie of bread and gossampine, lacke golde, and suche as bryng forth golde, are for the most part rough with mountaynes and rockes, and therefore barren: and thus they exercise marchandies without the vse of money. Reioysyng therefore with double gladnesse, aswel in that they sawe great lykenesse of golde, as also that fortune had offered them so fayre and fruitful a countrey, they sent for theyr felowes whom they had left before in the East syde of the gulfe of *Vraba*. Yet some say, that the ayre is there vnwholsome, because that part of the region lyeth in a lowe valley, enuironed with mountaynes and marysshes.

Golde founde in a thycket of reedes.

Brest plates of golde.

The golden regions are for the most part barren.

The seconde booke of the seconde Decade, of the supposed continent.

I Haue described to your holynesse where *Fogeda* with his companye (to whom the [illegible] tractes of *Vraba* was assigned to in[illegible]) entended to fasten theyr foote. Let [illegible] therefore leaue them of *Vraba* for [illegible], and returne agayne to *Nicuesa* whom the gouernaunce and Lieutenauntshyp of the moste large prouince of *Beragua* (beyng the West syde of the gulfe of *Vraba*) was appoynted. We haue declared howe *Nicuesa*, departyng with one Carauel and two Brigandines from *Vraba* the iurisdiction of his frend & companion *Fogeda*, directed his course Westwarde to *Beragua*, leauing the bygger shyppes somewhat behind hym, to folowe hym a farre of, but he tooke this deuice in an euyl houre, for he both lost his felowes in the nyght, and went past the mouth of the riuer *Beragua*, whiche he cheefely sought. One [illegible] *Olanus* a Cantabrian, and gouernour of one of the great [illegible], had the conduct of one of the Brigandines: he commyng behynde, learned of the inhabitauntes, whiche was the way Eastwarde to the gulfe of *Beragua*, ouerpassed and left behynde of *Nicuesa*. *Olanus* therfore directyng his course towarde the East, met with the other Brigandine, which had also wandered out of the way by reason of the darknes of the night. The gouernour of this Brigandine, was one *Petrus de Vmbria*. Thus both [illegible] of theyr meetyng, they consulted [illegible] to be [illegible] whiche way they coulde [illegible] theyr gouernour [illegible] his [illegible] after deliberation [illegible] iudged that *Nicuesa* could no more [illegible] to [illegible] hym in remembraunce of *Beragua*, then they them selues were [illegible] therof, hopyng also to fynde hym there. They sayled therfore towarde *Beragua*, where they founde within .xvi. myles distant, a ryuer whiche *Colonus* named *Lagartos*, because it nouryssheth great Lysardes, whiche in the Spanishe tongue are called *Lagartos*. These Lysardes are hurtful both vnto man and beast, and in shape much lyke vnto the Crocodiles of the ryuer *Nilus* in Egypt. In this ryuer they founde theyr companions and felowes of theyr errour, lying at anker with the great shyppes, whiche folowed behynde by the gouernours commaundement. Here the whole assemblie beyng carefull and disquieted by reason of the gouernours errour, after consultation, by the aduice of the captaynes of the Brigandines [illegible] had rased neere vnto the coastes of *Beragua*, they [illegible]. *Beragua*, in the language of the inhabitauntes [illegible], is as much to say, as the golden riuer. The [illegible] is also called by the same name, takyng name of the ryuer. In the mouth of this ryuer, the greatest vessels

cast

Lupus Olanus

Petrus de Vmbria.

The ryuer Lagartos.

The golden ryuer of Beragua.

togeather, and conueighed all theyr vitailes and other neces-saries to lande with theyr shyp boates, and elected *Lupus Olanus* to be theyr gouernour in steede of *Nicuesa* whom they had loste. By thaduise therfore of *Olanus* and the other vnder capytaines, that all hope of departure myght be taken from the souldyers which they had nowe brought thyther, and to make them the more wyllinge to inhabite that lande, they vtterly forsooke and caste of those shyppes beinge nowe rotten for age, and suffered them to be shaken and broosed of the surges of the sea. Yet of theyr soundeste plankes, wyth other newe, made of the trees of that Region (which they saye to be excedyng bigge and hygh) they framed a new carauell shortelye after, whiche they myght vse to serue for theyr necessitie. But *Beragua* was founde by the vnfortunate enterpryse of *Petrus de Vmbria.* For hee, beynge a man of prompte wit and apt forwardnesse to attempte thynges (in which sometyme fortune will beare a stroke notwithstanding our prouidence) tooke vppon hym thaduenture to searche the shore, to thintent to fynde a way for his felowes where they myght beste come alande. For this purpose, he chose hym .xii. maryners, and went aborde the shyp boate whiche serued the greatest shyppes.

The enterpryse & death of Petrus de Vmbria.

The flowyng of the sea, raged and rored there, with a horryble whorlyng, as we reade of the daungerous place of *Scylla* in the sea of Cicilie, by reason of the houge & ragged rockes reachyng into the sea, from whiche the waues reboundinge with vyolence, make a great noyse and roughnesse on the water, which roughnesse or reflowing, the Spaniardes call *Resacca.* In these daungerous wretched *Vmbria* wrestled a whyle, but in short space, a waue of the sea almoste as bygge as a mountayne, reboundyng from the rockes, ouerwhelmed the boate, and deuoured the same with the men, euen in the syght of their felowes: So that of them all, only one escaped by reason he was expert in swimming. For getting holde of the corner of a rocke, and sustaynyng the rage of the sea vntyll the next day when it waxed calme, and the shore was drye by the fall of the water, he escaped and resorted to his companye. But *Vmbria* with the other eleuen, were vtterlye caste awaye. The resydue of the companye, durst not committe them selues to the shyppe boates, but went alande with theyr [illegible]. Where remaynyng a fewe dayes, and saylyng along

The daungerous place of Scylla in the sea of Cicile.

along by the shore, they founde certayne vyllages of the inhabitauntes, which they call *Mamu*. Here they began to buylde a fortresse, and to sowe seedes after the manner of theyr countrey, in a certayne vale of fruitefull grounde, because in other places the region is barren. As these thynges were thus doing in *Beragua*, one of theyr companye standing vpon the top of a high rocke of especiall, and lyftyng his eyes towarde the West, began to crye, Lynnen sayles, lynnen sayles. And the neerer it drewe towarde hym, he perceiued it to be a shyp boate, commyng with a lytle sayle: yet receiued they it with muche reioycing, for it was the fysher boate of *Nicuesa* his Carauel, and of capacitie to cary only fyue men, and had nowe but three in it, whiche had stolne it from *Nicuesa*, because he refused to geue credite to them that he had passed *Beragua*, and left it behinde him Eastwarde. For they seeyng *Nicuesa* and his felowes to consume daylye by famine, thought that they would prooue fortune with that boate, yf theyr chaunce myght be to fynde *Beragua*, as in deede it was. Debatyng therefore with theyr felowes of these matters, they declared how *Nicuesa* erred and lost the Carauel by tempest, and that he was nowe wanderyng among the marysshes of vnknowen coastes, full of miserie and in extreme penurie of all thynges, hauyng nowe lyued for the space of threescore and tenne dayes, only with herbes and rootes, & seldome with fruites of the countrey, contented to drynke water, and yet that oftentymes faylyng, because he was instant to trauayle Westwarde by foote, supposyng by that meanes to come to *Beragua*. *Colonus* the fyrst fynder of this mayne lande, had coasted along by this tracte, and named it *Gracias Dei*, but thinhabitauntes call it *Cerabaro*. Through this region, there runneth a riuer, whiche our men named *Sancti Matthei*, distant from the West syde of *Beragua*, about an hundred and thyrtie myles. Here I let passe the name of this riuer, and of manye other places by the names whiche thinhabitauntes vse, because our men are ignoraunt thereof. Then *Lupus Olanus* the conductor of the shyppes of *Nicuesa*, [illegible] that he had receyued this [illegible] a [illegible]

The miserable case of Nicuesa.

The riuer of S. Matthei.

[illegible] whome at his commyng he cast in prison, and accused hym of treason, because he usurped the authoritie of the Lieuetenauntshyp, and that for the desyre he had to beare rule and be in authoritie, he tooke no care of his errours: also that he behaued him selfe negligently, demaundyng furthermore of hym, what was the cause of his so long delay. Lykewyse he spake to al the under officers sharpely, and with a troubled mind, and within fewe dayes after, commaunded them to trusse up theyr packes, and make them redy to depart. They desyred him to quyet hym selfe, and to forbeare them a whyle, untyl they had reaped the corne that they had sowen, whiche woulde shortly be rype: for all kynde of corne wareth rype there euery fourth moneth after it is sowen. But he utterly denyed to tarye anye whyle, but that he woulde foorthwith depart from that unfortunate lande, and plucked up by the rootes all that euer was brought into the gulfe of *Beragua*, and commaunded them to direct theyr course towarde the East. After they had sayled about the space of syxteene myles, a certaine young man, whose name was Gregorie, a Genues borne, and of a chylde brought up with *Colonus*, called to remembraunce that there was a hauen not farre from thence: and to prooue his sayinges true, he gaue his felowes these tokens, that is, that they shoulde fynde upon the shore, an anker of a lost shyppe halfe couered with sande, and under a tree next unto the hauen a spryng of cleare water. They came to the lande, founde the anker and the spryng, and commended the wytte and memorie of the young man, that he onlye among manye of the Maryners which had searched those coastes with *Colonus*, bare the thyng so well in mynde. This hauen *Colonus* called *Portus Bellus*. Where as in this voyage for lacke of vytualles, they were sometymes enforced to goe alande, they were euyl entreated of thinhabitantes: by reason whereof, theyr strengthes were so weakened with hunger, that they were not able to keepe warre against naked men, or scarcely to beare their harnesse on theyr backes: and therefore our men lost twentie of theyr companions, which were slayne with venemous arrowes. They consulted to leaue the one halfe of theyr felowes in the hauen of *Portus Bellus*, & the other part *Nicuesa* tooke with hym to [illegible] myles from

The rigorousnesse of Nicuesa.

Corne wareth rype euerye fourth moneth.

The commendation of a young man brought up with Colonus.

Portus Bellus.

Weakenesse of hunger.

Portus Bellus, he entended to buylde a fortresse harde by the sea syde, vpon the poynt or cape, whiche in tyme past Colonus named Marmor. but they were so feeble by reason of long hunger, that theyr strength serued them not to susteyne suche labour, yet he erected a lytle towne, able to resyst the fyrst assaulte of the inhabitauntes: this towne he called Nomen Dei. From the tyme that he left Beragua. what in the iourney among the sandie playnes, then also for hunger whille he buylded the towne, of the fewe whiche remayned alyue, he lost two hundred. And thus by litle and lytle, the multitude of seuen hundred, fourescore, and fyue men, was brought nowe to scarcelye one hundred. Whyle Nicuesa lyued with these fewe miserable men, there arose a contention among them of Vraba, as concernyng the Lieutenauntshyppe: for one Vascus Nunnez, by the iudgement of al men, trustyng more to his strength then wit, styrred vp certayne light felowes agaynst Ancisus, saying that Ancisus had not the kyngs letters patentes for that office, and that it was not sufficient that he was auctorised by Fogeda, and therefore forbode that he should execute the office of the Lieutenauntshyp, and wylled them to choose certayne of theyr owne companye, by whose counsayle and auctoritie they myght be gouerned. Thus being diuided into factions, by reason that Fogeda theyr captayne came not agayne, whom they supposed to be nowe dead of his venemous wound, they contended whether it were best to substitute Nicuesa in his place. The wysest sort, suche as were familier with Nicuesa, & could not beare the insolencie of Vascus Nunnez, thought it good that Nicuesa shoulde be sought out throughout all those coastes: for they had knowledge that he departed from Beragua, because of the barrennesse of the grounde, and that by the example of Ancisus, and suche other as had made shypwracke, it were possible that he myght wander in some secrete place, and that they coulde not be quiet in theyr myndes, vntyl they knewe the certayntie whether he with his felowes were aliue or dead. But Vascus Nunnez, fearyng lest at the commyng of Nicuesa, he shoulde not be had in auctoritie among his felowes, sayd they were mad men to thynke that Nicuesa lyued, and although he were alyue, yet that they had no neede of his helpe: for he auouched that there was none of his felowes, that were not

Cape Marmor.

Nomen Dei.

[illegible] towarde the Uiuersa. Whyle they were thus reasonyng to and fro, one *Rodericus Colmenaris* aryued in those coastes with two great shyppes, hauyng in them threescore freshe men, with great plentie of vyttualles and apparell. Of the nauigation of this *Colmenaris*, I entend to speake somewhat more. He therfore departed from the hauen of *Hispaniola*, called *Beata* (where they prepare and furnyshe them selues whiche make any voyage into these landes) about the Ides of October, in the yeere. 1510. and landed the.ix.of Nouember in a region in the large prouince of *Paria*, founde by *Colonus* betwene the hauen *Carthago*, and the region of *Cuchibacboa*. In this voyage, what by the roughnesse of the sea, and fiercenesse of the barbarians, he suffered many incommodities: for when his freshe water fayled, he sayled to the mouth of a certayne riuer which thinhabitantes cal *Gaira*, beyng apt to receiue shippes. This riuer had his course from the toppe of an exceedyng hygh mountayne couered with snowe, hygher then the whiche, al the companions of this captayne *Rodericus* say, that they neuer sawe: And that by good reason, yf it were couered with snowe in that region, which is not past ten degrees distant from the *Equinoctial* lyne. As they began to drawe water out of theyr shyp boate, a certayne kyng made towarde them, apparelled with vestures of gossampine cotton, hauyng twentie noble men in his company apparelled also: which thyng seemed straunge to our men, and not seene before in those partes. The kynges apparell hong loose from his shoulders to his elbowes, and from the gyrdle downewarde, it was much lyke a womans kyrtle, reaching euen to his heeles. As he drewe neere towarde our men, he seemed freendly to admonyshe them to take none of the water of that ryuer, affyrmyng it to be vnwholsome for men, and shewed them that not farre from thence, there was a ryuer, of good water. They came to the ryuer, and endeuouryng to come neere the shore, they were driuen backe by tempest. Also the burbulyng of the sand, declared the sea to be but shalow there. They were therefore enforced to returne to the fyrste ryuer where they myght safely cast anker. This kyng layde wayte for our men: for as they were fyllyng theyr barrelles, he set on them with about seuen hundred men (as our men iudged) armed after theyr manner, although they were naked

for

The nauigation of Rodericus Colmenaris.

An exceedyng high mountayne couered with snowe.

Apparelled men.

for only the kyng and his noble men [illegible]. They tooke away the shypboote, and broke it in manner to chips, they fiercely assaylyng our men with theyr venemous arrowes, that they slue of them fourtie and seuen, before they coulde couer them selues with their targets. For that poyson is of such force, that albeit the woundes were not great, yet they dyed therof immediatly, for they yet knewe no remedie agaynst this kynde of poyson, as they after learned of the inhabitauntes of *Hispaniola*: for this Ilande bryngeth foorth an hearbe which quencheth and mortifieth the violent poyson of the hearbe, wherwith theyr arrowes are infected, so that it be ministred in tyme. Yet of our companye whiche went for water, seuen escaped that conflycte, and hydde them selues in a hollowe tree, lurkyng there untyll nyght, yet escaped they not the handes of theyr enimies: for the shyppe departed from thence in the nyght season, and left them there, supposyng that they had ben slayne. Thus by manye suche perylls and daungers (which I lyghtly ouerpasse, because I wyll not be tedious to your holynesse) he aryued at the length at the hauen of *Vraba*, and cast anker at the East syde thereof, from whence not long before, our men departed to the West syde, by reason of the barrennesse of that soyle. When he had contineued a whyle in the hauen, and sawe no man styrryng, maruepled at the scilence of the places (for he supposed there to haue found his felowes) he could not coniecture what this should meane: and thereupon began to suspect that eyther they were dead, or that they had changed the place of theyr habitation. To knowe the certayntie hereof, he commaunded all the great ordinaunce, and other small gunnes whiche he had in his shyppes, to be charged, and fyers to be made in the night upon the toppes of the rockes. Thus the fyers beyng kyndled, he commaunded al the gunnes to be shot of at one instant, by the horrible noyse whereof, the gulfe of *Vraba* was shaken, although it were .xxiiii. myles distant, for so brode is the gulfe. This noyse was hearde of theyr felowes in *Dariena*, and they answered them agayne with mutuall fyers. Wherfore, by the folowyng of these fyers, *Colmenaris* brought his shippes to the West syde. Here those wretched and miserable men of *Dariena*, whiche nowe through [illegible]

Spanyardes slayne with venemous arrowes.

A remedie agaynst venemous arrowes.

The hauen of Vraba.

[illegible] theyr [illegible], by [illegible] Ancisus [illegible], liftyng vp theyr handes to heauen, with the teares runnyng downe theyr cheekes [illegible] Rodericus and his felowes with [illegible] of [illegible], as theyr present necessitie seemed to require: for whereas they were before his commyng, without vittailes, and almost naked, he brought them abundance of meate, drinke, and apparel. It resteth now (most holy father) to declare what cause of the dissention among them of *Vraba*, as concernyng the gouernaunce after the losse of theyr captaynes.

The thirde booke of the seconde Decade, of the supposed continent.

ALl the cheefe officers in *Beragua*, and suche as were most politike in counsayle, determined that *Nicuesa* should be sought out, yf by any meanes he coulde be founde. Wherupon they tooke from *Ancisus* the gouernour, refusyng the commyng of *Nicuesa*, a Brigandine whiche he made of his owne charges: and agreed, agaynst both the wyl of *Ancisus*, and the maister of fence *Vaschus Nunnez*, that *Nicuesa* should be sought forth to take away the stryfe as touching the gouernment. They elected therefore *Colmenaris* (of whom we spake before) to take this matter in hande, willing him to make diligent searche for *Nicuesa* in those coastes where they supposed he erred: for they hearde that he had forsaken *Beragua*, the region of an vnfruitefull grounde. They gaue him therfore commaundement to bring *Nicuesa* with hym, and further to declare vnto him that he should do [illegible] good seruice to [illegible], in takyng away the occasion of theyr seditions. *Colmenaris* [illegible] the [illegible] vpon hym the more gladly, because *Nicuesa* was his very frende, supposyng his commyng [illegible] be no lesse thankefull to [illegible] *Vraba*. Furni- [illegible] with [illegible] the Riuer with parte of the vitailes and other necessaries which he brought with hym before from *Hispaniola* to *Vraba*. Thus commyng along by all the coastes and goulfes neere thereabout, at the length, at the poynt called *Marmor*, he founde *Nicuesa*, of all lyuyng men most infortunate, in maner dryed vp with extreme hunger, filthy and horrible to beholde, with only threescore men in his company, left aliue of seuen hundred. They al seemed to hym so miserable, that he no lesse lamented theyr case, then yf he had found them dead. But *Colmenaris* comforted his frend *Nicuesa*, and embracyng hym with teares and chearefull wordes, releued his spirites, and further encouraged hym with great hope of better fortune, declaryng also that his commyng was looked for, and greatly desyred of all the good men of *Vraba*, for that they hoped that by his auctoritie, theyr discorde and contention shoulde be finished. *Nicuesa* thanked his frende *Colmenaris* after suche sorte as his calamitie required. Thus they tooke shyp together, and sayled directly to *Vraba*. But so variable and vnconstant is the nature of man, that he soone groweth out of vse, becommeth insolent and vnmyndfull of benefites after to muche felicitie: for *Nicuesa* after thus many teares and weepynges, after diuers bewaylynges of his infortunate destenye, after so many thankesgeuyng, yea after that he had fallen downe to the grounde and kyssed the feete of *Colmenaris* his sauiour, he began to quarel with hym before he came yet at *Vraba*, reprouing hym & them al for the alteration of the state of thynges in *Vraba*, and for the gatheryng of golde, affyrmyng that none of them ought to haue layde hande of any golde without the aduice of hym or *Fogeda* his companyon. When these sayinges and suche lyke, came to the eares of them of *Vraba*, they so styrred vp the myndes of *Ancisus* Lieuetenaunt for *Fogeda*, and also of *Vaschus Nunnez* of the contrary part, agaynst *Nicuesa*, that shortly after his aryuall with his threescore men, they commaunded hym with the ac- [illegible] to depart from thence: but this pleased not the better sort. Yet fearyng lest tumult shoulde be among the people, where *Vaschus* [illegible] *Nicuesa* [illegible]

Nicuesa is founde in a miserable case.

Insolencie after muche felicitie.

[illegible] Brigandine which remayned there: he tooke shippe in the Calendes of Marche, in the yeare. 1511. intendyng to goe to Hispaniola to complayne of the rashnesse of Vaschus Nunnez, and of the violence done to hym by Ancisus: But he entred into the Brigandine in an unfortunate houre, for he was never seene after. They suppose that the Brigandine was drowned with al the men therein. And thus unhappie Nicuesa fallyng headlong out of one miserie into another, ended his life more miserably then he lyued. Nicuesa beyng thus vylely rejected, and theyr vyttuals consumed which Colmenaris brought them, falling in maner mad for hunger, they were enforced lyke rauenyng woolues seekyng theyr pray, to inuade suche as dwelt about theyr confynes. Vaschus Nunnez therfore, their new captaine of their owne election, assemblyng togeather a hundred and thirtie men, and settyng them in order of battayle after his swoordplayers fashion, puffed up with pryde, placed his souldiers as pleased hym, in the forewarde and rerewarde, and some, as partizens, about his owne person. Thus assosiatyng with hym Colmenaris, he went to spoyle the kynges which were borderers therabout, and came fyrst to a region about that coast called Coiba (whereof we made mention before) imperiously and with cruell countenaunce commaundyng the kyng of the region, whose name was Careta (of whom they were never troubled as often as they passed by his dominions) to geue them vyttualles. But Careta denyed that he coulde geue them any at that tyme, alleagyng that he had oftentymes ayded the Christians as they passed by those coastes, by reason whereof, his store was nowe consumed: also that by the meanes of the continuall warre whiche he kept euer from his childes age with a kyng whose name was Poncha, borderyng upon his dominion, he and his familie were in great scarcenesse of al thynges. But Vaschus woulde admyt none of these excuses, and thereupon tooke Careta prisoner, spoyled his vyllage, and brought hym bounde with his two wyues and chyldren, and all his familie to Dariena. With this kyng Careta, they founde three of the subjectes of Nicuesa, which when Nicuesa passed by those coastes [illegible] for feare of punishment for theyr euill deser[illegible] [illegible] lying at anker: And when the [illegible] Careta

The death of Nicuesa.

Famine enforseth them to fal to spoylyng.

Careta kyng of Coiba.

Kyng Careta is taken and spoyled.

who

[illegible] eighteene monethes, and were [illegible] people of the countrey. Durynge this tyme, the [illegible] vittayles seemed vnto them delicate dishes & princely fare, especially because they enioyed the same without any [illegible] for wine and tyme, whiche two thynges moue and enforce men to suche harde shyftes and miseries, that in lyuyng they seeme not to lyue. Yet desyred they to returne to theyr olde cares, of suche force is education and naturall affection towarde them with whom we haue ben brought vp. The vyttayles which *Vascbus* brought from the vyllage of *Careta*, to his felowes left in *Dariena*, was rather somewhat to asswage theyr present hunger, then vtterly to take away theyr necessitie. But as touching *Ancisus*, beyng Lieuetenaunt for *Fogeda*, whether it were before these thynges, or after, I knowe not: but this I am sure of, that after the reiectyng of *Nicuesa*, many occasions were sought against *Ancisus* by *Vascbus* and his factionaries. Howsoeuer it was, *Ancisus* was taken, and cast in pryson, and his goodes confiscate: the cause hereof was (as *Vascbus* alleaged) that *Ancisus* had his commission of the Lieuetenauntshyp of *Fogeda* only, whom they said to be now dead, and not of the kyng, saying that he woulde not obey any man that was not put in office by the kyng him selfe by his letters patentes. Yet at the request of the grauest sort, he was somewhat pacified, and dealt more gentelly with hym, hauyng some compassion on his calamities, and thereupon commaunded him to be losed. *Ancisus* beyng at libertie, tooke shyppe to depart from thense to *Hispaniola*: but before he had hoysed vp his sayle, al the wisest sort resorted to him, humblye desyryng hym to returne agayne, promysyng that they woulde doo theyr diligence, that *Vascbus* being reconciled, he myght be restored to his full auctoritie of the Lieuetenauntshyp: but *Ancisus* refused to consent to theyr request, and so departed. Yet some there were that murmured that God and his angels shewed this reuenge vpon *Ancisus*, because *Nicuesa* was reiected through his counsayle. Howe so euer it be, the searchers of the newe landes [illegible] [illegible] by theyr owne follie, consumyng them selues with ciuile discorde, not weighing so great a matter, nor [illegible] [illegible], as the [illegible]

[illegible]

Margin notes:

[illegible] the se[illegible] of al myscheafe.

Ancisus, Lieuetenant for Fogeda, is cast in pryson.

Ancisus taketh his voyage to Hispaniola.

The reuenge of God.

The inconueniences of discorde.

[illegible] of the thyng requireth. In this meane tyme, they determined all with one agreement, to sende messengers into *Hispaniola* to the yong Admiral and viceroy, sonne and heyre to *Christophorus Colonus* the fynder of these landes, and to the other gouernours of the Ilande (from whom the newe landes receiue theyr ayde and lawes) to signifie vnto them what state they stoode in, and in what necessitie they liued, also what they had founde, and in what hope they were of greater thynges, if they were furnished with plentie of vyttualles and other necessaries. For this purpose they elected, at the assignement of *Vaschus*, one *Valdiuia*, beyng one of his faction, and instructed by hym agaynst *Ancisus*, and to be assystant with hym, they appoynted one *Zamudius* a Cantabrian, so that commaundement was geuen to *Valdiuia* to returne from *Hispaniola* with vittuals, & *Zamudius* was appoynted to take his voyage into Spayne to the kyng. They toke ship both togeather with *Ancisus*, hauyng in mind to certifie the king howe things were handled there, much otherwise then *Zamudius* information. I mee selfe spake with both *Ancisus* & *Zamudius* at their comming to the court. Whyle they were occupied about these matters, those wretched men of *Dariena* loosed *Careta* the king of *Coiba*, vpon condition that he shoulde ayde them in their warres agaynst his enimie and theyrs, kyng *Poncha*, bordering vpon his dominions. *Careta* made a league with them, promising that as they passed by his kingdome, he woulde geue them all things necessarie, & meete them with an armie of men, to goe forward with them to the battaile against *Poncha*. Theyr weapons are neyther bowes nor venomed arrowes, as we sayde thinhabitauntes to haue, whiche dwel eastward beyonde the gulfe. They fyght therefore at hande with long swordes (whiche they call *Macanas*) made of wood, because they haue no Iron. They vse also long staues lyke iauelyns, hardened at the endes with fyre, or typt with bone, also certayne slynges and dartes. Thus after the league made with *Careta*, both he and our men had certayne dayes appoynted them to till theyr grounde and sowe theyr seedes. This done, by the ayde of *Careta*, and by his conduction, they marched towarde the pallace of *Poncha*, who fled at their [illegible]

King Poncha.

Swordes of wood.

Kyng Careta [illegible] with the [illegible]

not helpe theyr felowes therewith, by reason of the farre distance of the place, although they had great plentie: for the vyllage of *Poncha* was more then a hundred myles dystant from *Dariena*, whereas was also none other remedie, but that the same shoulde haue ben carryed on mens backes to the sea syde, beyng farre of, where they left theyr shyppes in the whiche they came to the village of *Careta*. Here they founde certayne poundes weight of gold, grauen & wrought into sundry ouches. After the sackyng of this vyllage, they resorted toward the ships, intending to leaue the kynges of the inlande untouched at this tyme, and to inuade only them which dwelt by the sea coastes. Not farre from *Coiba*, in the same tracte, there is a region named *Comogra*, and the king thereof called *Comogrus*, after the same name. To this kyng they came fyrst next after the subuertion of *Poncha*, and founde his pallace situate in a fruiteful playne of .xii. leagues in bredth, at the rootes of the further syde of ỹ next mountaynes. *Comogrus* had in his courte a certaine noble man of neere consanguinitie to kyng *Careta*, whiche had fled to *Comogrus* by reason of certayne dissentions which was betwene *Careta* & hym, these noble men, they cal *Iura*. This *Iura* therefore of *Coiba*, met our men by the way, and conciled *Comogrus* to them, because he was wel knowen to our men, from the tyme that *Nicuesa* passed fyrst by those coastes. Our men therfore wente quietly to the pallace of *Comogrus*, beyng distant from *Dariena* thirtie leagues by a plaine way about the mountaynes. This kyng *Comogrus* had seuen sonnes, young men, of comely fourme and stature, which he had by sundry wyues. His pallace was framed of postes or proppes made of trees fastened together after a strange sort, and of so strong buildyng, that it is of no lesse strength then walles of stone. They whiche measured the length of the floore thereof, founde it to be a hundred and fyftie paces, and in bredth, fourescore foote, beyng roofed and paued with maruelous arte. They founde his storehouse furnished with abundance of delicate vittels, after the maner of theyr countrey, and his wyne sellar replenished with great vessels of earth and also of wood, fylled with their kinde of wine and syder, [illegible]

The region of Comogra, distant from Dariena .xxx. leagues.

Kyng Comogrus.

The kynges pallace.

[illegible]

[illegible] of [illegible] and [illegible] of other [illegible] and [illegible], as do the Almaynes, Flemynges, Englysshemen, & our Spanyardes which inhabite the mountaines, as the [illegible] and Asturians: lykewyse in the mountaynes of the Alpes, the Noricians, Sweuians, and Heluecians, make certeyne drynkes of barley, wheate, hoppes, and apples. They say [illegible] with *Comogrus* they dranke wines of sundry tastes, both whyte and blacke. But nowe you shal heare of a thyng more monstrous to beholde. Entryng therefore into the inner partes of the pallace, they were brought into a chamber hanged about with the carkasses of men, tyed with ropes of gossampine cotton. Beyng demaunded what they meant by that superstition, they answered that those were the carcasses of the father, graundfather, & great graundfather, with other the auncetours of theyr kyng *Comogrus*, declaryng that they had the same in great reuerence, and that they tooke it for a godly thyng to honour them religiously, and therefore appareled euery of the same sumptuously with gold and precious stones, accordyng unto theyr estate. After this sorte dyd the antiquitie honour theyr *Penates*, whiche they thought had the gouernance of theyr lyues. Howe they drye these carcasses upon certaine instrumentes made of wood, lyke unto hurdells, with a soft fyre under the same, so that only the skinne remayneth to hold the bones togeather, we haue described in the former Decade. Of *Comogrus* his seuen sonnes, the eldest had an excellent natural wyt. He therefore thought it good to flatter and please this wanderyng kinde of men (our men I meane) liuing only by shiftes and spoyle, lest being offended, and seeking occasions against him & his familie, they should handle hym as they dyd other which sought no meanes how to gratifie them: Wherefore, he gaue *Vascbus* and *Colmenaris* foure thousande ounces of golde artificially wrought, and also fiftie slaues, whiche he had taken in the warres: for suche, eyther they sell for exchaunge of other thynges, or otherwyse use them as them listeth, for they haue not the use of money. This golde with as muche more which they had in another place, our men weighed in the porche of *Comogrus* his palace, to separate the fift parte thereof, whiche portion is due to the kynges Exchequer: for it is decreed, that the fift part of both golde, pearles, and precious

Blacke wine.

The carcasses of men dryed.

The distribution of golde.

precious stones, shoulde be assigned to the kynges treasourie, and the residue to be diuided among them selues by composition. Here as brabblyng and contention arose among our men about the diuidyng of golde, this eldest sonne of kyng *Comogrus* beyng present, whom we praysed for his wysedome, commyng somewhat with an angrye countenaunce towarde hym whiche helde the ballaunces, he stroke them with his fyste, and scattered all the golde that was therein about the porche, sharpelye rebukyng them with woordes in this effecte. What is the matter, you Christian men, that you so greatly esteeme so lytle portion of golde more then your owne quietnesse, whiche neuerthelesse you entende to deface from these fayre ouches, and to melt the same into a rude masse. Yf your hunger of golde be so insatiable, that onlye for the desyre you haue thereto, you disquiete so manye nations, and you your selues also susteyne so many calamities and incommodities, lyuyng lyke banished men out of your owne countrey, I wyll shewe you a region flowyng with golde, where you may satisfie your rauenyng appetites: But you must attempt the thing with a greater power, for it standeth you in hand by force of armes to ouercome kings of great puissaunce, and rigorous defendours of theyr dominions. For besyde other, the great kyng *Tumanama* wyll come foorth agaynst you, whose kyngdome is most riche with golde, and distant from hence only syxe sunnes, that is, syxe dayes: for they number the dayes by the sunne. Furthermore, or euer you can come thither, you muste passe ouer the mountaynes inhabited of the cruell Canibales, a fierce kynde of men, deuourers of mans fleshe, lyuyng without lawes, wanderyng, and without Empire: for they also beyng desyrous of golde, haue subdued them vnder theyr dominion, whiche before inhabited the golde mynes of the mountaynes, and vse them lyke bondemen, usyng theyr labour in dyggyng and woorkyng their golde in plates and sundry images, lyke vnto these whiche you see here: for we do no more esteeme rude golde vnwrought, then we do cloddes of earth, before it be fourmed by the hande of the woorkeman to the similitude eyther of some vessell necessarie for our vse, or some ouche beautifull to be worne. These thynges doo we receyue of them for exchaunge of other of our

Young Comogrus his oration.

The hunger of golde.

A region flowyng with golde.

Kyng Tumanama.

Canibales.

The golde mines of the mountaynes.

Unwrought golde not esteemed.

[illegible], as of [illegible], whiche they haue [illegible], or by [illegible] and other thynges perteynyng to the fur[illegible] of householde, suche as [illegible] whiche inhabite the mountaynes, and especially for [illegible], whereof they stande in great neede, by reason of the barrennes of the mountaines. This iourney therefore must be made open by force of men, and when you are passyng ouer these mountaynes (poyntyng with his finger towarde the south mountaynes) you shal see another sea, where they sayle with shyppes as bygge as yours (meanyng the Canuels) vsyng both sayles and ores as you doo, although the men be naked as we are: all the way that the water runneth from the mountaynes, and al that syde lying towarde the South, bryngeth foorth golde abundauntly. As he sayd these woordes, he poynted to the vesselles in whiche they vse to serue theyr meate, affyrmyng that kyng *Tumanama*, and all the other kyngs beyond the mountaynes, had such & al other theyr householde stuffe of golde, and that there was no lesse plentie of gold among those people of the South, then of Iron with vs: for he knewe by relation of our men, whereof our swoordes and other weapons were made. Our captaynes marueylyng at the oration of the naked young man (for they had for interpreters those three men whiche had ben before a yeere and a halfe conuersaunt in the court of kyng *Careta*) pondered in theyr myndes, and earnestly consydered his sayinges, so that his rashnesse in scatteryng the golde out of the ballaunces, they turned to myrth and vrbanitie, commendyng his doyng and saying therin. Then they asked hym frendly, vpon what certaine knowledge he spake those thynges, or what he thought best herein to be done, yf they should bring a greater supply of men? To this young *Comogru[illegible]* staying a whyle with him selfe, as it were an Oratour preparing hym selfe to speake of some graue matter, and disposing his body to a iesture meete to perswade, spake thus in his mother tongue, Geue eare vnto me, O you Christians. Albeit that the gree[illegible] hunger of golde hath not yet vexed vs naked men, yet do we destroy one another by reason of ambition and desyre to rule. Hereof spryngeth mortal hatred among vs, and hereof commeth our destruction. Our predecessours kept warres, and so dyd [illegible] with princes beyng borderers about him.

Abundance of golde.

Householde stuffe of golde.

Naked people [illegible] ambition.

In

In the whiche warres, as we haue ouercome, so haue we ben ouercome, as doth appeare by the number of bondmen among vs, which we toke by the ouerthrowe of our enimies, of the whiche I haue geuen you fyftie. Lykewyse at another tyme, our aduersaries hauyng the vpper hande agaynst vs, ledde awaye many of vs captiue, for suche is the chaunce of warre. Also, among our familiers (whereof a great number haue ben captiues with them) beholde here is one whiche of long time led a payneful lyfe in bondage vnder the yoke of that kyng beyonde the mountaynes, in whose kyngdome is such abundance of gold. Of hym, and suche other innumerable, and lykewyse by the resort of free men on theyr side commyng to vs, and agayne of our men resortyng to them by safe conduct, these thynges haue ben euer as well knowen vnto vs, as our owne possessions: but that you may be the better assured hereof, and be out of al suspection that you shall not be deceiued, make me the guyde of this voyage, byndyng me fast, and keepyng me in safe custodie to be hanged on the next tree, yf you fynde my sayinges in anye poynt vntrue. Folowe my counsayle therefore, and sende for a thousande Christian men apt for the warres, by whose power we may, with also the men of warre of *Comogrus* my father, armed after our manner, inuade the dominions of our enimies: where both you may be satisfied with golde, and we for our conductyng and aydyng you in this enterpryse, shall thinke our selues abundantly rewarded, in that you shal helpe to deliuer vs from the iniuries and perpetuall feare of our enimies. After these wordes, this prudent young *Comogrus* helde his peace, and our men mooued with great hope and hunger of golde, began agayne to swalowe downe theyr spyttle.

A vehement perswasion.

A token of hunger.

The fourth booke of the seconde Decade, of the supposed continent.

After that they had taryed here a fewe dayes, and baptised *Comogrus*, with all his familie, and named hym by the name of Charles, after the kyng of Spayne, they returned to theyr felowes in *Dariena*, bryngyng with hym the hope of the thousande

Kyng Comogrus is baptised with his familie.

sande souldiers, whiche his sonne required to passe ouer those mountaynes towarde the South sea. Thus entryng into the vyllage whiche they had chosen to inhabite, they had knowledge that *Valdiuia* was returned within sixe monethes after his departure, but with no great plentie of vyttualles, because he brought but a smal shyppe: yet with hope that shortly after, there shoulde be sent them abundaunce of vyttualles, and a newe supplye of men. For yong *Colonus* the Admiral, and viceroy of *Hispaniola*, and the other gouernours of the Ilande, acknowledged that hytherto they had no respect to them of *Dariena*, because they supposed that *Ancisus* the Lieutenaunt had safely arryued there with his shyppe laden with vyttualles: wyllyng them from hencefoorth to be of good cheare, and that they shoulde lacke nothyng hereafter, but that at this present tyme they had no bigger ship wherby they myght send them greater plentie of necessaries by *Valdiuia*. The vyttuals therfore which he brought, serued rather somwhat to mitigate theyr present necessitie, then to satisfie theyr lacke. Wherefore, within a fewe dayes after *Valdiuia* his returne, they fel agayne into lyke scarcenesse: especially forasmuche as a great storme and tempest whiche came from the hygh mountaynes, with horrible thunder and lyghtnyng in the moneth of Nouember, brought with it suche a floodde, that it partly caryed away, and partly drowned al the corne and seedes which they had sowen in the moneth of September, in a fruitefull grounde before they went to kyng *Comogrus*. The seedes whiche they of *Hispaniola* call *Maizium*, and they of *Vraba* call *Hobba*, whereof they make theyr bread, whiche also we sayde to be rype thryse euery yeere, because those regions are not bytten with the sharpenesse of wynter by reason of theyr neerenesse to the Equinoctial lyne. It is also agreeable to the principles of natural philosophie, that this bread made of *Maizius* or *Hobba*, shoulde be more wholsome for the inhabitauntes of those countreys then bread made of wheate, by reason that it is of easier digestion: for whereas colde is wantyng, the natural heate is not dryuen from the outwarde partes into the inwarde partes and consequently, wherby digestion is made strengthened. [illegible] the increase of theyr seedes, [illegible] of both vyttualles

Horrible thunder and lyghtnyng in the moneth of Nouember.

and golde, they were enforced to seeke theyr meate further of, and therwith to signyfie to the gouernours of *Hispaniola* with what great necessitie they were oppressed, and what they had learned of *Comogrus* as concernyng the Regions towarde the South, willyng them in consideration thereof, to aduertise the kyng to send them a thousande souldiers, by whose helpe they myght by force make waye through the mountaynes, diuidyng the sea on both sydes, if they coulde not bryng the same to passe quietly. The same *Valdiuia* was also sent on this message, caryyng with hym to the kynges treasurers (hauing theyr office of receipt in *Hispaniola*) three hundred poundes weyght of golde, after eyght ounces to the pounde, for the fyft portion due to the kynges excheker. This pound of eight ounces, the Spaniardes call *Marcha*, whiche in weight amounteth to fyftye peeces of golde called *Castellani*, but the Castilians call a pounde *Pesum*. We conclude therefore, that the summe hereof, was .xv. thousand of those peeces of gold called *Castellani*. And thus is it apparent by this accompt, that they receiued of the barbarous kinges, a thousande and fyue hundred poundes, of eyght ounces to the pounde: all the whiche they founde readye wrought in sundrye kyndes of ouches, as cheynes, braselets, tablets, and plates, both to hang before theyr brestes, and also at theyr eares, and nosethryls. *Valdiuia* therfore tooke shypping in the same Carauell in the which he came last, and returned also before the thyrde day of the Ides of January, in the yeere of Christe M. D. XI. What chaunced to hym in this voyage, we wyll declare in place conuenient. But let vs now returne to them whiche remayned in *Vraba*. After the dismissyng of *Valdiuia*, beyng pricked forwarde with outragious hunger, they determined to searche the inner partes of that gulfe in sundry places. The extreeme angle or poynt of the same gulfe is distant from the enterance thereof, about fourescore myles. This angle or corner, the Spaniardes call *Culata*. *Vascbus* hym selfe came to this poynt with a hundred men, coasting along by the gulfe with one brygandine and certayne of the boates of those regions, whiche the Vrabians call *Vru*, lyke vnto them whiche the inhabitauntes of *Hispaniola* call *Canoas*. From this poynt, there falleth a ryuer from the East into the gulfe, ten tymes bigger then the ryuer of *Dariena*, whiche the so falleth into the same. Saylyng along by the ryuer about the space of thyrtie myles (for they cal it niene leagues) and somewhat enclynyng towarde the ryght hande Southwarde, they founde certayne vyllages of thinhabitauntes, the kyng whereof was called *Dabaiba*. Our men also were certified before, that *Cemacchus* the kyng of *Dariena*, whom they put to flyght in the battayle, fledde to this *Dabaiba*, but at the commyng of our men, *Dabaiba* also fledde. It is thought that he was admonyshed by *Cemacchus*, that he shoulde not abyde the brunte of our men. He folowed his counsayle, forsooke his villages, and left all thynges desolate: yet our men founde heapes of bowes and arrowes, also muche housholde stuffe, and many fysshyng boates. But those marysshe groundes were neyther apt for sowyng of seedes, or plantyng of trees, by reason whereof, they founde there fewe suche thynges as they desyred, that is, plentie of vyttualles: for the inhabitauntes of this region haue no bread, but such as they geat in other countreys neare about them by exchange for their fyshe, onlye to serue theyr owne necessitie: yet founde they in the houses of those whiche fledde, golde wrought and grauen, amountyng to the summe of seuen thousande of those peeces, whiche we sayde to be called *Castellani*: also certaine Canoas, of the whiche they brought away two with them, and great plentie of theyr housholde stuffe, with certaine bundels of bowes & arrowes. They say, that from the marysshes of that riuer, there come certayne battes in the nyght season, as bygge as turtle doues, inuadyng men, and bytyng them with a deadly wounde, as some of them testifie whiche haue ben bytten of the same. I mee selfe communing with *Ancisus* the Lieuetenant whom they reiected, and among other thynges askyng hym of the venemous bytyng of these battes, he tolde me that he hym selfe was bytten by one of them on the heele, his foote lyyng vncouered in the nyght, by reason of the heate in sommer season, but that it hurte hym no more, then if he had ben bitten by any other beast not venemous. Other say, that the bytyng of some of them is venemous: yet that the same is healed incontinently, yf it be washed with water of the sea. *Ancisus* tolde me also, that the venemous woundes made by the Canibales arrowes infected with poyson, are healed by washyng with water of the sea, and also by cauterising [illegible]

Marysshe groundes.

Ancisus bitten of a Batte.

with what frense, and that he had experience therof in the region of *Caribana*, where many of his men were so wounded. They departed therefore from the poynt of the gulfe of *Vraba*, not wel contented, because they were not laden with vittualles. In this theyr returne, there arose so great a tempest in that wyde gulfe, that they were enforced to cast into the sea al the houshold stuffe, whiche they tooke from the poore wretches whiche liued only by fysshyng. The sea also swalowed vp the two boates that they tooke from them, wherewith the men were lykewyse drowned. The same tyme that *Vascbus Nunnez* attempted to searche the poynt of the gulfe towarde the south, euen then by agreement, dyd *Rodericus Colmenaris* take his voyage toward ẏ mountaines by the east, with threescore men, by the riuer of the other gulfe. About fourtie myles distant from the mouth of the other ryuer, (for they cal it twelue leagues) he founde certayne vyllages situate vpon the bankes of the ryuer, whose *Chiui* (that is) kyng, they cal *Turui*. With this kyng dyd *Colmenaris* yet remayne, when *Vascbus* after his returne to *Dariena* saylyng by the same ryuer, came to hym. Here refresshyng theyr whole companye with the vittuals of this *Turui*, they departed from thence togeather. Other fourtie myles from hence, the ryuer encompasseth an Ilande inhabited with fysshermen. In this, because they sawe great plentie of trees whiche beare *Cassia fistula*, they named the Ilande *Cannafistula*. They found in it .lx. villages of ten cotages apeece. On the ryght syde of the Ilande there runneth another riuer, whose chanel is of depth sufficient to beare Brigandines. This riuer they called *Riuum Nigrum*, frō the mouth wherof, about .xv. miles distant, they found a towne of fiue .C. houses seuered, whose *Chebi* (that is) kyng, was called *Abenamachei*. They al forsooke theyr houses, as soone as they heard of our mens commyng: but when they saw that our men pursued them, they turned againe, & ran vpon them with desperate mindes, as men driuen from their owne possessions. Theyr weapons are swordes of wood, & long staues lyke iauelins, hardened at the ende with fyre: but they vse neyther bowes nor arrowes, nor any other of the inhabitauntes of the West syde of the gulfe. The poore naked wretches were easely dryuen to flyghte with our weapons. As our men folowed them in the chase, they tooke the kyng *Abenamachei*, and [illegible]

A tempest.

King Turui.

The Ilande of Cannafistula.

certaine of his noble men. A common souldier of ours, whom the kyng had wounded, commyng to hym when he was taken, cut of his arme at one stroke with his swoorde: but this was done vnawares to the captaynes. The number of the Christian men whiche were here, was about an hundred and fyftie: the one halfe whereof the captaynes left here, and they with the resdue rowed vp the riuer agayne, with twelue of the boates of those regions, whiche they cal *Vru*, as they of *Hispaniola* cal them *Canoas* as we haue sayde. From the ryuer of *Riuus Niger*, and the Ilande of *Cannafistula*, for the space of threescore and ten myles, leauyng both on the right hande and on the left, many riuers falling into it bygger then it selfe, they entred into one, by the conductyng of one of the naked inhabitauntes, beyng appoynted a guyde for that purpose. Uppon the banke of this ryuer next vnto the mouth of the same, there was a kyng called *Abibeiba*, who because the region was ful of marysshes, had his pallace buylded in the toppe of a hygh tree, a new kind of buildyng, and seldome seene: but that lande bryngeth forth trees of such exceedyng height, that among theyr branches a man may frame large houses: as we reade the lyke in diuers auctours, howe in many regions where the Ocean sea riseth and ouerfloweth the lande, the people were accustomed to flee to the hygh trees, and after the fall of the water, to take the fyshe left on the lande. This maner of buyldyng, is to lay beames crosse ouer the branches of the trees, fast bounde togeather, and thereupon to rayse theyr frame, strongly made agaynst wynde and weather. Our men suppose that they builde theyr houses in trees, by reason of the great floods and ouerflowyng of riuers, whiche oftentymes chaunce in those regions. These trees are of suche heyghe, that the strength of no mans arme, is able to hurle a stone to the houses [illegible]ded therein. And therfore do I geue the better credit to Pli[illegible], and other auctours, whiche write that the trees in some places in *India* are so high by reason of the fruitefulnes of y ground, abundance of water, and heate of the region, that no man is able to shoote ouer them with an arrowe: and by iudgement of all men, it is thought that there is no fruitefuller grounde vnder the sunne, then this is whereof we nowe entreate. Our [illegible] measuryng manye of these trees, founde them to be of suche

King Abibeiba dwelleth in a tree.

The rysyng of the Ocean sea.

Trees of marueilous height.

Plinie.

Fruitefull grounde.

suche bignes, that seuen men, yea sometimes eight, holdyng hande in hande with theyr armes stretched foorth, were scarsely able to fathame them about: yet haue they theyr cellers in the grounde, well replenyshed with such wynes wherof we haue spoken before. For albeit that the vehemencie of the winde is not of power to cast downe those houses, or to breake the braunches of the trees, yet are they tossed therewith, and swaye somwhat from syde to syde, by reason whereof, the wyne shoulde be muche troubled with mouing. All other necessarye thinges, they haue with them in the trees. When the kyng or any other of the noble men, dyne or suppe in these trees, theyr wynes are brought them from the cellers by theyr seruauntes, whiche by meanes of exercise, are accustomed with no lesse celerytie to runne up and downe the staires adherente to the tree, then doo our wayting boyes uppon the playne grounde fetche us what wee call for from the cobbarde besyde our dyning table. Our men therefore came to the tree of kyng *Abibeiba*, and by thinterpretoures called hym foorth to communication, geuing hym signes of peace, and thereuppon wyllyng hym to come downe. But he denyed that he woulde come out of his house, desyring them to suffer hym to lyue after his fashion: but our men fell from fayre woordes to threatning, that except he woulde descende with all his familie, they woulde eyther ouerthrowe the tree, or elles set it on fyre. When he had denied them agayne, they fell to hewing the tree with theyr axes. *Abibeiba* seeing the chippes fall from the tree on euery syde, chaunged his purpose, and came downe with only two of his sonnes. Thus after they had entreated of peace, they communed of geatheryng of golde. *Abibeiba* annswearred that he had no golde, and that he neuer had any neede therof, nor yet regarded it any more then stones. But when they were instante uppon hym, he sayde unto them, If you so greatly desyre golde, I wyll seeke for some in the next mountaynes, and bryng it unto you: for it is plentifully engendred in those mountaynes. Then he appoynted a daye when he woulde bryng this golde. But *Abibeiba* came neyther at the day, nor after the day appointed. They departed therefore from thence well refreshed with [illegible] and wyne, but not with golde [illegible] *Abibeiba* [illegible],

his

Abibeiba, the kyng of the tree, yeeldeth to Valchus.

Golde no more esteemed then stones.

his [illegible] as concernyng the golde mynes and the Canibales, as they hearde before of kyng *Comogrus*. Saylyng yet further about thyrtie myles, they chaunced vpon certayne cotages of the Canibales, but vtterly voyde without men or stuffe: for when they had knowledge that our men wandered in the prouinces neere about them, they resorted to the mountaynes, caryinge all theyr goodes and stuffe with them.

Canibales.

The fyfte booke of the seconde Decade, of the supposed continent.

In the meane tyme whyle these thynges were done along by the shores or bankes of the ryuer, a certayne Decurian, that is, a captayne ouer tenne, of the companye of those which *Vaschus* and *Colmenaris* had left for a garryson in *Rino Nigro*, in the dominion of kyng *Abinamachei*, whether it were that he was compelled through hunger, or that his fatal day was nowe come, he attempted with his souldiers to searche the countreys neere thereabout, and entred into the vyllage of a king called *Abraiba*. This captaynes name was *Raia*, whom *Abraiba* slue with two of his felowes, but the residue fledde. Within a fewe dayes after, *Abraiba* hauyng compassion on the calamitie of his kynsman and neyghbour *Abenamacheius*, beyng dryuen from his owne possessions (whose arme also we sayd before that one of the souldiers cut of at the riuer of *Rine Nigro*) and now remaynyng with *Abraiba*, to whom he fled by stealth after he was taken, went to *Abibeiba* thinhabitour of the tree, who had nowe likewyse forsaken his countrey for feare of our men, and wandered in the desolate mountaynes and woods. When he had therfore founde hym, he spake to hym in this effect, What thyng is this, oh unfortunate *Abibeiba*? or what nation is this that so tyrannously oppresseth us, that we can not enioy our quiet libertie? howe long, howe long I say, shall we suffer theyr crueltie? were it not much better for us to dye, then to abide suche iniuries and oppressions as you, as *Abinamacheius* our kinsman, as *Comogrus*, as *Careta*, as *Poncha*, as I and other princes of our order haue susteyned? [illegible] thyng be more intollerable, then to see our wyues,

our

our chyldren, and our subiectes, to be ledde away captiues, and our goodes to be spoyled euen before our faces? I take the gods to witnesse, that I speake not so much for mine owne part, as I do for you, whose case I lament: for albeit they haue not yet touched me, neuertheles by the example of other, I ought to thinke that my destructiō is not farre of. Let vs therfore (if we be men) trye our strength, & proue our fortune agaynst them which haue dealt thus cruelly with *Abenamacheius*, and driuen him out of his countrey, let vs set on them with al our power, and vtterly destroy them. And if we can not slay them al, yet shal we make them afraide either to assayle vs agayne, or at the least diminishe their power: for whatsoeuer shal befall, nothyng can chaunce worse vnto vs then that which we nowe suffer. When *Abibeiba* heard these wordes, & such other lyke, he condescended to do in al things as *Abraiba* woulde require: whereupon they appoynted a day to bryng theyr conspiracie to passe, but the thyng chaunced not accordyng to their desyre: for of those whiche we sayd to haue passed to the Canibals, there returned by chaunce to *Riuus Niger*, the night before the day appoynted to worke their feate, thirtie men, to the ayde of them whiche were left there, yf any sedition should rise as they suspected. Therfore at the dawning of the day, the confederate kyngs, with fyue hundreth of theyr ditionaries armed after theyr maner, besieged the village with a terrible alarome, knowyng nothing of the newe men whiche came thither the same nyght. Here our target men came foorth against them, and first assayled them a farre of with theyr arrowes, then with theyr pykes, and last with theyr swoordes: but the naked seelye soules, perceiuyng a greater number of theyr aduersaries then they looked for, were soone dryuen to flyght, and slayne for the most parte lyke scatteryng sheepe. The kynges escaped, they slue many, and tooke many captiues, whiche they sent to *Dariena*, where they vsed them for labourers to tyll and sowe theyr grounde. These thynges thus happyly atchyued, and that prouince quieted, they returned by the ryuer to *Dariena*, leauyng theyr thyrtie men for a garrison, vnder the gouernance of one *Furatado* a capitayne. This *Furatado* therfore sent from *Riuo Nigro*, where he was appoynted gouernour, xx. of his felowes, and one woman, with xxiiii. captiues, to *Vascbus* and his companye, in

Men good ynough yf they had iron.

Captiues.

A garryson of thirtie men.

one of the byggest *Canoas* of that prouince. As they rowed downe by the ryuer, there came foorth sodenly ouerthwart the ryuer agaynst them foure great *Canoas*, which ouerthrewe theyr boate, and slue as many of them as they coulde come by, because they were vnprepared, suspecting no such thyng. Our men were all drowned and slaine, except two, which hid them selues among certeyne fagottes that swamme on the water, in the whiche they laye lurkyng, and so escaped to theyr felowes in *Dariena*: who by them beyng aduertysed hereof, beganne to cast theyr wyttes what this thyng myght meane, being no lesse solicitate for them selues, then meditatyng in what daunger theyr felowes had ben in *Riuo Nigro*, excepte by good fortune, those thirtie newe men whiche were sent to them, had come to the vyllage the nyght before the conspiracie shoulde haue ben wrought. Consultyng therefore what was best to be doone herein, at the length with diligent searchyng, they had intelligence that fyue kynges, that is to wytte, *Abibeiba* the inhabitour of the tree, and *Cemaccus* dryuen from his vyllage which our men nowe possessed, *Abraiba* also and *Abenamacheius*, kynsemen, with *Dabaiba* the kyng of the fysher men, inhabyting the corner of the gulfe whiche we called *Culata*, were al assembled to conspire the Christian mens destruction at a daye assigned: whiche thyng had surely come to passe, if it had not ben otherwyse hyndered by Gods prouidence. It is therefore ascrybed to a myracle, and truely not vnworthyly, if we waye howe chaunce detected and betrayed the counsayle of these kynges. And because it is worthy to be heard, I wyll declare it in fewe wordes. *Vascus Nunnez* therefore, who rather by power then by election, vsurped the gouernance in *Dariena*, beyng a maister of fence, and rather a rashe ruffler then a politike captaine (although fortune somtime fauoureth fooles) among many women whiche in diuers of these regions he had taken captiue, had one, which in fauour and beutie excelled all other. To this woman her brother often tymes resorted, who was also dryuen out of his countrey with king *Cemacchus*, with whom he was very familyer, and one of his cheefe gentelmen. Among other communication whiche he had with his syster whom he loued entierly, he vttered these wordes, My deare and welbeloued syster, gyue eare to my sayinges, and kepe most secretelye

Eightene Spanyardes slayne and drowned.

The kinges which conspired the death of the Christians.

A straunge chaunce.

Women can kepe no counsayle.

that

that whiche I wyll declare unto you, yf you desyre your owne wealth and myne, and the prosperitie of our countrey and kynsefolkes. The insolencie and crueltie of these men whiche haue dryuen vs out of our possessions, is so int[illegible]ble, that the princes of the lande are determyned no longer to susteyne theyr oppressions. By the conducting therefore of fyue kynges (whiche he named in order) they haue prepared a hundred great *Canoas*, with fyue thousande men of warre by lande and by sea, with vitails also in the village of *Ticbiri*, sufficient to mantayne suche an army: declaryng further, that the kynges by agreement, had diuyded among them the goodes and heades of our men, and therefore admonyshed her, at the day appoynted by some occasion to conueigh her selfe out of the way, lest she shoulde be slayne in the confusion of the battayle: For the souldier victourer, is not woont to spare any that commeth in his rase. And thus shewing his syster the day assigned to the slaughter, he departed. But the young woman (for it is the swoorde that women feare, and obserue more then the grauitie of *Cato*) whether it were for the loue or feare that she had to *Vascbus*, forgetting her parentes, her kynsfolkes, her countrey, and all her freendes, yea and al the kynges into whose throtes *Vascbus* had thruste his swoorde, she opened al the matter unto hym, and concealed none of those thinges which her undiscrete brother had declared to her. When *Vascbus* therfore had hearde the matter, he caused *Fuluia*, (for so had they named her) to sende for her brother, who came to her immediatly, was taken, & enforced to tel the whole circumstances of the matter: wherupon he playnely confessed, that king *Cemaccbus* his lord and maister, sent those foure Canoas to the destruction of our men, and that these new conspiracies were attempted by his counsaile: likewise that *Cemaccbus* sought the destruction of *Vascbus* him selfe, when he sent him .xl. men, under pretence of frendshyp, to tyll and sowe his grounde, after the maner of the countrey, geuing them in commaundement to slay *Vascbus* at *Marris*, whither he resorted to comforte his labourers, as the maner is of al good husbandes, yet durst they at no tyme execute their [illegible] commaundement upon hym, because *Vascbus* came [illegible] a foote or unarmed, but was accustomed [illegible] with a iauelyn in his hande, and [illegible]

An armie of an hundred Canoas, and fyue .M. men.

Triumph before victorie.

Affection corrupteth true iudgement.

The conspiracie of the kynges is detected.

Kyng Cemacchus conspireth the death of Vaschus.

a swoorde by his syde. Wherfore *Cemacchus* being frustrate of his particuler counsayle, tooke this last thing in hande, to his owne destruction and his neighbours: for the conspiracie being detected, *Vascus* called threescore and tenne souldiers, commaunding them to folowe hym, but declared nothing unto them whither he went, or what he entended to do. He went forwarde therfore fyrst toward *Cemacchus*, which lay from hym only tenne myles: but he had knowledge that he was fledde to *Abraiba*, the kyng of the marysshes of *Culata*. Yet searching his village, he founde a noble man, a ruler under hym, and also his kynsman, whom he tooke prysoner, with many other of his familiers and frendes both men and women. The same houre that he set forwarde to seeke for *Cemacchus*, *Rodericus Colmenaris* rowed up the ryver with foure of theyr byggest *Canoas*, and threescore men, by the conduction of the maydes brother who brought hym to the village of *Tichiri*, in ye which we sayd al their victuals to remaine which were prepared for theyr armye. *Colmenaris* therfore sacked the village, and possessed all their victuals, and wine of sundry colours, likewise tooke the governour therof prisoner, and hanged him on the tree in whiche he dwelt him selfe, commaundyng hym to be shotte through with arrowes in the syght of thinhabitauntes, and with hym foure other rulers to be hanged on gibbets, to the example of other rebelles. This punyshment thus executed uppon the conspiratours, stroke the hartes of all thinhabitauntes of the province with such feare, that there is not nowe a man that dare styrre his fynger agaynst the wrath of our men. They lyve nowe therefore quietly, and the other kyngs by theyr example do the gladlyer lyve in subiection, with lesse offence bearyng the yoke which they can by no meanes shake of.

Vaschus pursueth the kings with threescore and ten men.

Colmenaris sacketh the village of Tichiri.

Fyve rulers hanged & shot through with arrowes.

The syxte booke of the seconde Decade, of the supposed continent.

These thynges thus fynysshed, assemblyng al theyr company togeather, they determined with one consent, that a messenger shoulde forthwith be sent to *Hispaniola* (from whence they have theyr lawes and ayde) to declare the whole ordre of al these affayres, fyrste fyrst to the Admiral and gouernour of the Ilande, and afterwarde to the Kyng of Spayne, and to perswade hym to sende those thousande men whiche young *Comogrus* sayde to be expedient to passe ouer the mountaynes, lying betwene them and the golden regions toward the South. *Vascbus* hym selfe dyd greatlye affect this embassage: but neither would the residue of his felowes electe hym therto, nor his factionaries suffer hym to departe, aswell for that thereby they thought they should be left desolate, as also that they murmured, that if *Vascbus* should once go from them, he woulde neuer returne to suche turmoyles and calamities, by the example of *Valdiuia* and *zamudius*, who had ben now absent sence the moneth of January, in so much that they thoughe they woulde neuer come agayne: but the matter was otherwyse then they tooke it, as I wyll shewe in his place, for they were perished. At the length after many scrutinies, they elected one John *Quicedus*, a graue man, wel in yeeres, and treasourer of the kynges Exchequer in those prouinces: they had conceiued a good opinion of this *Quicedus*, that all thynges shoulde be well brought to passe by his meanes, aswell for his wysdome, as also that they were in good hope of his return, because he had brought his wife with hym to those regions, whom he left with his felowes for a pledge of his comming againe. When they had thus elected *Quicedus*, they were againe of diuers opinions whom they might ioyne with him for assistance, affirming that it were a daungerous thing to committe so weightie a matter to one mans handes, not that they mistrusted *Quicedus*, but because the life of man is fraile, & the chaunge of the ayre perillous, especially to them, hauyng now of long time ben accustomed to the temperature neere vnto the *Equinoctial*, if they should be compelled to returne to ÿ North, with alteration of ayre & diet. They thought it therfore good to appoynt a companion to *Quicedus*, that if by chaunce the one should faile, thother might remaine, & that if they both escaped, the king should geue ÿ better credit to the relation of both. After long consultation therfore, they chose *Rodericus Colmenaris*, a man of good experience, of whom we haue oftentimes made mention: for from his youth he had trauailed ouer al *Europe* by lande and by sea, and was present at the voyages of al things in Italie agaynst the Frenchmen, of whose maners also they

Iohan. Quicedus is sent to Spayne.

[illegible]

A wife is a hinderaunce.

had no small hope, because he had many farmes, and had tilled and sowne much grounde in *Dariena*, by the increase whereof, he myght get much gold by selling the same to his felowes. He left therfore the charge of al his affayres in *Dariena* with his partner *Alphonsus Nannez*, a iudge of the lawe, who also was lyke to haue ben chosen procuratour of this voyage before *Colmenaris*, yf one had not put them in remembraunce that he had a wife at *Matritis*, fearing lest being ouercome with her teares, he woulde no more returne. *Colmenaris* therfore, a free man, & at libertie, being associate assystant with *Quicedus*, they tooke shyppyng together in a Brigandine, the fourth day of the Calendes of Nouember, in the yeere of Christe. 1512. In this voyage, beyng tossed with sundry tempestes, they were by the violence of the winde cast vpon the West coastes of that large Iland, which in the fyrst Decade we called *Cuba*, supposed to haue ben firme land. They were sore oppressed with hunger, for it was nowe three monethes synce they departed from theyr felowes: by reason whereof, they were enforced to take lande, to prooue what ayde they coulde get among the inhabitauntes. Theyr chaunce therefore was to arryue in that part of the Ilande, where *Valdiuia* was dryuen aland by tempest. But oh you wretched men of *Dariena*, tary for *Valdiuia*, whom you sent to prouide to helpe your necessities, prouyde for your selues rather, and trust not to them whose

The death of Valdiuia.

fortune ye knowe not. For when he arryued in *Cuba*, the inhabitantes slue hym with al his felowes, and left the Carauel wherin they were caryed, torne in peeces, and halfe couered with sande on the shore, where *Quicedus* and *Colmenaris* fyndyng the fragmentes thereof, bewayled theyr felowes myssfortune: but they founde none of theyr carcasses, supposyng that they were eyther drowned, or deuoured of the Canibales, which oftentimes make incursions into that Ilande to hunt for men. But at the length, by two of the Ilande men which they had taken, they had knowledge of *Valdiuia* his destruction, and that the inhabitauntes the more greedily attempted the same, for that they had heard by the babblyng of one of his felowes, that he had great plentie of golde: for they also take pleasure in the beautie of golde, whiche they [illegible] artificially into sundry ouches. Thus our men stric[illegible] for the small welfare of theyr felowes, [illegible]

Sport of laughyng, [illegible] of the tongue.

and

and in vayne seekyng reuenge for theyr iniuries, determined to forsake that unfortunate lande, departyng from those couetous naked barbarians, with more sorowe and necessitie then they were in before. Or euer they had passed the South syde of *Cuba*, they fel into a thousande mysfortunes, and had intelligence that *Fogeda* arryued therabout, leadyng a miserable lyfe, tossed and turmoyled with tempestes, and vexed with a thousande perplexities: so that departyng from thence almost alone, his felowes beyng for the most part al consumed with maladies and famine, he came with much difficultie to *Hispaniola*, where he dyed by force of the poyson of his venemous wounde which he had receiued in *Vraba* as we haue sayde before. But *Ancisus* electe Lieutenant, sayled by al those coastes with much better fortune: for as he hym selfe tolde me, he founde prosperous wyndes in those parties, and was wel enterteyned of thinhabitantes of *Cuba*, but this specially in the dominion of a certayne kyng whose name was *Commendator*: for wheras he desyred of the Christian men whiche passed by, to be baptised, demaundyng the name of the gouernour of the Ilande next vnto *Hispaniola*, beyng a noble man, and a knyght of the order of *Galatraua*, of whiche order, all are called *Commendatores*, this kings desyre was to be named after him. Kyng *Commendator* therefore freendly receiued *Ancisus*, & gaue him great abundance of al thinges necessarie. But what *Ancisus* learned of theyr religion during the tyme of his remaynyng there, I haue thought good to aduertise your holynesse. You shal therfore vnderstande, that certayne of our men saylyng by the coastes of *Cuba*, left with kyng *Commendator* a certayne poore Maryner beyng diseased, who in short space recoueryng his health, and hauyng nowe somewhat learned theyr language, began to growe into great estimation with the kyng and his subiectes, insomuche that he was oftentimes the kynges Lieutenant in his warres agaynst other princes his borderers. This mans fortune was so good, that al thynges prospered well that he tooke in hande: and albeit that he were not learned, yet was he a vertuous and well meanyng man, accordyng to his knowledge, and dyd religiously honour the blessed virgin, bearyng euer about with hym her picture fayre paynted vpon paper, and sowed in his apparell nere vnto his hart, signifying vnto the

kyng

The calamities and death of *Fogeda*.

Maladies and famine.

The prosperous voyage of *Ancisus*.

A king of *Cuba* baptised by the name of *Commendator*.

A marueylous hystorie howe God wrought miracles by the simple fayth of a Maryner.

Be not rashe in iudgement.

kyng, that this holynes was the cause of al his victories: perswadyng hym to doo the like, and to cast away all his *Zemes*, which were none other then the similitudes of euill spirites, most cruell enimies and deuourers of our soules, and to take vnto him the holy virgin and mother of God to be his patronesse, if he desyred all his affayres aswel in warre as in peace to succeede prosperously: also that the blessed virgyn woulde at no tyme fayle hym, but be euer redye to helpe him and his, if they woulde with deuout hartes call vppon her name. The maryner had soone perswaded the naked nation, and thereuppon gaue the king (who demaunded the same) his pycture of the virgin, to whom he buylded and dedicated a chapell and an alter, euer after contemning and rejecting his *Zemes*. Of these *Zemes* made of gossampine cotton, to the similitudes of spirites walking in the nyght, which they oftentimes see, and speake with them familyerly, we haue spoken sufficiently in the nynth booke of the first Decade. Furthermore, according to the institution of this maryner, when the sonne draweth towarde the fall, this king *Commendator* with al his famyly, both men and women, resort dayly to the saide chapell of the virgin Marie, where kneeling on theyr knees, and reuerently bowing downe theyr heades, holdyng theyr handes ioyned together, they salute the image of the virgin with these wordes, *Aue Maria, Aue Maria*, for fewe of them can reherse any more wordes of this prayer. At *Ancisus* his being there, they tooke hym and his felowes by the handes, and ledde them to this chapell with reioysing, saying that they woulde shewe them maruelous thinges. When they were entred, they poynted with theyr fyngers to the Image of the virgyn, al to be set and honged about with ouches and iewels, and many earthen pottes, fylled some with sundry meates, and some with water, rounde about all the tabernacle: for these thinges they offer to the image in the steede of sacrifice, according to theyr olde superstition towarde theyr *Zemes*. Being demaunded why they dyd thus, they answered, Lest the image should lacke meate, [illegible] they most certainly [illegible] they doo eate & drinke. [illegible] that they haue had of the [illegible] the blessed virgyn, it is [illegible]

A Chappell buylded to the pycture of the virgin Marie.

One superstitious religion turned into an other, holdeth still many thinges of the first.

a thing worthy to be heard, and most assuredly to bee taken for a trueth: for by the report of our men, there is such feruent godly loue and zeale in these simple men toward the holy virgin, that to them being in the daunger of warre agaynst theyr enimies, they doo in maner (yf I may so terme it) compel her to descende from heauen to helpe them in theyr necessities. For such is the goodnes of God, that he hath left vnto men in maner a pryce whereby we may purchase hym with his holy angels & sayntes, that is to witte, burnyng loue, charitie, and zeale. Howe therfore can the blessed virgin at any time be absent from them which call for her helpe with pure faith and feruent loue? *Commendator* him selfe, with al his noble men and gentelmen, doo testifie with one voyce, that in a foughte battayle in the whiche this maryner was capitaine, bearing with him this picture of the virgin Marie, the *Zemes* of theyr enimies turned their backes, and trembled in the presence of the virgins image, and in the sight of them all: for euerye of them bryng theyr *Zemes* to the battaile, hoping by theyr helpe to obteine the victorie. Yea they say further, that durying the time of the battaile, they saw not only an Image, but a liuely woman clothed in fayre and white apparel, aydyng them against theyr enimies: which thing also the enimies them selues acknowledged, confessyng that on the contrary part, she appeared to them shakyng a scepter in her hande with threatenyng countenaunce, whiche caused theyr hartes to shake and faint for feare: but after that this Maryner departed from them, being taken into a shyppe of certayne Christians passyng by those coastes, *Commendator* declared that he with al his subiectes, continually obserued his institutions: insomuch that beyng at contention with another prince, whiche of theyr *Zemes* were most holy and of greatest power, the matter grewe to such extremitie, that they tryed it with hande strokes: and that in all these attemptes, the blessed virgin neuer fayled hym, but was euer present in the brunt of the battayle, and gaue hym easie victorie with a smal power of men, against a maine armie of his enimies. Beyng demaunded with what wordes they cryed vpon the virgin Mary when they assayled theyr enimies, they answered that they had learned no other wordes of the Maryners doctrine, but *Sancte Maria adiuua nos. Sancte Maria adiuua nos.* That is, holy Mary

Zeale without knowledge is neuer godly.

Marke this blyndnesse.

This ignorance is to be lamented.

The deuil dissembleth to keepe his in blyndnesse styll.

A notable lye of a papistical heretike.

One blasphemie vpon another.

Marie helpe vs, holy Marie helpe vs, and this also in the Spanishe tongue: for he had left these wordes in the mouthes of all men. Whyle they murthered and destroyed them selues thus on both sydes, they fell to entreatie of peace, and agreed to trye the matter, not hande to hande by combatte of certayne chosen for both parties, as the maner was among the Romanes and diuers other nations in the old tyme, or by any sleight or policie, but that two young men shoulde be chosen, for eche partie one, with theyr handes bounde faste behynde them in the playne fyelde, bothe parties beyng sworne to acknowledge that *Zemes* to be the better, which fyrst loosed the bandes of the young man which stoode bounde for the tryall of his religion. Thus diuidyng them selues, and placyng the sayd young men before them in the syght of them all, with theyr handes fast bounde by theyr enimies, the contrary parte called fyrst on theyr *Zemes* (that is the deuyl, to whose similitude theyr Images are made) who immediately appeared in his lykenesse aboute the young man that stoode bounde in the defence of Satans kyngdome. But as soone as *Commendator* with his companye cryed *Sancta Maria adiuua nos, Sancta Maria adiuua nos,* forthwith there appeared a fayre virgin clothed in whyte, at whose presence the deuyl vanquished immediatly. But the virgin, hauing a long rod in her hande, & putting the same on the bandes of the young man that stoode for *Commendator*, his handes were loosed immediatly in the syght of them all, and his bandes founde about the handes of hym that stoode for the other partye, insomuch that they them selues founde hym double bounde. But for all this, were not the enimies satisfyed, quarelling that this thyng was done by some sleyght or deuise of man, & not by the power of the better *Zemes*. And thereuppon requyred, for the auoydyng of all suspection, that there myght be eyght graue and sage men appoynted, for eche side foure, which should bynde the men in the syght of them all, and also geue iudgement whether the thing were done without craft or guyle. Oh pure simplicitie and constant fayth: oh golden and blessed confidence. *Commendator* and his familiers, doubted not to graunt theyr enimies theyr request, with lyke fayth wherewith the diseased woman obteyned health of the [illegible], and wherby Peter feared not to walke on the sea

The deuyll appeareth in his lykenesse.

What likenes?

A strange myracle not to be credited.

Another myracle.

Wise men.

Math. viiii. This is another matter.

sea at the syght of his maister Christ. These young men therfore were bounde in the presence of these eight graue men, and were placed within theyr lystes in the syght of both parties. Thus vpon a signe geuen, when they called vpon theyr *Zemes*, there appeared in the sight of them al, a deuil with a long taile, a wide mouth, great teeth, and hornes, resemblyng the similitude of the image whiche the kyng beyng enimie to *Commendator* honored for his *Zemes*. As the deuyl attempted to loose the bandes of his client, the blessed virgin was immediatly present as before at the cal of *Commendator* & his subiects, & with her rodde loosed the bandes of her suppliant, whiche were agayne likewyse founde fast tyed about the handes of hym that stoode for the contrarye part. The enimies therfore of *Commendator*, beinge stricken with great feare, and amased by reason of this great myracle, confessed that the *Zemes* of the virgin was better then theyr *Zemes*: for the better proofe whereof, these pagans being borderers to *Commendator*, whiche had euer before ben at continuall warre and enmitie with hym, when they had knowledge that *Ancisus* was arryued in those coastes, they sent Ambassadours vnto hym, to desire him to sende them priestes, of whom they might be baptised: wherupon he sent them two which he had there with hym at that present. They baptised in one day an hundred and thyrtie of thinhabitantes, sometime enimies to *Commendator* but nowe his frendes, and ioyned with hym in aliance. All suche as came to be baptised, gaue the priestes of theyr owne liberalitie, either a cocke or a henne, but no capons, for they can not yet skill howe to carue theyr cocke chickens to make them capons. Also certayne salted fishes, and newe fyne cakes made of theyr bread: likewise certayne foules franked and made fatte. When the priestes returned to the shyppes, syxe of these newe baptised men accompanyed them laden with vitualls, wherewith they kepte a ioyful Easter: for on the Sunday, two dayes before saynt *Lazarus* day, they departed from *Dariena*, and touched at that tyme only the cape or angle of *Cuba*, neere vnto the East syde of *Hispaniola*. At the request of *Commendator*, *Ancisus* left with hym one of his companye, to the intent to teache hym and his subiectes, [illegible] the [illegible] of the angell, whiche [illegible] to be so much

The deuyl appeareth againe

The virgin Mary in her owne person ouercometh the deuyl.

The priestes rewarde.

Who name you Capons?

[illegible] of the blessed virgin, as they can rehearse the [illegible] of that prayer. Thus *Ancisus* takyng his leaue of kyng *Commendator*, directed his course to *Hispaniola*, from which he was not farre. Shortly after, he tooke his voyage to Spayne, and came to *Valladoleto* to the kyng, to whom he made greeuous complaynt of the insolencie of *Vaschus Nunnez*, insomuche that by his procurement the kyng gaue sentence agaynst hym. Thus muche haue I thought good (most holy father) whereof to aduertise your holynesse, as concernyng the religion of these nations, not only as I haue ben enstructed of *Ancisus* (with whom I was dayly conuersaunt in the Court, and vsed hym familiarlye) but also as I was enfourmed of diuers other men of great auctoritie, to the intent that your excellencie may vnderstande howe docible this kynd of men are, and with what facilitie they may be allured to embrace our religion: but this can not be done sodenly, yet we haue great cause to hope that in short time they wyl be al drawen by litle and litle, to the Euangelical lawe of Christe, to the great encrease of his flocke. But let vs nowe returne to the messengers or procuratours as concernyng the affayres of *Dariena*.

[illegible] voiage to Spayne.

Ancisus complayneth of Vaschus.

Marke to whō this fayned miraculous storie was written.

The seuenth booke of the seconde Decade, of the supposed continent.

FRom *Dariena* to *Hispaniola*, is eyght dayes saylyng, and sometimes lesse with a prosperous winde: yet *Quicedus* and *Colmenaris* the procuratours of *Dariena*, by reason of tempestes & contrary windes, could scarcely sayle it in a hundred dayes. When they had taryed a fewe dayes in *Hispaniola*, and had declared the cause of the commyng to the Admirall and the other gouernours, they take shipping in two marchant shippes, beyng [illegible], whiche were also accustomed to sayle to and fro betweene Spayne and the Ilande of *Hispaniola*. They departed from *Dariena* (as we sayde before) the fourth day of the [illegible] in the yere of Christ. 1512. and came not [illegible] the Calendes of May in the yeare folowyng, [illegible] 1513. [illegible] the court.

Iohn

Iohannes Fonseca (to whom at the beginnyng the charge of these affayres was committed, whom also for his faythfull seruice towarde the kyng, your holynesse created general Commissarie in the warres agaynst the Moores) receiued them honourably, as men commyng from the newe worlde, from naked nations, and landes vnknowen to other men. By the preferment therefore of the Byshop of *Burges*, *Quicedus* and *Colmenaris* were brought before the kyng, and declared theyr legacie in his presence. Suche newes and presentes as they brought, were dilectable to the kyng and his noble men, for the newnesse and strangenesse therof. They also soiourned with me oftentymes. Theyr countenaunces do declare the intemperatnesse of the ayre and region of *Dariena*, for they are yelowe, lyke vnto them that haue the yelowe gaundies, and also swolne: but they ascribe the cause hereof, to the hunger whiche they susteyned in tymes past. I haue ben aduertised of the affayres of this newe worlde, not only by these procuratours of *Dariena*, and *Ancisus*, and *Zamudius*, but also by conference with *Baccia* the lawyer, who ran ouer a great part of those coastes: lykewyse by relation of *Vincentius Annez*, the patrone of the shyps, and *Alphonsus Nignus*, both being men of great experience, and wel trauailed in those parties, beside many other, of whom we haue made mention in other places, for there came neuer any from thence to the court, but tooke great pleasure to certifie me of al thynges, eyther by worde of mouth or by wrytyng. Of many thynges therefore whiche I learned of them, I haue geathered such as to my iudgment seme most worthy to satisfie them that take delyte in histories. But let vs nowe declare what folowed after the commyng of the procuratours of *Dariena*. Therfore, before theyr arryual, there was a rumor spred in the court, that the cheefe gouernours and Lieuetenantes *Nicuesa* and *Fogeda*, also *Iohannes de la Cossa* (a man of such reputation, that by the kinges letters patentes he was named the great maister of the kyngs shyppes) were al peryshed by mischaunce: and that those fewe whiche yet remayned alyue in *Dariena*, were at contention and discorde among them selues, so that they neither endeuoured theyr diligence to allure those symple nations to our fayth, nor yet had regarde to searche the natures [illegible]

The procuratours of Dariena are honourably receiued at the court.

The great master of the kings ships.

determined to sende a newe capitayne thyther, which shoulde restore and set al thynges in good order, and put them out of aucthoritie whiche had usurped the Empire of those prouinces without the kynges speciall commaundement. To this office, was one *Petrus Arias* assigned, a man of great prowesse, and a citizen of *Segouia*, but when the procuratours of *Dariena* had publyshed in the courte howe great a matter it was, and of what moment, many laboured earnestly to the kyng, to take the office out of his handes: but the Bishop of *Burges*, beyng the kynges cheefe chaplayne, and one of the Commissioners appoynted by hym in these matters, beyng aduertised hereof, came immediatly to the king, and spake to hym in this effect: May it please your hyghnesse to understande (most catholique prynce) that wheras *Petrus Arias*, a man of valiant courage and great seruice, hath offred him selfe to aduenture his life in your maiesties affaires, under uncertayne hope of gayne, and most certayne perils, yet that notwithstandyng, some other haue ambiciously maliced his felicitie and preferment, laboring for the office wherto he is elected. It may please your grace herein, so to shew him your fauour, and permit hym to enioy his sayde office, as your maiestie do knowe hym to be a woorthy and meete man for the same, hauyng in tyme past had great experience of his prowesse and valyantnesse, aswel in behauyng him selfe, as orderyng his souldiers, as your hyghnesse may the better consyder, yf it shal please you to call to remembraunce his doynges in the warres of Aphrica, where he shewed him selfe both a wise Captaine, and a valiant souldier. As concernyng his manners and usages otherwayes, they are not unknowen to your maiestie, under whose wyng he hath of a chylde ben brought up in the Courte, and euer founde faythfull toward your highnesse. Wherfore, to declare my opinion, under your graces fauour (whom it hath pleased to appoynt me a Commissioner in these affayres) I thynke it were ungodly that he shoulde be put from his office at the suite of any other, especially beyng therto moued by ambition and couetousnesse, who perchaunce would proue them selues to be the same men in the office, if they should obteyne it, as they now shew them selues in the ambitious desyring of the same. When the Bishop had sayd these woordes, the kyng confirmed the election of *Petrus Arias*, in more

Petrus Arias is elected gouernour of Dariena.

The oration of the Byshop of Burges, in the defence of Petrus Arias.

The warres of Aphrica.

more ample matter then before, wyllyng the byshop to appoynt hym a thousande and two hundred souldiers at his charges, makyng hym a warrant to the officers of his Exchequer, to delyuer hym money in prest for the same purpose. *Petrus Arias* therfore beyng thus put in office, and auctorised by the kinges letters patentes vnder his brode seale, chose a great number of his souldiers in the court, and so departed from *Valiadoleto*, about the Calendes of October, in the yere. 1513. and sayled first to Ciuile, beyng a very ryche citie, and wel replenished with people, where by the kynges magistrates, he was furnyshed with men and vyttualles, and other necessaries parteynyng to so great a matter: for the kyng hath in this citie erected a house, seruyng only for the affayres of the Ocean, to the whiche al they that goe or come from the newe landes and Ilandes, resorte to geue accomptes, aswel what they cary thyther, as what they bryng from thence, that the kyng may be truely answered of his custome of the fyft part, both of golde and other thynges, as we haue sayde before. This house they cal the house of the Contractes of *Indi*. *Petrus Arias* founde in Ciuile aboue two thousand young men, whiche made great suite to goe with hym, lykewyse no smal number of couetous olde men, of the whiche, many offered them selues to goe with him of their owne charges without the kings stipende. But lest the ships shoulde be pestered with to great a multitude, or lest vittuals shoulde fayle them, the libertie of free passage was restrayned. It was also decreed that no stranger myght passe without the kynges licence. Wherefore I doo not a lytle maruayle at *Aloisius Cadamustus* a Venetian, and wryter of the Portugales voyages, that he was not ashamed to wryte thus of the Spanyardes nauigations: we went, we sawe, we dyd: whereas he neuer went, nor any Venetian sawe, but he stole certayne annotations out of the three first bookes of my fyrst Decade, wrytten to Cardinal *Ascanius* & *Archimboldus*, supposyng that I would neuer haue publyshed the same. It myght also happen that he came by the copie therof at the handes of some ambassadour of Venice, for I haue graunted the copie to many of them, & was not daungerous to suffer them to communicate the same to other. Howsoeuer it be, this gentleman *Aloisius Cadamustus* seemeth not to chalenge vnto hym the frute of an other mans labour.

A house in Ciuile appoynted to the affayres of India.

Perularia.

The Portugales inuentions.

Of the inuentions of the Portugales (whiche surely are woonderful) whether he haue written that which he hath seene (as he saith) or likewise bereaued other men of the iust commendations of theyr trauayles, I wyl not iudge, but am content to let hym lyue after his manner. Among the company of these souldiers, there were none embarked but such as were licenced by the king, except a few Italians, Genues, who by frendshyp and suite were admitted for the Admiralles sake young *Colonus*, sonne and heyre to *Christophorus Colonus*, the fyrst fynder of those landes. *Petrus Arias* therfore toke shipping in the riuer *Betis* (now called *Guadalquevir*) running by the citie of Ciuile, about the begynnyng of the yeere of Christ. 1514. But he loosed anker in an euyl houre, for such a tempest folowed shortly after his departure, that it rent in peeces two of his ships, and so tossed the other, that they were enforced to heaue ouerboorde part of theyr vyttualles to lyghten them. All suche as escaped, sayled backe agayne to the coastes of Spayne, where, beyng newly furnysshed and refresshed by the kynges officers, they went forward on theyr voyage. The master Pylote of the gouernours shyp, was *Iohannes Vesputius* a Florentine, the neuiew of *Americus Vesputius*, who left him as it were by discent of inheritaunce, thexperience of the Maryners facultie, and knowledge of the sea, carde, and compasse. But we were aduertised of late by certayne whiche came from *Hispaniola*, that they had passed the Ocean with more prosperous winde: for this marchaunt shyppe commyng from *Hispaniola*, founde them landing at certaine Ilands neere therabout. But in the meane time, whyle my importunate callers on, *Galeacens Butrigarius*, and *Iohannes Cursius*, men studious by al meanes to gratifie your holynesse, ceassed not to put me in remembraunce that they had one in a redines to depart into Italy, & taried only to cary with him vnto your holines these my fayre *Nereides*, although rudely decked, lest I shoulde bestow much tyme in vayne, I haue let passe many things, & wil reherse only such as seeme in my iudgement moste worthy memory, although somwhat disordered, as occasion hath serued. So it is therefore, that this *Petrus Arias* hath a wife named *Helisabetha Boadilla*, beyng niese by the brothers syde to the marques of *Boadilla*, whiche rendred the citie of *Segouia* to Fernando and Helisabeth princes of Spayne, at suche time as the

The nauigation of Petrus Arias.

A shipwracke.

Americus Vesputius.

A notable example of a valiant woman.

Portu-

Portugales inuaded the kyngdome of Castile, by reason wherof, they were encouraged fyrst to resyst, and then with open warre to assayle and expulse the Portugales, for the great treasure which the kyng Henry brother to queene Helisabeth had geathered togeather there. This marquesse, while she liued, did euer shewe a manly and stoute mynde, both in peace and warre, so that by her counsayle, many noble thinges were brought to good effecte in Castile: vnto this noble woman the wyfe of *Petrus Arias* was niese by her brothers syde. She, folowyng the magnanimitie of her aunt, perceiuyng her husband nowe furnyshyng hym selfe to depart to the vnknowen coastes of the newe worlde, and those large tractes of lande and sea, spake these wordes vnto hym: My most deare and welbeloued husbande, we ought not nowe to forgeat that from our young yeeres we haue ben ioyned togeather with the yoke of holy matrimonie, to thintent that we shoulde so lyue togeather, and not asunder, duryng the tyme of our natural lyfe: wherefore for my part, to declare my affection herein, you shal vnderstande, that whither soeuer your fatall destenie shall dryue you, eyther by the furious waues of the great Ocean, or by the manyfolde and horrible daungers of the lande, I wyl surely beare you company: there can no peryll chaunce to me so terrible, nor any kynde of death so cruell, that shal not be muche easyer for me to abyde, then to liue so farre separate from you. It were muche better for me to dye, and eyther to be cast into the sea, to be deuoured of the fyshes, or on the lande to the Canibales, then with continual mournyng and bewaylyng, to liue in death, and dye lyuyng, whyle I consume in lookyng rather for my husbandes letters, then for hym selfe. This is my ful determination, not rashly, nor presently excogitate, nor conceiued by the lyght phantasie of womans brayne, but with long deliberation and good aduisement. Nowe therefore choose to whether of these two you wyll assent, eyther to thruste your swoorde in my throte, or to graunt me my request. As for the children which god hath geuen vs as pledges of our inseparable loue (for they had foure sonnes, and as many daughters) shall not stay me a moment: let vs leaue vnto them such goodes and possessions as haue ben left vs by our parentes and freendes, whereby they may lyue among the worshypfull of theyr order:

The wyfe of Petrus Arias.

for other thynges I take no care. When this noble matrone of manly vertue had finished those woordes, her husbande seeyng the constant mynde of his wyfe, and her in a redynesse to do accordyng to her woordes, had no hart to denye her louyng petition, but embracing her in his armes, commended her intent, and consented to her request. She folowed hym therfore, as did *Ipsicratea* her *Mithridates*, with her heare hangyng loose about her shoulders: for she loued her husband, as dyd *Halicarnassea* of *Caria* hers, being dead, and as dyd *Artemisia* her *Mausolus*. We haue also had aduertisment since theyr departure, that she (beyng brought vp as it were amōg soft fethers) hath with no lesse stoute courage susteyned the roringes and rages of the Ocean, then dyd eyther her husbande, or any of the Maryners brought vp euen among the sourges of the sea. But to haue sayde thus muche hereof, this shall suffice: let vs nowe speake of other thynges no lesse worthy memorie. Therfore, wheras in the first Decade we haue made mention of *Vincentius Annez Pinzonus*, ye shal vnderstand, that he accōpanied *Christophorus Colonus* the Admiral in his first voyage, and afterwarde made an other voyage of his owne charges with only one shyppe. Agayne, the fyrst yeere after the departyng of the Capitaynes *Nicuesa* and *Fogeda*, he ran ouer those coastes from *Hispaniola*, and searched al the South syde of *Cuba*, from the East to the West, and sayled rounde about that Ilande, whiche to that day, for the great length thereof, was thought to haue ben part of the continent or firme land, although some other say that they dyd the lyke. *Vincentius Annez* therefore, knowyng nowe by experience that *Cuba* was an Ilande, sayled on further, and founde other landes Westwarde from *Cuba*, but suche as the Admiral had first touched. Wherfore, beyng in manner encompassed with this newe lande, turning his course towarde the left hande, and rasing the coastes of that lande by the East, ouerpassing also the mouthes of the gulfes of *Beragua*, *Vraba*, and *Cuchibacboa*, he arryued at the region whiche in the first Decade we called *Paria* and *Os Draconis*, and entred into the great gulfe of freshe water, which *Colonus* discouered, beyng replenyshed with great abundance of fyshe, and famous by reason of the multitude of Ilandes lying in the same, beyng distant Eastwarde from *Curiana* about an hundreth and thirtie myles, in the which tracte,

are

are the regions of *Cumana* and *Manacapana*, whiche alſo in the
ſixt booke of the fyrſt Decade we ſayd to be regions of the large
prouince of *Paria*, where many affyrme to be the greateſt plentie
of the beſt pearles, and not in *Curiana*. The kynges of theſe regions (whom they cal *Chiacones*, as they of *Hiſpaniola* cal them
Cacici) beyng certified of the comming of our men, ſent certayne
ſpyes to enquire what new nation was arryued in theyr coaſtes,
what they brought, and what they would haue, and in the meane
tyme furnyſhed a number of theyr *Canoas* (whiche they call *Chi-
chos*) with men armed after theyr manner: for they were not
a lytle aſtonyſhed to beholde our ſhippes with the ſayles ſpread,
whereas they vſe no ſayles, nor can vſe but ſmall ones yf they
woulde, by reaſon of the narowneſſe of theyr Canoas. Swar-
myng therefore about the ſhyppe with theyr Canoas (whiche
we may wel cal *Monoxyla*, becauſe they are made of one whole
tree) they feared not to ſhoote at our men, beyng yet within their
ſhyppes, and keepyng them ſelues vnder the hatches, as ſafely
as yf they had ben defended with ſtone walles. But when our
men had ſhotte of certayne peeces of ordinaunce agaynſt them,
they were ſo diſcomfited with the noyſe and ſlaughter thereof,
that they droue them ſelues to flyght. Being thus diſparcled, our
men chaſed them with the ſhip boate, toke many, and ſlue many.
When the kynges heard the noyſe of the gunnes, and were certified of the loſſe of theyr men, they ſent ambaſſadours to *Vincentius Agnes* to entreate of peace, fearyng the ſpoyle of theyr
goodes, and deſtruction of theyr people, yf our men ſhould come
alande in theyr wrath and furie. They deſyred peace therefore,
as coulde be coniectured by theyr ſignes and poyntynges: for
our men vnderſtoode not one worde of theyr language. And for
the better proofe that they deſyred peace, they preſented our men
with three thouſande of thoſe weyghtes of golde that the Spanyardes call *Caſtellanum Aureum*, whiche they commonly call *Pe-
ſum*. Alſo a great barrel of wood ful of moſte excellent maſcu-
line Frankencenſe, weighing about two thouſande and ſixe hundred poundes weight, after eight ounces to the pounde: whereby they knewe that that lande brought foorth great plentie of
Frankencenſe, for there is no entercourſe of marchaundies
betwene the inhabitauntes of *Paria* and the Sabeans, being ſo
farre

Plentie of pearles.

The vſe of gunnes.

Great abundance of gold & frankencenſe. *Olibanum.*

Sabea is a countrey in Arabia, which bringeth foorth Frankencenſe.

[illegible], wheras also they of *Paria* knowe nothyng without theyr owne coastes. With the golde and Frankencense whiche they presented to our men, they gaue them also a great multitude of theyr peacockes, both cockes and hennes, dead and alyue, aswel to satisfie theyr present necessitie, as also to carry with them into Spayne for encrease, lykewyse certayne carpettes, couerlettes, table clothes, and hangyngs, made of Gossampine silke, finely wrought after a strange deuice, with pleasant and variable colours, hauyng golden belles, and such other spangles and pendauntes, as the Italians call *Sonaglios*, and the Spanyardes *Cascaueles*, hangyng at the pursles therof. They gaue them furthermore speakyng popyngayes of sundry colours, as many as they would aske: for in *Paria* there is no lesse plentie of popyngayes, then with vs of doues or sparows. Thinhabitants of these regions, both men & women, are apparelled with vestures made of gossampine cotton, the men to the knees, and the women to the calfe of the legge. The fashion of theyr apparel is simple and playne, muche lyke vnto the Turkes: but the mens is double, and quilted, like that which the Turkes vse in the warres. The princes of *Paria* are rulers but for one yeere: but theyr auctoritie is no lesse among the people both in peace and warre, then is thauctoritie of other kyngs in those regions. Their villages are buylded in compasse, along by the bankes of al that great gulfe. Fyue of theyr princes came to our men with theyr presentes, whose names I thought worthy to be put in this historie, in remembrance of so notable a thyng, *Chiaconus Chiauaccha* (that is, the prince of *Chiauaccha*, for they cal princes or kings *Chiaconus*) *Chiaconus Pintiguanus*, *Chiaconus Chamailaba*, *Chiaconus Polomus*, and *Chiaconus Potto*. The gulfe beyng first found of the Admiral *Colonus*, they cal *Baia Natiuitatis*, because he entred into the same in the day of ye natiuitie of Christ, but at that time he only passed by it without any further searchyng, and *Baia* in the Spanyshe tong, signifieth a gulfe. When *Vincentius* had thus made a league with these princes, folowyng his appoynted course, he founde many regions toward ye East, desolate by reason of diuers floods and ouerflowynges of waters: also many standyng pooles in diuers places, and those of exceedyng largenesse. He ceassed not to folowe this tracte, vntil he came to the poynt or cape of that moste

Rulers for one yeere.

The great gulfe of Paria.

[illegible]

most long lande. This poynt seemeth as though it woulde inuade the mount *Atlas* in *Aphrica*: for it prospecteth towarde that part of Aphrike, which the Portugales cal *Caput bonæ Sperantiæ*. The poyntes or capes of the mount *Atlas*, are rough and sauage, neere unto the sea. The cape of *Bona Speranza*, geathereth thyrtie and foure degrees of the South pole, called the pole Antartike, but that poynt only seuen degrees. I suppose this lande to be that, whiche I fynde in olde wryters of Cosmographie to be called the great Ilande Atlantike, without any further declaryng eyther of the situation, or of the nature thereof.

The great Ilande Atlantike.

The eight booke of the seconde Decade, of the supposed continent.

WHen John the king of Portugale liued, whiche was predecessour to him that nowe raigneth, there arose a great contention betweene the Castilians and the Portugales, as concernyng the dominion of these newe founde landes. The Portugales, because they were the fyrst that durst attempt to searche the Ocean sea synce the memorie of man, affirmed that al the nauigations of the Ocean, ought to parteyne to them only. The Castilians argued on the contrary part, that whatsoeuer God by the ministration of nature hath created on the earth, was at the begynnyng common among men, and that it is therfore lawful to euery man to possesse such landes as are voyde of Christian inhabitours. Whyle the matter was thus uncertaynelye debated, both parties agreed that the controuersie shoulde be decyded by the byshop of Rome, and plighted fayth to stande to his arbitrement. The kyngdome of Castile was at that tyme gouerned by that great queene *Helisabeth* with her husband: for the Realme of Castile was her dowrie. She also and the kyng of Portugale, were cosyn germanes of two systers, by reason whereof, the dissention was more easyly pacified. By the assent therfore of both parties, Alexander the bishop of Rome, the .vi. of that name, by [illegible] of his leaden bull, drewe a right lyne from the [illegible] the South, an [illegible] leagues Westwarde, with-

Contention betweene the Castilians & Portugales for the newe landes.

The bishop of Rome diuideth the landes.

[illegible] the paralels of these Ilandes whiche are called *Capas Viride*, or *Cabouerde*, within the compasse of this lyne (although some denye it) falleth the poynt of this lande whereof we haue spoken, whiche they cal *Capus Sancti Augustini*, otherwyse called *Promontorium Sancti Augustini*, that is, saint Augustines cape or poynt: and therefore it is not lawful for the Castilians to fasten foote in the begynnyng of that land. *Vincentius Annez* therefore departed from thence, beyng aduertised of the inhabitantes, that on the other syde of the hygh mountaynes towarde the South, lying before his eyes, there was a region called *Ciamba*, whiche brought forth great plentie of golde. Of certayne captiues whiche he tooke in the gulfe of *Paria* (whiche certaynely perteyneth to the dominion of Castile) he brought some with him to *Hispaniola*, and left them with the young Admirall to learne our language: but he hym selfe repayred to the court, to make earnest suite to the kyng, that by his fauour he myght be gouernour of the Iland of *Sancti Iohannis* (otherwise called *Buricbena*, being distant from *Hispaniola* only .xxv. leagues) because he was the fyrst finder of golde in that Ilande. Before *Vincentius* made suite for this office, one Don Christopher, a Portugale, the sonne of the countie of *Camigna*, was gouernour of the Ilande, whom the Canibales of the other Ilandes slue, with al the Christian men that were in the same, except the Bishop and his familiers, whiche fled and shyfted for them selues, forsakyng the churche and al the ornamentes thereof: for your holynesse hath consecrated fiue byshops in these Ilands, at the request of the most catholique king. In *Sancto Dominico* the chiefe citie of *Hispaniola*, *Garsia de Padilla*, a regular Fryer of the order of saint Fraunciss, is byshop. In the towne of Conception, doctor *Petrus Xuares* of *Deza*, and in the Ilande of saint Iohn or *Buricbena*, *Alphonsus Mansus* a licenciate, being both obseruantes of the institution of saint Peter. The fourth is Fryer Barnarde of *Mesa*, a man of noble parentage, borne in *Toledo*, a preacher, & bishop of the Ilande of *Cuba*. The fift is *Iohannes Cabedus*, a fryer preacher, whom your holynesse [illegible] minister of Christe, to teache the Christian fayth among the inhabitantes of *Dariena*. The Canibales shal shortlye [illegible], and the blood of our men shalbe reuenged, and [illegible] because [illegible] they haue committed

The golden region of Ciamba.

The Ilande of S. Iohannis.

Fyue byshops of the Ilande made by the bishop of Rome.

 this

this abominable slaughter of our men, they came agayne from theyr owne Ilande of *Sancta crux* (otherwise called *Ay Ay*) to the Ilande of *Sancti Iohannis*, and slue a kyng whiche was a frende to our men, and ate hym, and al his family, utterly subvertyng his village, upon this occasion, that violating the law of hostage, he had slayne seuen Canibales whiche were left with hym by composition to make certayne Canoas, because the Ilande of *Sancti Iohannis* beareth greater trees, and apter for that purpose, then doth the Iland of *Sancti crux*, the cheefe habitatiō of the Canibales. These Canibales yet remaynyng in the Iland, certaine of our men saylyng from *Hispaniola*, chaunced upon them. The thyng beyng understoode by the interpretours, our men quarellyng with them, and callyng them to accompt for that mischeuous deede, they immediatly directed theyr bowes and venemous arrowes against them, and with cruell countenances threatned them to be quiet, lest it shoulde repent them of theyr commyng thyther. Our men fearyng theyr venemous arrowes (for they were not prepared to fyght) gaue them signes of peace. Beyng demaunded why they destroyed the vyllage, and where the king was with his familie, they answered, that they rased the vyllage, and cut the kyng with his familie in peeces, and ate them in the reuenge of theyr seuen workmen: and that they had made faggottes of theyr bones, to cary them to the wiues and chyldren of theyr slayne workemen, in wytnesse that the bodyes of theyr husbandes and parentes lay not unreuenged, and therewith shewed the faggottes of bones to our men, who beyng astonyshed at theyr fiercenesse and crueltie, were enforced to dissemble the matter, and holde theyr peace, quarellyng no farther with them at that tyme. These and suche other thynges doo dayly chaunce, the whiche I do let passe, lest I should offende the eares of your holynesse with such bloody narrations. Thus haue we sufficiently digressed from the regions of *Beragua* and *Vraba*, beyng the cheefest foundations of our purpose. We wyll now therfore entreate somewhat of the largenesse and depth of the ryuers of *Vraba*: also declare both what they and the landes which they runne through do bryng foorth: lykewyse of the greatnesse of the lande from the East to the West, and of the breadth therof from the South to the North, and what theyr opinion and hope

The Canibales of the Iland of Sancta Crux.

The ryuers of Vraba.

hope is of thynges yet vnknowen in the same. We wyll therefore begyn at the newe names, wherwith the Spanyardes haue named these prouinces, synce they were vnder the dominions of the Christians.

The nienth booke of the second Decade, of the supposed continent.

BEragua therfore they called *Castella Aurea*, that is, golden Castile, and *Vraba* they named *Andalusia noua*, that is, newe Andalusia. And lyke as of many Ilandes whiche they subdued, they chose *Hispaniola* for the cheefe place of theyr habitation: so in the large tracte of *Paria*, they appoynted theyr colonie or bidyng place in the two regions of *Vraba* and *Beragua*, that al suche as attempt any voyages in those coastes, may resorte to them, as to safe portes to be refresshed when they are weerie or dryuen to necessitie. Al our seedes and plantes do now marueylously encrease in *Vraba*, lykewyse blades, settes, slippes, graffes, suger canes, and suche other as are brought from other places to those regions, as also beastes and foules, as we haue sayd before: O marueylous fruitefulnesse. Twentie dayes after the seede is sowen, they geather rype cucumbers, and such lyke, but Colwoortes, Beetes, Lettuse, Borage, are rype within the space of ten dayes. Gourdes, Melones, and Pompions, within the space of .xxviii. dayes. *Dariena* hath many natiue trees and fruites, of diuers kindes, with sundry tastes, & holsome for the vse of men, of the which I haue thought it good to describe certaine of the best. They nourishe a tree whiche they call *Guaiana*, that beareth a fruite muche resemblyng the kinde of Citrones which are commonly called Limones, of taste somwhat sharpe, myxt with sweeteness. They haue also abundance of nuts of pinetrees, and great plentie of Date trees, which beare fruites bigger then the Dates that are knowen to vs, but they are not apt to be eaten for theyr to much sowrenesse. Wylde & barren Date trees grow of them selues in sundry places, the braunches wherof they vse for broomes, and eate also the buddes of the same. *Guananana* being hygher and bygger then the orange-tree, bryngeth foorth a great fruite

The fruitefulnesse of Vraba.

The fruitefulnes of Dariena

fruite as bygge as pome Citrons. There is another tree much like to a chestnut tree, whose fruite is like to the bigger sorte of fyge, beyng holsome and of pleasant taste. *Mameis*, is another tree that bryngeth forth fruite as bygge as an orange, in taste nothing inferior to the best kindes of Melones. *Guanana*, beareth a fruite lesse then any of the other, but of sweete sauour like spice, and of delectable taste. *Honos* is another tree, whose fruite both in shape and taste is muche lyke to prunes, but somewhat bygger: they are surely perswaded that this is the *Myrobalane* tree. These growe so abundantly in *Hispaniola*, that the hogges are fedde with the fruite therof, as with mast among vs. The hogges like this kynde of feedyng so wel, that when these fruites ware ripe, the swineheards can by no meanes keepe them out of the woods of these trees, by reason whereof, a great multitude of them are become wilde. They also affirme, that in *Hispaniola* swines flesh is of muche better taste and more whollsome then mutton: for it is not to be doubted, but that diuers kindes of meates doo engender sundry tastes and qualities in such as are nourished therwith. The most puissant prince *Ferdinandus*, declared that he had eaten of another fruite brought from those landes, being full of scales, with keyes, much lyke a pineapple in fourme and colour, but in tendernes equal to melow pepons, and in taste exceedyng al garden fruites: for it is no tree, but an hearbe, much like vnto an archichoke, or *Acantho*: The king him selfe gaue the cheefest commendation to this. I haue eaten none of these fruits: for of a great number which they brought from thence, only one remayned vncorrupted, the other being putrified by reason of the long voyage. Al suche as haue eaten of them newly geathered in their natiue soyle, do marueylously commende theyr sweetenesse and pleasaunt taste. They dygge also out of the grounde certayne rootes growyng of them selues, whiche they call *Betatas*, muche lyke vnto the nauie rootes of Millane, or the great puffes or mushromes of the earth. Howsoeuer they be dressed, eyther fryed or sodde, they geue place to no suche kynde of meate in pleasant tendernes. The skinne is somwhat tougher then eyther the nauies or mushromes, and of earthy colour, but the inner meate therof is very white: These are nourished in gardens, as we sayd of *Iucca* in the first Decade. They are also eaten rawe, and

Swynes flesshe of better taste & more holsome then mutton.

Fruites putrified on the sea.

Betatas.

and haue the taste of roste chestnuts, but are somewhat sweeter. We haue spoken sufficiently of trees, herbes, and fruites, we wyl nowe therfore entreate of thynges sensitiue. The landes and desolate pastures of these regions, are inhabited and deuoured of wylde and terrible beastes, as Lions, Tygers, and suche other monsters as we nowe knowe, and haue ben described of olde auctours in tyme past. But there is specially one beast engendred here, in which nature hath endeuoured to shew her cunnyng: This beast is as bygge as an Oxe, armed with a long snoute lyke an Elephant, and yet no Elephant, of the colour of an oxe, and yet no oxe, with the hoofe of a horse, and yet no horse, with eares also muche lyke vnto an Elephant, but not so open, nor so much hangyng downe, yet muche wyder then the eares of any other beast. Of the beast which beareth her whelpes about with her in her second belly as in a purse (beyng knowen to none of the olde wryters) I haue spoken in the fyrst Decade, which I doubt not to haue come to the handes of your holynesse. Let vs nowe therefore declare what resteth of the floodes and ryuers of *Vraba*. The riuer of *Dariena* falleth into the gulfe of *Vraba*, with a narow chanel, scarcely able to beare the Canoas or Lighters of that prouince, and runneth by the village where they chose theyr dwellyng place, but the ryuer in the corner of the gulfe whiche we sayde that *Vascbus* passed by, they founde to be .xxiiii. furlonges in breadth (which they call a league) and of exceedyng deapth, as of two hundred cubits, fallyng into the gulfe by diuers mouthes. They say that this riuer falleth into the gulfe of *Vraba*, lyke as the ryuer *Ister* (otherwyse called *Danubius*, and *Danowe*) falleth into the sea Pontike, and *Nilus* into the sea of Egypt, wherefore they named it *Grandis*, that is, great: whiche also they affyrme to nouryshe many and great Crocodiles, as the old wryters testifie of *Nilus*, and especially as I haue learned by experience, hauyng sayled vp and downe the riuer of *Nilus*, when I was sent Ambassadour to the Souldane of Alcayr, at the commaundement of the most catholique kyng. What I may therefore geather out of the wrytynges of so many learned aucthours as concernyng the riuer of *Nilus*, I knowe not: for they say that nature hath geuen two ryuers of that name to water the lande, whether they wyl them to spryng out of the mountaynes of the moone

Lions and Tygers.

A strange beast.

The ryuers of Vraba.

A league is xxiiii. furlonges.

Danubius.

A Crocodile is muche lyke a Newte, but of exceedyng bygnesse.

moone or the same, or out of the tops of the rough mountaines of *Ethiopia*, affyrmyng one of the same to fall into the goulfe of Egypt toward the North, and the other into the south Ocean sea. What shal we say in this place? Of that *Nilus* in Egypt there is no doubt. The Portugales also which sayle by the coastes of the Ethiopians called *Nigritæ*, and by the kyngdome of *Melinda*, passyng under ỳ Equinoctial lyne, among theyr marueylous inuentions haue found another toward the South, and earnestly affirme the same to be also deriued from the mountaynes of the moone, and that it is another chanel of *Nilus*, because it bryngeth forth Crocodiles, whereas it hath not ben read before time, that any other riuer nourished Crocodiles sauing only *Nilus*. This riuer the Portugales cal *Senega*. It runneth through the region of the *Nigritas*, beyng very fruiteful toward the North shore, but on the South syde sandie and rough. Crocodiles are also engendred herein. What shal we then say of this thirde? yea I may wel say the fourth: for I suppose them also to be Crocodiles, which *Colonus* with his company found, armed with scales as hard as shelles, in the ryuer called *Delagartos*, wherof we haue made mention before. Shal we say that these ryuers of *Dariena* also and *Vraba*, haue theyr original from the mountaynes of the moone, wheras they spryng out of the next mountaynes, and can by no meanes haue the same original with *Nilus* in Egypt, or that in *Nigrita*, or els that in the kyngdome of *Melinda*, from whence so euer they are deryued, whereas these other (as we haue sayde) spring out of the next mountaynes, which diuide another South sea, with no great distance from the North Ocean. Wherefore, it appeareth by experience of such as haue trauailed the world in our tyme, that other waters besyde the riuer of *Nilus* in Egypt, may lykewyse bryng foorth Crocodiles. In the Marysshes also and fennes of the regions of *Dariena*, are founde great plentie of Phesantes and Peacockes (but not of variable colours) with manye other kyndes of byrdes and foules vnlyke vnto ours, aswel apt to be eaten, as also to delyte the eares of men with pleasaunt noyse. But our Spanyardes, because they are ignoraunt in fowlyng, take but fewe. Also innumerable popingayes of sundry kyndes are founde chattering in the groues of those fennie places. Of these there are some equall to Ca-

Ni pons

A philosophical discourse as concerning thoriginal of springes and ryuers.

The breadth of the lande at Vraba, from the North Ocean to the South sea.

[illegible] in bryghtnesse, and some as whyte as snowe. But of the diuersitie of popyngiayes, we haue spoken sufficiently in the fyrste Decade: for in the rase of this large lande, *Colonus* hym selfe brought and sent to the courte a great number of euery kynde, the whiche it was lawfull for all the people to beholde, and are yet dayly brought in lyke manner. There remayneth yet one thyng moste worthy to be put in hystorie, the whiche, I had rather to haue chaunced into the handes of *Cicero* or *Liuie*, then into myne: for the thyng is so maruelous in my estimation, that I fynde my wytte more entangled in the discription hereof, then is sayde of the henne when she seeth her young chycken intrapped in towe or flaxe. The breadth of that lande from the North Ocean to the south sea, is only syxe dayes iourney, by relation of the inhabitauntes. The multitude therfore and greatnesse of the riuers on the one syde, and on the other syde the narownesse of the lande, bryng me into suche doubt howe it can come to passe, that in so lytle a space of three dayes iourney, measuryng from the high toppes of those mountaynes, I doo not vnderstande howe so many and so great ryuers may haue recourse vnto this North sea: for it is to be thought, that as many do flowe towarde thinhabitantes of the south. These riuers of *Vraba* are but small, in comparison of many other in those coastes: for the Spanyardes say, that in the tyme of *Colonus*, they founde and passed by an other riuer after this, whose goulfe fallyng into ye sea, they affirme to be litle lesse then a hundred myles in the fyrst coastes of *Paria*, as we haue sayde elsewhere: for they say, that it falleth from the toppes of high mountaynes with so swyft and furious a course, that by the violence and greatnesse therof, it dryueth backe the sea, although it be rough & enforced with a contrary wynde. They al affirme lykewyse, that in al the large tracte therof, they felt no sowre or salt water, but that all the water was freshe, sweete, and apt to be dronke. Thinhabitauntes call this ryuer *Maragnonum*, and the regions adiacent to the same, *Mariatambal*, *Camamorus*, and *Paricora*: beside those riuers whiche I haue named before, as *Darien*, *Grandis*, *Dabaiba*, *Beragua*, *Sancti Mathei*, *Boius gatti*, *Delagartos*, & *Gaira*, they whiche of late haue searched those coastes, haue founde many other. Deliberatyng therfore with me selfe, from whense those mountaynes, beyng so narowe

narowe and neare vnto the sea on both sydes, haue suche great holowe caues or dennes of such capacitie, and from whence they are fylled, to cast foorth suche abundance of water: hereof also askyng them the opinions of the inhabitauntes, they affirme them to be of diuers iudgementes herein, alleaging fyrst the greatnes of the mountaynes to be the cause, whiche they say to be verye high, whiche thyng also *Colonus* the first fynder thereof affirmeth to be true, addyng thereunto that the paradise of pleasure is in the tops of those mountaynes whiche appeare from the gulfe of *Paria* & *Os Draconis*, as he is fully perswaded. They agree therfore that there are great caues within these mountaynes, but it resteth to consyder from whence they are fylled. If therfore al the riuers of freshe waters, by the opinion of many, do so flowe out of the sea, as dryuen and compelled through the passages or pores of the earth, by the ponderous weyght of the sea it selfe, as we see them breake foorth of the sprynges, and directe theyr course to the sea agayne, then the thyng is lesse to be marueyled at here, then in other places: for we haue not read that in any other place, two suche seas haue enuironed any lande with so narowe lymyttes: for it hath on the ryght syde the great Ocean, where the sunne goeth downe on the left hande, and another on the other syde where the sunne ryseth, nothyng inferiour to the fyrste in greatnesse, for they suppose it to be myxte and ioyned as al one with the sea of East India. This lande therfore beyng burdened with so great a weyght on the one syde, & on the other, (yf this opinion be of any value) is enforced to swalowe vp such deuoured waters, and agayne to cast foorth the same in open sprynges and streames. But yf we shall denye that the earth draweth humours of the sea, and agree that all fountaynes or sprynges are engendred of the conuersion or turnyng of ayre into water, distilling within the holow places of the mountaines (as the most part thinke) we wyll geue place rather to thauctoritie of them whiche stycke to those reasons, then that our sense is satisfied of the ful trueth thereof. Yet do I not repugne, that in some caues of mountaynes, water is turned into ayre: for I mee selfe haue seene, howe in the caues of manye mountaynes in Spayne, in maner showres of rayne to fall continually, and that the [illegible]

The sea.

The lande enclosed with two seas.

Conuersion of ayre into water in the caues of mountaynes.

certayne riuers by the sydes of the mountaynes, wherewith all suche trees as are planted on the steepe or foote of the mountaynes, as vines, oliue trees, and suche other, are watered, and this especially in one place: as the right honorable Lodouike the Cardinal of Aragonie, most obsequious to your holynesse, and two other bishops of Italy, whereof the one is *Siluius Pandonus*, and the other an Archbishop (whose name and title I do not remember) can beare me witnesse: for when we were togeather at *Granata*, lately deliuered from the dominion of the Moores, and walked for our pastyme to certaine pleasant hilles (by the whiche there ranne a fayre ryuer) while Cardinal Lodouike occupied hym selfe in shootyng at byrdes whiche were in the bushes neere vnto the ryuer, I & thother two bishops determined to clime the mountaynes, to searche the original and spryng of the ryuer: for we were not farre from the toppes thereof. Folowyng therfore the course of the ryuer, we founde a great caue, in which was a continual fal of water, as it had ben a showre of rayne, the water whereof, fallyng into a trenche made with mans hande, encreaseth to a ryuer, and runneth downe by the sydes of the mountaynes. The lyke is also seene in this famous towne of *Valladoleto* (where we nowe soiourne) in a certaine greene close, not past a furlong distant from the walles of the towne. I graunt therefore, that in certayne places, by conuersion of the ayre deawe into water, within the caues of suche mountaynes, many springes and riuers are engendred: but I suppose that nature was not solicitate to bryng foorth suche great floods by this so small industrie. Two reasons therfore do founde best to my iudgement: wherof the one is, the often fal of rayne: the other, the continual autume or spryng tyme which is in those regions, being so neere vnto the Equinoctial, that the common people can perceiue no difference betweene the length of the day and the nyght throughout all the yeere, where as these two seasons are more apt to engender abundance of rayne, then eyther extreme wynter, or feruent sommer. An other reason in effect much like vnto the fyrst, is this: If the sea be ful of pores, and that by the pores therof, beyng opened by the south wyndes, we shal consent that vapours are lyfted vp, whereof the watery cloudes are engendred, this lande muste nedes be moysted with moe showres then any o- [illegible] ther.

(The) often fal of rayne and con(tinu)all spryng tyme.

The Equinoctiall.

The pores of the sea, and the south wynde.

ther, yf it be as narowe as they say, and enuironed with two mayne seas collaterally beatyng on the same: howsoeuer it be, I can not but geue credite to the report of suche worthy men as haue recourse to those regions, and can no lesse then declare the same, albeit it may seeme incredible to some ignorant persons, not knowing the power of nature, to whom, Plinie was perswaded, that nothing was impossible. We haue therefore thought it good to make this discourse by the way of argument, lest on the one syde, men of good learnyng and iudgement, and on the other syde, suche as are studious to finde occasions of quarelyng in other mens wrytynges, shoulde iudge vs to be so vndiscrete, lightly to geue credite to euery tale, not being consonant to reason: but of the force and great violence of those freshe waters, whiche repulsyng the sea, make so great a gulfe (as we haue sayde) I thynke the cause thereof to be the great multitude of floods and riuers, whiche beyng geathered togeather, make so great a poole, and not one ryuer, as they suppose. And forasmuch as the mountaines are exceeding high and steepe, I thinke the violence of the fall of the waters to be of suche force, that this conflict betweene the waters, is caused by thimpulsion of the poole, that the salt water can not enter into the gulfe. But here perhaps some wyll marueyle at me, why I should marueyle so muche hereat, speakyng vnto me scornefully, after this manner: Why doth he so marueyle at the great riuers of those regions? Hath not Italie his *Eridanus*, named the kyng of ryuers of the old wryters? Haue not other regions also the lyke? as we reade of *Tanais, Ganges*, and *Danubius*, which are sayde so to ouercome the sea, that freshe water may be drawen fourtie myles within the same. These men I would satisfie with this aunswere. The famous ryuer of *Padus* in Italie (whiche they nowe call *Po*, and was of the Greekes called *Eridanus*) hath the great mountaynes called *Alpes*, diuiding Fraunce, Germanie, and Pannonie, from Italie, lying at the backe therof, as it were bulwarkes agger, full of moysture, and with a long tracte receiuyng *Ticinum*, with innumerable other great ryuers, falleth into the sea Adriatike: The lyke is to be sayde of the other. But these ryuers [illegible] [illegible]

The fludde Eridanus.

and some there are whiche affirme this lande to be very large in other places, although it be but narowe here. There commeth also to my remembraunce another cause, the whiche although it be of no great force, yet do I entende to wryte it. Perhaps therefore the length of the lande reachyng farre from the East to the West, if it be narowe, may be a helpe hereunto: for as we reade, that the ryuer *Alpheus* passeth through the holowe places under the sea, from the citie of *Elis* in *Peloponeso*, and breaketh forth at the fountayne or spryng *Arethusa* in the Iland of *Sicilia*, so is it possible that these mountaines may haue such long caue[illegible] parteynyng unto them, that they may be the [illegible] of the water passing through the landes beyng farre distant, and that the same waters commyng by so long a tracte, may in the way be greatly encreased, by the conuersion of ayre into water, as we haue sayde. Thus much haue I spoken freely, permitting both to them which do frendly interprete other mens doynges, and also to the malitious scorners, to take the thing euen as them lysteth, for hytherto I can make no further declaration hereof, but when the trueth shalbe better knowen, I wil do my diligence to commit the same to wrytyng. Nowe therfore, forasmuch as we haue spoken thus muche of the breadth of this lande, we entende to describe the length and fourme of the same.

The ryuer Alpheus.

Longe caues in the mountaines.

The tenth booke of the seconde Decade, of the supposed continent.

That lande reacheth foorth into the sea, euen as doth Italy, although not lyke the legge of a man, as it doth. But nowe I compare a Pigmean or a dwarfe, to a Giant: for that part thereof whiche the Spanyardes haue ouer runne, from the sayd East poynt which reacheth towarde the sea Atlantike, (the ende not beyng yet founde towarde the West) is more then eyght tymes longer then Italie. And by what reason I am moued to say eyght tymes, your holynesse shall understande. From [illegible] they re- [illegible] your [illegible] these

The length and forme of the Iland.

thinges in the Latine tongue, I did my endeuour that al things myght come foorth with due tryal and experience: whereupon I repayred to the Bishop of *Burges*, beyng the cheefe refuge of this nauigation. As we were therfore secretely togeather in one chamber, we had many instruments parteining to these affaires, as globes, and many of those maps whiche are commonly called the shipmans cardes, or cardes of the sea. Of the which, one was drawen by the Portugales, wherunto *Americus Vespucius* is said to haue put to his hande, beyng a man most expert in this facultie, and a Florentine borne, who also vnder the stipende of the Portugales, had sayled towarde the South pole many degrees beyonde the Equinoctiall. In this carde we founde the first front of this lande to be broder then the kynges of *Vraba* had perswaded our men of theyr mountaynes. To another, *Colonus* the Admiral, while he yet lyued, and searched those places, had geuen the beginning with his owne handes: wherunto *Bartholomeus Colonus* his brother and Lieuetenaunt had added his iudgement, for he also had sayled about those coastes. Of the Spanyardes lykewyse, as many as thought them selues to haue anye knowledge what parteyned to measure the land & the sea, drewe certayne cardes in parchment as concernyng these nauigations. Of all other, they moste esteeme them whiche *Iohannes de la Cossa* the companion of *Fogeda* (whom we sayde to be slayne of the people of *Caramairi* in the hauen of *Carthago*) and another expert pylote called *Andreas Moralis*, had set foorth. And this aswel for the great experience which they both had (to whom these tractes were aswel knowen as the chambers of theyr owne houses) as also that they were thought to be cunninger in that part of Cosmographie, which teacheth the discription and measuring of the sea. Conferring therfore al these cardes togeather, in euery of the whiche was drawen a lyne, expressing not the myles, but leagues, after the maner of the Spanyardes, we tooke our compasses, & began to measure the sea coastes after this order. From that poynt or fronte whiche we sayde to be included within the lyne parteynyng to the Portugales iurisdiction, beyng drawen by the paralleles of the Ilandes of *Cabouerde*, but a hundred leagues [illegible] West [illegible]

[illegible] M iii [illegible]

Cardes of the sea.

The carde of Americus Vespucius.

The carde of Colonus.

The carde of Iohannes de la Cossa.

The carde of Andreas moralis.

The maner of measuring the cardes.

entraunce of the riuer *Maragnonum*: and from thence to *Os Draconis*, seuen hundred leagues, but somwhat lesse by the discription of some, for they doo not agree in al poyntes exquisitely. A league. The Spanyardes wyl that a league conteyne foure myles by sea, and but three by lande. From *Os Draconis*, to the cape or poynt of *Cuchibacoa*, whiche being passed, there is a gulfe on the left hande, we measured three hundred leagues in one Carde, & much thereabout in another. From this poynt of *Cuchibacoa*, to the region of *Caramairi*, in whiche is the hauen *Carthago* (whiche some cal *Carthagena*) we found about a hundred & seuentie leagues. From *Caramairi* to the Iland *Fortis*, fyftie leagues. From thence to the gulfes of *Vraba*, among the whiche is the vyllage called *Sancta Maria Antiqua*, where the Spanyardes haue appoynted theyr habitation, only .xxxiii. leagues. From the ryuer of *Vraba* in the prouince of *Dariena*, to ye riuer of *Beragua*, where *Nicuesa* had intended to haue fastened his foote, if God had not otherwyse decreed, we measured a hundred and thirtie leagues. From *Beragua*, to that riuer, which we said of *Colonus* to be called *Sancti Matthei*, in the which also *Nicuesa* loosing his Carauel, wandered in great calamities, we founde in our Cardes only a hundred and fourtie leagues: Yet many other whiche of late tyme haue come from these partes, haue described many mo leagues in this tract from the ryuer of *Sancti Matthei*, in whiche also they place diuers ryuers, as *Aburema*, with the Iland called *Scutum Catiba*, lying before it, whose kyngs name is *Facies combusta*. Likewise another ryuer called *Zobraba*, after that, *Vrida*, and then *Duraba*, in the which golde is founde. Furthermore, many goodly hauens, as *Cerabaro* and *Hiebra*, so called of the inhabitauntes. And thus yf your holynesse wyll conferre these numbers togeather, you shall fynde in this accompt, a thousand, fyue hundred, twentie and fiue leagues, which amount to fyue thousande & seuen hundred myles, from the poynt of *Sancti Matthei*, whiche they cal *Sinum perditorum*, that is, The gulfe of ye lost men. But we may not leaue here: for after this, one *Astur Ouetensis*, otherwyse named *Iohannes Dias de Solis*, borne in *Nebrissa* (whiche bryngeth foorth many learned men) sayling from this riuer towarde the West, ouerranne many coastes and leagues, but the middest of that shore bendeth [illegible] the North, and is not therefore directly placed in that

The nauigation of Iohannes Dias.

with

with the other, yet may we geather by a diameter or right lyne, about three hundred leagues. Hereby may you geather what is the length of this lande, but of the breadth, perhaps we shal hereafter haue further knowledge. Let vs nowe speake somewhat of the varietie of the degrees of the eleuation of the pole starres. This lande therefore, although it reache foorth from the East into the West, yet is it crooked, and hath the poynt bendyng so towarde the South, that it looseth the syght of the North pole, and is extended beyonde the Equinoctial lyne seuen degrees towarde the South pole: but the poynt hereof, parteyneth to the iurisdiction of the Portugales, as we haue sayde. Leauing this poynt, and saylyng towarde *Paria*, the North starre is seene againe, & is so much the more lifted vp, in how much the region enclineth more towarde the West. The Spanyardes therfore haue diuers degrees of eleuations, vntyll they come to *Dariena*, being theyr cheefe station and dwelling place in those landes: for they haue forsaken *Beragua*, where they founde the North pole eleuate .viii. degrees, but from hence, the land doth so much bend towarde the North, that it is there in manner equal with the degrees of the straightes of Hercules pyllers, especially yf we measure certaine landes founde by them toward the North syde of *Hispaniola*, among the which there is an Iland about three .C. and .xxv. leagues frō *Hispaniola*, as they say which haue searched the same, named *Boiuca*, or *Agnaneo*, in the which is a continuall spring of running water, of such marueilous vertue, that ẏ water thereof being drunke, perhaps with some diet, maketh olde men young agayne. And here must I make protestation to your honesse, not to thynke this to be sayde lyghtly or rashly, for they haue so spread this rumour for a trueth throughout al the courte, that not onlye al the people, but also many of them whom wysedome or fortune hath diuided from the common sort, thynke it to be true: but yf you shal aske my opinion herein, I wyl answere, that I wyll not attribute so great power to nature, but that God hath no lesse reserued this prerogatiue to hym selfe, then to searche the hartes of men, or to geue substaunce to priuation, (that is) beyng, to no beyng, except we shall beleeue the fable of *Colchis* of *Eson* renouate, to be as true as the wrytynges of *Sibylla Erythrea*. Albeit perhaps the scoles of Phisicians and

The eleuation of the pole.

The iurisdiction of the Portugales.

Hercules pyllers.

The Ilande Boiuca or Agnaneo.

The renouation of age.

A water of marueilous vertue.

and natural philosophers, wyll not muche spcke to affyrme, that by the vse of certayne secrete medicines and dyet, the accidentes of age (as they cal them) may be long hydden and deferred, whiche they wyl to be vnderstoode by the renouation of age. And to haue sayde thus much of the length and breadth of these regions, and of the rough and hugious mountaynes, with theyr waterye caues, also of the diuers degrees of that lande, I thinke it sufficient. But I thought it not good to let passe what chaunced to these miserable men among theyr generall calamities. I remember that when I was a chylde, me thought my bowelles grated, and that my spirites were marueylously troubled for very pitie, when I read in the poete Virgyl, howe *Achemenides* was left of *Vlysses* vpon the sea bankes among ẏ giantes called *Cyclopes*, where for the space of many dayes from the departyng of *Vlysses*, vntyl the comming of *Eneas*, he eate none other meate, but only berries and hawes. But our vnfortunate Spanyardes, whiche folowed *Nicuesa* to inhabite *Beragua*, would haue esteemed hawes & berries for great delicates. What should I heare speake of the head of an asse bought for a great pryce, and of such other extremities as men haue suffered in townes besieged? After that *Nicuesa* had determined to leaue *Beragua* for the barrennesse of the soyle, he attempted to searche *Portum Bellum*, and then the coastes of the poynt called *Marmor*, yf he myght there fynde a place more fortunate to inhabite. In this meane tyme, so greeuous famine oppressed his souldiers, that they neyther absteined frō eating of mangie dogges, which they had with them, aswel for theyr defence as for huntyng (for in the warre agaynst the naked people, dogges stoode them in great steade) nor yet sometyme from the slaine inhabitauntes: for they found not there any fruitful trees, or plentie of foules, as in *Dariena*, but a barren ground, and not meete to be inhabited. Here certaine of the souldiers made a bargayne with one of their felowes for the pryce of a leane dogge, who also was almost dead for hunger: they gaue the owner of the dogge many of those peeces of gold which they cal *Pesos*, or golden Castellans. Thus agreeing of the pryce, they flayed the dogge to be eaten, and cast his mangie skinne, with the bones of the head hangyng thereto, among the bushes. The [illegible], a certayne footeman of theyr companye, chaunced

ced

Margin notes:

The accidentes of age may be hydden.

Extreme hunger.

This was at the siege of Hierusalem.

Many dogges eaten.

A mangie dog deare solde.

ced to fynde the skynne being nowe full of maggottes and stynkyng. He brought it home with hym, sodde it, and eate it. Many resorted to hym with theyr dysshes for the brothe of the sodde skynne, profering hym for euerye dysshefull a piece of golde. An other founde two toades, and sodde them, which a sycke man bought of hym for two fine shurtes, curiously wrought of lynnen intermyxed with golde. Certayne other wanderyng about to seeke for vittuals, found in a pathway in the myddest of a feelde, a dead man, of the inhabitantes, which had ben slaine of his owne company, and was nowe rotten and stynkyng. They drewe hym a syde, dismembred hym secretely, rosted hym, and ate hym, therewith asswagyng theyr hunger, as yf they had ben fedde with pheasauntes. One also, whiche departing from his companions in the nyght season, went a fysshyng among the reedes of the marysshes, lyued only with slyme or mudde for the space of certayne dayes, untyl at the length creepyng, & almost deade, he founde the way to his felowes. And thus these miserable men of *Veragua*, vexed with these and suche other afflictions, were brought from the number of seuen hundreth, threescore and ten souldiers, scarsely to fourtie, beyng nowe also added to the company of them in *Dariena*. Fewe were slayne of thinhabitauntes, but the resydue consumed by famine, breathed out theyr wery soules, openyng a way to the newe landes for suche as shal come after them, appeasyng the fury of the barbarous nations, with the price of theyr blood. Consyderyng therfore, after these stormes, with what ease other men shall ouerrunne and inhabite these landes, in respect to the calamities that these men haue suffered, they shall seeme to goe to bryde feastes, where all thynges are redy prepared agaynst theyr commyng. But where *Petrus Arias* arryued with the kynges nauie and newe supply of men, to this houre I knowe no certantie. What shal chaunce heareafter, I wyl make diligent inquisition, if I shal understand this to be acceptable to your holynes. Thus I byd you farewel: from the courte of the most Catholyke kyng, the daye before the nones of December, in the yeere of Christ. 1514.

Brothe of a mangie dogs skynne.

Toades eaten.

A dead man eaten.

Note.

Petrus Arias whō the Spanyardes call Pedrarias.

The

www.ingramcontent.com/pod-product-compliance
Lightning Source LLC
Chambersburg PA
CBHW020858230426
43666CB00008B/1235
* 9 7 8 3 7 4 4 7 9 7 1 6 0 *